Linux on HP Integrity Servers

System Administration for
Itanium-Based Systems

Marty Poniatowski

Hewlett-Packard® Professional Books

HP-UX

Cooper/Moore	HP-UX 11i Internals
Fernandez	Configuring CDE
Madell	Disk and File Management Tasks on HP-UX
Olker	Optimizing NFS Performance
Poniatowski	HP-UX 11i Virtual Partitions
Poniatowski	HP-UX 11i System Administration Handbook and Toolkit, Second Edition
Poniatowski	The HP-UX 11.x System Administration Handbook and Toolkit
Poniatowski	HP-UX 11.x System Administration "How To" Book
Poniatowski	HP-UX 10.x System Administration "How To" Book
Poniatowski	HP-UX System Administration Handbook and Toolkit
Poniatowski	Learning the HP-UX Operating System
Rehman	HP-UX CSA: Official Study Guide and Desk Reference
Sauers/Ruemmler/Weygant	HP-UX 11i Tuning and Performance
Weygant	Clusters for High Availability, Second Edition
Wong	HP-UX 11i Security

UNIX, LINUX, WINDOWS, AND MPE I/X

Mosberger/Eranian	IA-64 Linux Kernel
Poniatowski	UNIX User's Handbook, Second Edition
Stone/Symons	UNIX Fault Management

COMPUTER ARCHITECTURE

Evans/Trimper	Itanium Architecture for Programmers
Kane	PA-RISC 2.0 Architecture
Markstein	IA-64 and Elementary Functions

NETWORKING/COMMUNICATIONS

Blommers	Architecting Enterprise Solutions with UNIX Networking
Blommers	OpenView Network Node Manager
Blommers	Practical Planning for Network Growth
Brans	Mobilize Your Enterprise
Cook	Building Enterprise Information Architecture
Lucke	Designing and Implementing Computer Workgroups
Lund	Integrating UNIX and PC Network Operating Systems

SECURITY

Bruce	Security in Distributed Computing
Mao	Modern Cryptography: Theory and Practice
Pearson et al.	Trusted Computing Platforms
Pipkin	Halting the Hacker, Second Edition
Pipkin	Information Security

WEB/INTERNET CONCEPTS AND PROGRAMMING

Amor	E-business (R)evolution, Second Edition
Apte/Mehta	UDDI
Chatterjee/Webber	Developing Enterprise Web Services: An Architect's Guide
Kumar	J2EE Security for Servlets, EJBs, and Web Services
Mowbrey/Werry	Online Communities
Tapadiya	.NET Programming

OTHER PROGRAMMING

Blinn	Portable Shell Programming
Caruso	Power Programming in HP OpenView
Chaudhri	Object Databases in Practice
Chew	The Java/C++ Cross Reference Handbook
Grady	Practical Software Metrics for Project Management and Process Improvement
Grady	Software Metrics
Grady	Successful Software Process Improvement
Lewis	The Art and Science of Smalltalk
Lichtenbelt	Introduction to Volume Rendering
Little/Maron/Pavlik	Java Transaction Processing
Mellquist	SNMP++
Mikkelsen	Practical Software Configuration Management
Norton	Thread Time
Tapadiya	COM+ Programming
Yuan	Windows 2000 GDI Programming

STORAGE

Thornburgh	Fibre Channel for Mass Storage
Thornburgh/Schoenborn	Storage Area Networks
Todman	Designing Data Warehouses

IT/IS

Anderson	mySAP Tool Bag for Performance Tuning and Stress Testing
Missbach/Hoffman	SAP Hardware Solutions

IMAGE PROCESSING

Crane	A Simplified Approach to Image Processing
Gann	Desktop Scanners

About Prentice Hall Professional Technical Reference

With origins reaching back to the industry's first computer science publishing program in the 1960s, and formally launched as its own imprint in 1986, Prentice Hall Professional Technical Reference (PH PTR) has developed into the leading provider of technical books in the world today. Our editors now publish over 200 books annually, authored by leaders in the fields of computing, engineering, and business.

Our roots are firmly planted in the soil that gave rise to the technical revolution. Our bookshelf contains many of the industry's computing and engineering classics: Kernighan and Ritchie's *C Programming Language*, Nemeth's *UNIX System Administration Handbook*, Horstmann's *Core Java*, and Johnson's *High-Speed Digital Design*.

PH PTR acknowledges its auspicious beginnings while it looks to the future for inspiration. We continue to evolve and break new ground in publishing by providing today's professionals with tomorrow's solutions.

Linux on HP Integrity Servers
System Administration for
Itanium-Based Systems

Marty Poniatowski

www.hp.com/hpbooks

PRENTICE
HALL
PTR

PEARSON EDUCATION
Prentice Hall Professional Technical Reference
Upper Saddle River, NJ 07458
www.PHPTR.com

Library of Congress Cataloging-in-Publication Data
A CIP catalog record of this book can be obtained from the Library of Congress
LOC Number: 2004107332

Publisher, HP Books: *William Carver*
Executive Editor: *Jill Harry*
Cover Design: *Sandra Schroeder*
Editorial Assistant: *Brenda Mulligan*
Manufacturing Buyer: *Dan Uhrig*
Marketing Manager: *Stephane Nakib*
Senior Project Editor: *Sarah Kearns*
Copy Editor: *Sheri Cain*

Published by Pearson Education
Publishing as Prentice Hall Professional Technical Reference
Upper Saddle River, New Jersey 07458

PRENTICE
HALL
PTR

Prentice Hall PTR offers excellent discounts on this book when ordered in quantity for bulk purchases or special sales. For more information, please contact: U.S. Corporate and Government Sales, 1-800-382-3419, corpsales@pearsontechgroup.com. For sales outside the U.S., please contact: International Sales, 1-317-581-3793, international@pearsontechgroup.com.

Printed in the United States of America
First Printing

ISBN 0-13-140000-2

Pearson Education LTD.
Pearson Education Australia Pty, Limited
Pearson Education South Asia Pte. Ltd.
Pearson Education Asia Ltd.
Pearson Education Canada, Ltd.
Pearson Educación de Mexico, S.A. de C.V.
Pearson Education—Japan
Pearson Malaysia, S.D.N B.H.D.

Contents

Foreword

Linux has proven to be a true phenomenon that the technology world sees rarely, if ever. By itself and at a high level, the technology that makes up the Linux operating system has been implemented before, either in the multiple UNIX implementations over the years or other commercial grade operating systems such as VMS and others.

The real phenomenon is the open source development process. The community development process is the reason that Linux has moved from interest and participation exclusively by hobbyists and computer scientists to that of end users who need truly scalable, commercial grade operating systems.

Never before has a single common operating system been used to solve problems at the very low end, scaled through 64-bit systems to large-scale, high-performance clusters to mainframe class architectures and all the way to the data center, while encompassing most any application in between.

No single operating system has been capable of spanning that wide range. No single operating system has gone across so many architectures.

To bring an operating system from no commercial relevance to the fastest growing technology in the commercial world in less than three years has much to say about the process in itself and the participation of the diverse community.

The strength of the open source model has gotten the attention of most all of the commercial vendors in the IT space. This has contributed to a change in the makeup of the community who participates in Linux development.

There are many more developers who now contribute within the process on a full-time basis while being paid by those commercial, proprietary vendors. Certainly the engineers with a passion for open source, as well as engineers who work for commercial Linux vendors such as Red Hat, still contribute heavily to the process, but the combination has helped drive what's getting attention from the community to more high-end enterprise features. It has also allowed for a wider range of hardware to be tested and ported to, as well as much larger workloads by the commercial applications.

You can see how this process, with such diverse participation and now with access to all hardware (e.g., HP Itanium-based Integrity Servers) and workloads, has allowed for Linux to mature in such a short timeframe. It is essentially not one company that is maturing the operating systemóas is the case with a proprietary operating systemóbut rather the industry as a whole. The only thing that makes this possible is the openness of the process itself combined with the operating mantra of "let the best technology win" when decisions need to be made on implementation directions by the community.

Arguably, the Linux kernel is the largest open source project to ever be assembled. It is also now easy to say that it is the most successful. We are now starting to see the success of the kernel project and the open source development process as the catalyst in driving other open source projects that are focused on other pieces of the computing infrastructure.

These technologies are starting to find their way into the enterprise in commercial grade use and applications; whether in storage or application servers, open source is now becoming mainstream in the commercial environment. The success of Linux has proved the model. I am confident that we will continue to see more of the commercial computing infrastructure built on open source in the years to come.

This book covers Red Hat Enterprise Linux on HPís Integrity Servers. This high-end product line further demonstrates that Linux has truly moved into the enterprise. Marty Poniatowski does an excellent job of providing information to get you up and running quickly with Red Hat Linux on HP Integrity Servers so that you can reap the benefits of Linux in your data center.

Paul Cormier
Executive Vice President, Engineering
Red Hat, Inc.

Preface

ABOUT THIS BOOK

Linux on HP Integrity Servers covers the Linux operating system on HP Itanium®-based systems, called the Integrity server family, running Red Hat Enterprise Linux (RHEL).

This book starts out with extensive coverage of booting HP Integrity servers. These servers can run multiple operating systems so the boot process is important to understand. The boot process is substantially different than it is on HP Precision Architecture-based systems, called the HP 9000 family. The Extensible Firmware Interface (EFI) is an important part of booting HP Integrity servers, so I spend a significant amount of time on EFI in Chapter 1.

I then cover loading Linux on an HP Integrity system in Chapter 2. The installation is done in console-only mode since you may very well have an HP server without a graphics display on it. The graphics-based installation is nearly identical to that of loading an IA-32 system with Linux, so I didn't want to cover the same information that appears in many other Linux books. To load Linux on an HP Integrity server, you first load the *HP Enablement Kit for Linux,* which is a set of tools that provide a framework for installing, configuring, and recovering a Linux distribution on our Integrity servers. The kit is completely distribution agnostic, meaning that it is independent of a Linux distribution. You'll be loading Red Hat Enterprise Linux (RHEL) only in this book, but other Linux distributions can be loaded on some Integrity servers so the LEK needs to be independent of a specific Linux distribution. The **elilo** program you'll use to boot-strap the Integrity server is provided as part of the *HP Enablement Kit for Linux.*

This book then covers many additional system administration topics in the subsequent chapters.

The versions of Linux that run on Integrity that are used in this book are types of the Red Hat Enterprise Linux (RHEL) family, including versions RHEL 3 and RHEL 2.1. The three members of the RHEL family are Advanced Server, Enterprise Server, and Workstation. The primary difference in these releases, at the time of this writing, has to do with their high- end capabilities. In the examples in this book I use RHEL Advanced Server because it supports greater than two CPUs, a lot of memory, and Itanium- based systems. There are also examples on IA-32 based systems that use other Red Hat releases. There are many Linux background chapters which apply to all Linux systems so the hardware platform, either Integrity servers or IA-32, is not important.

Although the term Itanium is used throughout this book, the current implementation of Itanium is Itanium 2. I just shortened the name to Itanium for easier reading. You may also see the old name of IA-64 appear occassionally in screen shots, but I won't use IA-64 in my text.

Other Linux distributions run on HP Integrity systems such as SuSE Linux enterprise server. I used Red Hat because this release was available at the time I began writing the book and many of my customers were evaluating Integrity servers running Red Hat. In addition to Linux, HP-UX, Windows Server 2003, and OpenVMS run on HP Integrity servers. Some of the book's examples show the boot process in which Linux, Windows, and HP- UX are all loaded on the same HP Integrity server. Different operating systems run in different hard partitions, called Node Partitions (nPartitions) on HP Integrity servers. This capability is new at the time of this writing and will be enhanced dramatically by HP in the coming months and years.

This is the first revision of this book, but to keep up with the many advancements that will take place, you can expect several revisions to the book. I want to receive your feedback on this book and topics that you'd like to see covered in future revisions. Please send your thoughts to me at the following email address:

marty.poniatowski@hp.com

Linux Components

This how-to book doesn't have a lot of background information in any of the chapters. This book illustrates how to get important tasks done. The next few pages provide some Linux background that covers the structure of Linux. Figure P-1 is a high-level depiction of a Linux system.

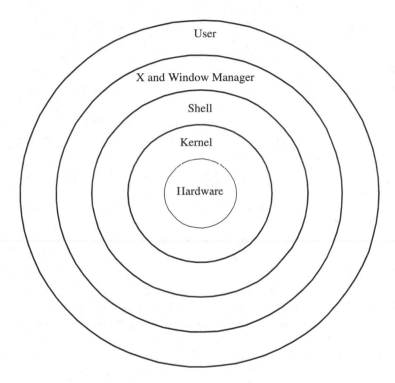

Figure P-1 High-Level Linux System Structure

Before describing this figure, note that everyone has a somewhat different way of viewing the components of Linux. This figure contains the most important components from a user perspective.

At the heart of Figure P-1 is the hardware. Linux, in its many forms, now runs on many different types of hardware. I have melded the Integrity and IA-32 hardware on which Linux runs throughout this book and have pointed out the areas of Red Hat Enterprise Linux (RHEL) that are peculiar to HP Integrity servers.

The next circle from the center of this diagram is the kernel. The kernel performs many functions including management of devices, memory, and processes; scheduling and execution of all commands; and containment of drivers that control system hardware. The kernel is an aspect of the system that system administrators spend a lot of time maintaining. When a new device is configured, a device driver may have to be added to the kernel to support the new device. There is also substantial tuning that can be performed to the kernel to optimize system performance for the application(s) running on the Linux system. Users have only indirect interaction with the kernel through the commands you issue that work their way to the kernel.

The next circle is the shell. The shell takes commands from you and starts the process of executing the commands. In addition to passing commands to more inner layers of the system, the shell also allows you to run commands in the background and run shell programs.

The next circle is the X Window System and the window manager that you run. There is a chapter in the book covering both GNOME and KDE. You usually don't see the graphical user interface as a separate circle in such Linux diagrams, because most of the work done in a graphical user interface works its way down to a shell command. Because most Linux users use a graphical user interface, this warrants its own circle.

The final circle is the user. As a system administrator, you have access to all the components in the diagram.

Another way to view Linux is on a distribution basis. Figure P-1 shows Linux in a generic way. You won't be using a generic Linux: you'll be using a specific distribution, such as Red Hat Enterprise Linux (RHEL) Advanced Server on your HP Integrity servers. Figure P-2 breaks down Linux components in the way in which you'd view them as part of a distribution.

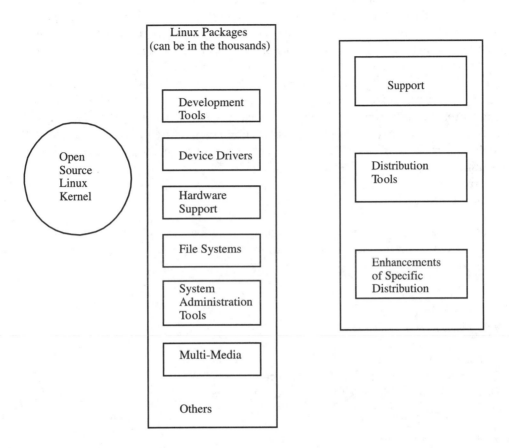

Figure P-2 High-Level Linux Distribution

The high-level depiction of a Linux distribution in Figure P-2 has several components. On the far left is the Linux kernel, which is open-source software and serves as the basis for any Linux distribution. The center components consist of open source modules as well as distribution-specific enhancements. There may be, for instance, open-source system administration tools as well as distribution-specific adminstration tools that are part of a release. The components on the right are those specific to a distribution, such as the support available.

An additional consideration with Itanium and operating systems is byte ordering. This is often referred to as the endian of an architecture or operating system. Itanium doesn't care about byte ordering and can support both byte ordering methods. Operating systems that store the most significant byte in the leftmost position are big endian. Operating systems that store the most significant byte in the rightmost position are little endian. Linux is a little endian operating system. Linux and Windows are little endian and HP- UX is big endian. All these operating systems run on HP Integrity servers.

Some examples in this book use the "retail" release of Red Hat version 8.x. The "retail" releases of Red Hat, such as 8.x, have been replaced by Fedora. Fedora Project is a Red Hat-sponsored and community-supported open-source project. Fedora Core 2 is available at the time of this writing.

Relevant URLs

There are many Web sites that can assist you in your Linux system administration endeavors. I have listed some of the more prominent Linux-related Web sites below as they existed at the time of this writing:

Extensible Firmware Interface:
http://www.intel.com/technology/efi

Technical documentation, including most all HP documents.
Of particular interest at this site are documents on *HP Linux Enablement Kit*, and documents on HP Integrity servers:
http://www.docs.hp.com

Information on Itanium:
http://www.hp.com/go/itanium

IT Resource Center
(This is essential for every HP-UX administrator):
http://www.itrc.com

Linux kernel archive:
http://www.kernel.org

RPM home page for package managment:
http://www.rpm.org

Red Hat Linux manuals:
http://www.redhat.com/docs/manuals/

The Linux Documentation Project:
http://www.tldp.org

GNOME desktop environment site:
http://www.gnome.org/

Linux on Itanium:
http://www.gelato.org

An excellent iptables "how to" document:
 http://www.linxguruz.org/iptables/howto

Software depot home page:
http://www.software.hp.com

Instant Capacity on Demand (iCOD):
http://www.hp.com/go/icod

The International Association of HP Computing Professionals:
http://www.interex.org

Register name servers at:
http://www.icann.org/registrars/accredited-list.html

Information on Perl, including sites to download Perl:
http://www.perl.com

The Perl Journal:
http://www.tpj.com

Site devoted to managing and promoting open source:
http://www.opensource.org

Linux documentation site:
http://www.linuxdoc.org

Office suite software:
http://www.openoffice.org/

Web-based management software:
http://www.webmin.com

Rute's Linux tutorial:
http://rute.2038bug.com/index.html

Online Manual Pages

Many times in this book, I refer to the online manual pages supplied with Linux. You can get the online manual page for a command by issuing **man** *command_name*. You can view an online manual page from a specific section by specifying the *section* number. To view the signal man page in section seven, you would issue the following command:

man 7 signal

This produces the signal(7) man page. If you were to type just man signal, the signal(2) man page would be produced; that is, the man page for signal in section *2 would be shown.*

Also, see /usr/share/doc where most Linx documentation is kept. /usr/ share/doc/ *<pkg-name> contains information about packages.*

Acknowledgments

There were too many people involved in helping me with this book to list each and every one. I have, therefore, decided to formally thank those who wrote sections of this book and those who took time to review it. I'm still not sure whether it takes more time to write something or review something that has been written to ensure it is correct.

Stephen Geary

Stephen is the executive champion and sponsor of this book and played an active role in getting it published.

Stephen Geary, Director, Worldwide Linux R&D, is responsible for overseeing HP's Linux technical strategy, Linux support for HP's Integrity Servers, integrated Linux-based solutions for various markets, and HP's Open Source Program Office. Stephen also has direct responsibly in developing HP's overall Linux and Open Source strategies. Stephen has active roles with the Open Source Development Lab (OSDL) and the Linux Standards Base (LSB). Steve chairs the Data Center Linux Steering Group and is a member of the Carrier Grade Steering Group for the Carrier Grade Linux effort.

Stephen has been with HP for 15 years working in various capacities tied to either HP-UX or Linux. Prior to working for HP, Stephen worked for General Motors as a Fuel Systems Engineer in Flint, Michigan. He holds two bachelor's degrees: bachelors of science degree in mechanical engineering from Michigan Technological University and a bachelors degree in computer science from Colorado State University, Fort Collins, Colorado.

The Author - Marty Poniatowski

Marty has been a Solution Architect with Hewlett-Packard Company for 17 years in the New York area. He has worked with hundreds of Hewlett-Packard customers in many industries, including Internet startups, financial services, and manufacturing.

Marty has been widely published in computer-industry trade publications. He has published over 50 articles on various computer-related topics. In addition to this book, he is the author of 13 other Prentice Hall books. *Marty holds an M.S. in Information Systems from Polytechnic University (Brooklyn, NY), an M.S. in Management from the University of Bridgeport (Bridgeport, CT), and a B.S. in Electrical Engineering from Roger Williams University (Bristol, RI).*

Before joining Hewlett-Packard Marty was the manager of a design group at startup Canaan Computer Corporation. His first position was as an Electrical Design Engineer on military computer systems at United Technologies Corporation performing both integrated circuit and board-level design.

Phil Anderson

Phil assisted with many facets of publishing this book including lining up expert Linux on Integrity reviewers. This book would not have been published without Phil's involvement.

Phil has been with HP since 2001. Prior to HP, Phil's career spanned from software development to product management at AT&T Bell Laboratories, Citigroup, and an internet startup company. Since joining HP, Phil has focused on business planning and product marketing of Linux on Integrity (Itanium-based) servers. He is currently part of the worldwide marketing team for Linux on the HP Integrity server family.

Glen Foster

Glen reviewed every chapter of this book to ensure that all the Linux on Integrity server information is correct. Glen spent a tremendous amount of time reviewing this book, and it could not have been published if it weren't for his herculean effort.

Glen came back to HP just prior to the 2002 merger vote that eventually combined Hewlett-Packard and Compaq Computer Corp. into the industry-leading company it is today. Before his return to HP, Glen was most recently the Director of Quality Assurance for Red Hat, Inc., and prior to that, Director of Quality Assurance for Softway Systems, Inc. Glen is now the lead of the QA department of the Linux and Open Source Lab, concentrating on Integrity hardware and firmware and making Linux distributions a safer and more cost-effective offering for HP's customers.

Elizabeth Zinkann

Elizabeth reviewed all the chapters in this book.

Elizabeth is a Contributing Editor and Review Columnist for *Sys Admin Magazine, The Journal for UNIX System Administrators*. Her articles have also appeared in *Performance Computing, Linux Magazine*, and *Network Administrator*. As an independent computer consultant, she has built Linux servers, maintained computers utilizing Linux, Solaris, Macintosh, and Windows environments, and taught UNIX, shell programming, and Internet essentials. In a former life, she also programmed communications features for both domestic and international databases at AT&T Network Systems.

Steven M. Wolff

Steven supplied the valuable command summaries that appear in Chapter 1.

Steven came to HP as a result of HP's acquisition of Convex in 1995. At Convex, he was a customer engineer supporting European customers mainly in Athens, Greece. After joining HP, he worked in Worldwide Technical Expert Center (WTEC) HW supporting the V-Class and then in Event Management Labs (EML) labs authoring the Superdome Level 300 Hardware course. He is currently in the Mission Critical Solution Center Organization working for the Superdome Support Team supporting North American Superdome Customers. Steven is also a HPUX Certified System Administrator.

Bill Garcia

Bill Garcia was a user of Linux several years ago, well before the operating system was popular. Bill provided me with expert assistance when writing this book, as well as access to the Integrity servers in his lab.

Bill is a Member of HP Partner Technical Services Organization, assisting Independent Software Vendors (ISVs) certify their applications on Integrity servers. In this role, Bill manages a lab with many Integrity servers and works directly with ISVs. Bill has held numerous positions in his many years with Hewlett Packard.

Ranald Adams

Ranald is a long-time Linux user and one of the first technical experts in the field to run Linux on Integrity systems and helped with the development of this book.

Ranald is a Solution Architect at Hewlett-Packard in the Microsoft Partner Organization, where he concentrates on providing Microsoft-based solutions for HP customers, primarily on HP Integrity servers. Prior to his life at Hewlett-Packard, Ranald was a Designer, Engineer, and Senior IT Manager in the Music, Entertainment, New Media and DotCom industries where he worked both sides of the fence - creating content and implementing business infrastructure to support and deliver it - using most of the major OS and hardware platforms. Ranald has been using Linux, OpenBSD, and other Open Source solutions since 1993 to solve real-world problems in the environments for which he is responsible.

Brian Allen

Brian was one of the original HP Solution Architects in the field to work with Linux on Integrity servers and provided assistance in creating this book.

Brian joined HP directly from college in 1979 as a Customer Engineer supporting large business computer customers in the Northeast. Over the years, Brian had many roles at HP including an Area Technical Support Engineer, factory-based Software Support Engineer, and Senior Technical Consultant in HP's Professional Services Organization. This range of experience is one of Brian's greatest assets that customers continue to benefit from in his current roles as a Solution Architect for HP's Corporate Financial Accounts program.

Marty Paul

Marty Paul contributed to and reviewed several chapters in this book.

Marty is a Senior System Analyst in the Engineering and Deployment Services Group of Pitney Bowes in Danbury, CT. He has worked with nearly all HP hardware, including HP Superdome systems running hard and virtual partitions. He is now testing HP Integrity servers running Linux, Windows, and HP-UX. Marty has been in the IT industry for 20 years and has supported a number of systems, including six years as an HP-UX expert.

Reviewers and Contributors

In all, there were about 25 reviewers of this book. I'm not sure what makes someone agree to review a book. You don't get the glory of a contributing author, but it is just as much work. I would like to thank the many people who devoted a substantial amount of time to reviewing this book to ensure that I included topics important to new system administrators and covered those topics accurately. In particular, I would like to thank Bradley Chapple and Adam Schwartz of HP for their review and assistance with the EFI- related material. I also want to thank Steve Stichler and his team for contributing information on MC/ServiceGuard for Linux and for reviewing the MC/ServiceGuard portion of this book.

Chapter 1

Booting: EFI and Management Processor

This chapter covers booting an HP Integrity (Itanium-based) server. Booting an Integrity server requires that you become familiar with two levels of firmware. The first level is HP's implementation of Intel's EFI (Extensible Firmware Interface), *POSSE* (Pre-OS System Environment). The second is HP's independent support processor for the system console, the *Management Processor* (MP). Although functionality varies from one platform to another the topics in this chapter apply to all HP Integrity servers at the time of this writing. The systems used throughout this chapter include a variety of two and four-way Integrity servers.

This chapter covers the following topics:

• EFI and POSSE

• Management Processor (MP)

In addition to providing background on these topics, this chapter also provides many examples of running commands and analyzing output for both POSSE and MP.

At the end, you can use an excellent series of tables as a quick reference for many boot-related commands.

EFI and POSSE

EFI is an interface between your operating systems and platform firmware. POSSE is the HP implementation of EFI that contains additional commands beyond the ones available through EFI alone. You'll use the EFI acronym in this chapter, but you should be aware that some HP documentation may use POSSE. EFI is a component that is independent of the operating system and provides a shell for interfacing to multiple operating systems The interface consists of data tables that contain platform-related information along with boot and runtime service calls that are available to the operating system and its loader. These components work together to provide a standard environment for booting multiple operating systems.

If you are interested in finding out more about EFI than what's documented here, take a look at Intel EFI Web site. At the time of this writing, EFI information can be found at *http://www.intel.com/technology/efi.*

As you can see in Figure 1-1, EFI on HP Integrity servers contains several layers. The hardware layer contains disk with an EFI partition, which in turn has in it an operating system loader. This layer also contains one or more operating system partitions.

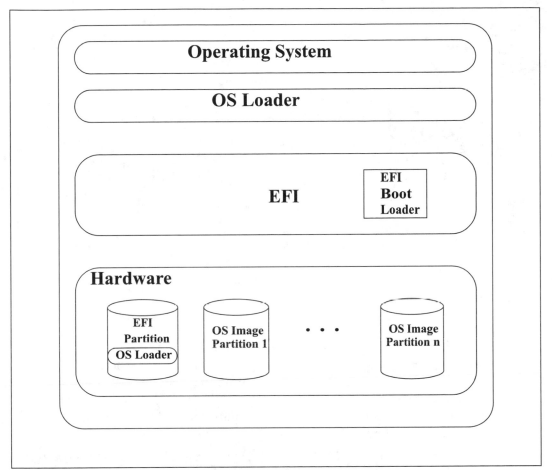

Figure 1-1   EFI on HP Integrity Servers

In addition, the EFI system partition itself consists of several different components as shown in Figure 1-2.

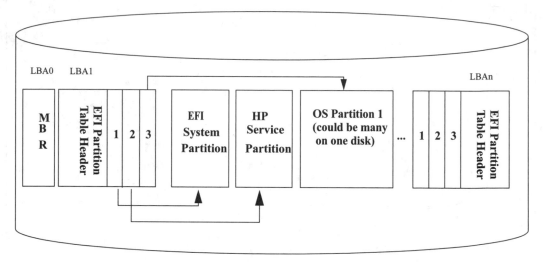

Figure 1-2   EFI System Partition

The Logical Block Addresses (LBAs) are shown across the top of the diagram. The Master Boot Record (MBR) is the first LBA. There is then a partition table. Three partitions are shown on this disk. Note that multiple operating system partitions can be loaded on the same disk. At the time of this writing, Windows Server 2003 and Linux can be loaded on the same disk. The EFI partition table on the right is a backup partition table.

Booting an operating system with EFI on an Integrity servers involves several steps. Figure 1-3 depicts the high-level steps.

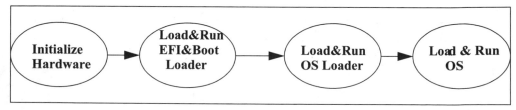

Figure 1-3   Load and Run an Operating System

The first step is to initialize the hardware. This takes place at the lowest level (BIOS) before EFI or the operating systems play any part in the process. Next, the EFI and boot loader are loaded and run. After an operating system is chosen, the operating system loader is loaded and run for the specific operating system being booted. Finally, the operating system itself is loaded and run. There are no specific operating systems cited in Figure 1-3 because the process is the same regardless of the operating system being loaded. In the examples in this book, Linux, HP-UX, and Windows are used and all these operating systems would load in the same manner.

Working with EFI

Traversing the EFI menu structure and issuing commands is straight forward. You make your desired selections and then traverse a menu hierarchy. To start EFI, when the system self test is complete, hit any key to break the normal boot process. The main EFI screen appears. Figure 1-4 shows the EFI Boot Administration main screen from which you can make various boot-related selections.

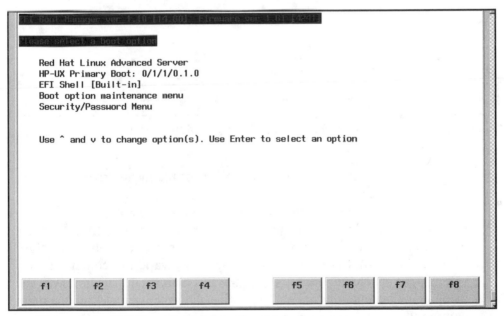

Figure 1-4   EFI Boot Administration Main Screen

Figure 1-4 shows that there are two operating systems installed on this Integrity server - an *HP-UX Primary Boot* and a *Red Hat Linux Advanced Server*. Either of these can be booted. From the main screen, you can also choose either *EFI Shell [Built-in], Boot option maintenance menu,* or *Security/Password menu.* The first item shown in the EFI main screen is the default. Use the arrow keys to scroll and highlight a selection. After the item you need is highlighted, press *Enter* to select it. For example, if you were to select *Boot option maintenance menu,* you would see a screen resembling the one shown in Figure 1-5.

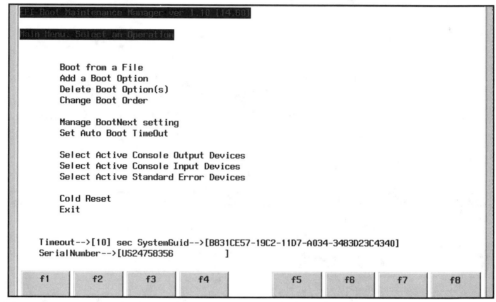

Figure 1-5   EFI Boot Maintenance Manager Main Menu

Figures 1-4 and 1-5 give you a feeling for the menu-driven nature of EFI and EFI selections.

One of the important things a system administrator might need to know is a given system's device mappings. To view mappings using EFI, you need to get to a console-like EFI *Shell>* prompt. To do so, you must select *EFI Shell* in Figure 1-4. Once at the prompt, there are a variety of commands that you can run - including **map**. **map** is the EFI command that shows device mapping on the Integrity server. This listing shows the output from the **map command**:

```
Shell> map
fs0 : Acpi(HWP0002,100)/Pci(1|0)/Scsi(Pun0,Lun0)/HD(Part1,Sig8E89981A-0B97-11D7-9C4C
                                                                    - AF87605217DA)
fs1 : Acpi(HWP0002,100)/Pci(1|0)/Scsi(Pun1,Lun0)/HD(Part1,Sig7C0F0000)
blk0: Acpi(HWP0002,0)/Pci(2|0)/Ata(Primary,Master)
blk1: Acpi(HWP0002,100)/Pci(1|0)/Scsi(Pun0,Lun0)
blk2: Acpi(HWP0002,100)/Pci(1|0)/Scsi(Pun0,Lun0)/HD(Part1,Sig8E89981A-0B97-11D7-9C4C
                                                                    - AF87605217DA)
blk3 : Acpi(HWP0002,100)/Pci(1|0)/Scsi(Pun0,Lun0)/HD(Part2,SigC9D59DF0-0BA7-11D7-9B31
                                                                    - FBA1AECDAF7E)
blk4 : Acpi(HWP0002,100)/Pci(1|0)/Scsi(Pun0,Lun0)/HD(Part3,SigC9D7945C-0BA7-11D7-9B31
                                                                    - FBA1AECDAF7E)
blk5 : Acpi(HWP0002,100)/Pci(1|0)/Scsi(Pun1,Lun0)
blk6 : Acpi(HWP0002,100)/Pci(1|0)/Scsi(Pun1,Lun0)/HD(Part1,Sig7C0F0000)
blk7 : Acpi(HWP0002,100)/Pci(1|0)/Scsi(Pun1,Lun0)/HD(Part2,Sig7C0F0000)
```

The device mappings can be difficult to read. Much of the information is intended for programmers and technicians. As a system administrator, however, you need to know which entries correspond to which devices and which entries are for your partitions and file systems. To determine that, let's take a look at each entry.

As you probably guessed, file systems begin with *fs* and block devices begin with *blk* in this listing. To understand these entries however, let's look at them individually. To make their meaning clearer, I've grouped the entries differently than they originally appeared in the EFI listing previously shown.

Red Hat Advanced Server disk and related entries:
blk1 physical disk
blk2 is first partition on *blk1*
blk3 is second partition on *blk1*
blk4 is third partition on *blk1*
fs0 is first file system on *blk1*

HP-UX 11i disk and related entries:
blk5 physical disk
blk6 is first partition on *blk5*
blk7 is second partition on *blk5*
fs1 is first file system on *blk5*

Let's analyze one of the block (blk) entries:

```
blk1 : Acpi(HWP0002,100)/Pci(1|0)/Scsi(Pun0,Lun0)
```

blk is the label assigned to the physical drive and the *1* is the number of the physical drive (*blk* can also be a partition on a physical drive as we'll see shortly). *Acpi(HWP0002,100)* first shows a device type of *HWP0002* with a PCI host number of *100*. This PCI host number is often called the *ROPE*. The *ROPE* is the circuitry that handles I/O for the PCI interface. Although this information is most often used by programmers, it is sometimes handy to know the *ROPE* since it also defines the I/O card slot. The following types of devices are the most common:

HWP0001: Single I/O Controller Single Block Address w/o I/O Controller in the namespace.
HWP0002: Logical Block Address (LBA) device.
HWP0003: AGP LBA device.

After the *ROPE* we find a *Pci* entry. This entry indicates that the device/slot number is *1* and the function number is *0*.

The *Scsi Pun* (physical unit) will be either *0* or *1* depending on which is the SCSI address of the disk. The *Lun* (logical unit) will always be *0* in this case because you're not assigning any *Logical Units* on the disks. Now, let's look at the blk2 entry:

```
blk2 : Acpi(HWP0002,100)/Pci(1|0)/Scsi(Pun0,Lun0)/
HD(Part1,Sig8E89981A-0B97-11D7-9C4C-AF87605217DA)
```

The *blk2* entry is a partition on the *blk1* device. All of the information is the same for the two entries except for the additional partition-related information beginning with *Part1*. *Part1* indicates this is the first partition on physical device *blk1* with an EFI signature beginning with *Sig*. *blk3* and *blk4* are additional partitions that we created when we loaded Advanced Server on this disk and created three partitions. The first group ends with the *fs0* entry:

```
fs0 : Acpi(HWP0002,100)/Pci(1|0)/Scsi(Pun0,Lun0)/
HD(Part1,Sig8E89981A-0B97-11D7-9C4C-AF87605217DA)
```

Notice that the *fs0* line also matches *blk1* and *blk2* from a path perspective. This is a file system readable by EFI; hence, it begins with *fs*.

To summarize, what we see is a physical device *blk1* that has on it an EFI partition *blk2* and a file system *fs0*. All three of these are listed as separate entries in EFI. In addition, *blk3* and *blk4* are partitions on the same physical device *blk1*.

The same applies to physical unit 1, which is *Pun1*. This is *blk5*. It too has two partitions at *blk6* and *blk7*. *fs1* is the file system that is on disk. This is the HP-UX disk in our configuration:

```
blk0 : Acpi(HWP0002,0)/Pci(2|0)/Ata(Primary,Master)
```

The *blk0* device in the list is the DVD-ROM. The *Ata* (Advanced Technology Attachment) is the official name that *American National Standards*

Institute group X3T10 uses for what the computer industry calls *Integrated Drive Electronics* (IDE) - in this case, a DVD-ROM.

Table 1-1 summarizes the fields that we analyzed for all the entries. Keep in mind that some of this information, such as the *Acpi* data, is most often necessary to help analyze the system in the event of a problem.

Table 1-1   Description of EFI Device Mappings Field

Item	Description
blkn	Physical drive or a partition on a physical drive. A physical drive can be a hard disk drive or a removable media drive. A *Partn* in parenthesis is shown in the examples when there is a partition on a disk drive.
Acpi(Device,X)	The device type is the first entry in the parenthesis. The second entry, *X*, is the PCI host number. *Acpi* is Advance Configuration and Power Interface.
Pci(D|F)	This indicates PCI-related information. *D* is the PCI device/slot number and *F* is the PCI function number.
Scsi(Pun.Lun)	The physical characteristic of the disk which is SCSI. The *Pun* is the SCSI number and the *Lun* is the LUN number on the physical device.
HD(Part,Sig)	The partition *Part* and EFI Signature *Sig* on the partition.

Keep in mind that the file system numbers may change when you remap devices or when components are added or removed, such as a DVD device.

There are many more EFI commands that you may want to use in addition to **map**. Table 1-2 summarizes many of the most used EFI commands. We'll take a look at some of them in the next section.

Table 1-2   Commonly Used EFI Commands

EFI Command[a]	Description
Commands Found in All Menus	
map	Produce a device map list (**map -r** rescans the bus)
info boot	Boot from specified Path

EFI Command[a]	Description
help *command*	Display help for specified command or menu (**help bch** is handy)
reset	Reset the system (to allow reconfiguration of complex)
exit (at the EFI shell)	Return to the Main Menu
Commands Found on the MAin Menu	
EFI Boot Manager "Change Boot Order"	Display or modify a path (In "Boot option maintenance menu" and then "Change Boot Order," select the desired boot path and use "u" or "d" to move up or down.)
bcfg	search for boot devices
more, plus many commands offer a [-b] parameter to cause 25 line breaks	Display or change scrolling capability
Commands Found on the COnfiguration Menu	
autoboot	Display or start the auto start flag
info boot	Display or set processor Boot Identifier
EFI Boot Manager	Display boot-related information
autoboot	Seconds allowed for boot attempt
cpuconfig	Config/Deconfig Processor
autoboot	Display or set boot tests execution
time	Read or set the real time clock
Commands Found on the Information Menu	
info all	Display all system information
info boot	Display boot-related information
info cache	Display cache information
info chiprev	Display revision number of major VLSI
MP command <df>	Display FRU information
info fw	Display firmware version for PDC, ICM, and Complex
info io	Display firmware version for PDC, ICM, and Complex

EFI Command[a]	Description
info mem	Display memory information
info cpu	Display processor information
SERvice	Service-related commands
errdump clear	Clear (zero) the contents of PIM
mm	Read memory locations scope of page deallocations
PDT	Display or clear the Page Deallocation (Processor Internal Memory)
errdump mca	Display PIM information (Processor Internal Memory)
more [-b]	Display or change scrolling capability

[a] An interesting aspect of the EFI commands is that you can accomplish many of the same functions running BCH commands on PA-RISC systems. To those of you who have PA-RISC system experience, you'll see many of the same functions performed in EFI.

Using EFI, you can control the boot-related setup on your Integrity server. Because of the number of operating systems you can run on Integrity servers, you'll use this interface often to coordinate and manage them.

EFI Command Examples

As previously mentioned, traversing the EFI menu structure and issuing commands is straightforward. When the system boots, you are given the option to interrupt the autoboot. (If you don't interrupt it, the autoboot will load the first operating system listed which, in our case, is *Red Hat Advanced Server.*) At system startup, the EFI Boot Manager presents the boot option menu (as shown in the following output). Here, you have five seconds to enter a selection before *Red Hat Linux Advanced Server* is started:

```
EFI Boot Manager ver 1.10 [14.60] Firmware ver 1.61 [4241]

Please select a boot option

    Red Hat Linux Advanced Server
    HP-UX Primary Boot: 0/1/1/0.1.0
    EFI Shell [Built-in]
```

```
Boot option maintenance menu
Security/Password Menu


Use ^ and v to change option(s). Use Enter to select an option
Default boot selection will be booted in 5 seconds
```

You can use the arrow, or the *u* and *d* keys, to move up and down respectively. We used the ‡ key (down arrow) to select *EFI Shell [Built-in]*. This brought us to the *Shell>* prompt. From there, we can issue EFI commands. Similarly, once your at the *Shell>* prompt, help is always available. To get a listing of the classes of commands available in *Shell>*, simply enter **help** and press Enter:

```
Shell> help
List of classes of commands:

boot           -- Booting options and disk-related commands
configuration  -- Changing and retrieving system information
device         -- Getting device, driver and handle information
memory         -- Memory related commands
shell          -- Basic shell navigation and customization
scripts        -- EFI shell-script commands

Use 'help <class>' for a list of commands in that class
Use 'help <command>' for full documentation of a command
Use 'help -a' to display list of all commands
```

When using Linux from a network connection from another system you may have to use the ^ and *v* to move up and down the menu structure respectively.

You can also issue *help* requests for any EFI commands at any level. For example, if you want to know more about your current cpu configuration, you would start with **help configuration** to determine the help command for cpu configuration, and then **help cpuconfig**:

```
Shell> help configuration
Configuration commands:

cpuconfig  -- Deconfigure or reconfigure cpus
date       -- Displays the current date or sets the date in the system
err        -- Displays or changes the error level
esiproc    -- Make an ESI call
errdump    -- View/Clear logs
info       -- Display hardware information
monarch    -- View or set the monarch processor
palproc    -- Make a PAL call.
salproc    -- Make a SAL call
time       -- Displays the current time or sets the time of the system
ver        -- Displays the version information

Use 'help <command>' for full documentation of a command
Use 'help -a' to display list of all commands

Shell> help cpuconfig
cpu    Specifies which cpu to configure

CPUCONFIG [cpu] [on|off]
```

```
on|off Specifies to configure or deconfigure a cpu

Note:
    1. Cpu status will not change until next boot.
    2. Specifying a cpu number without a state will display
       configuration status.

Examples:
  ^ To deconfigure CPU 0
    fs0:\> cpuconfig 0 off
    Cpu will be deconfigured on the next boot.

  * To display configuration status of cpus
    fs0:\> cpuconfig
    PROCESSOR INFORMATION

                        Proc              Arch   Processor
      CPU     Speed     Rev   Model Family Rev    State
      ---  ----------   ----  ----- ------ ----  -------------
        0    560 MHz     B1     0     31     0   Sched Deconf
        1    560 MHz     B1     0     31     0         Active
Shell>
```

As a result of having issued this *help cpuconfig,* we now know how to manipulate the CPUs in our system. The following output shows what happens when you issue the *cpuconfig* command with a few options:

```
Shell> cpuconfig

PROCESSOR INFORMATION

                    Proc              Arch   Processor
  CPU     Speed     Rev   Model Family Rev    State
  ---  ----------   ----  ----- ------ ----  -------------
    0   1000 MHz     B3     0     31     0         Active
    1   1000 MHz     B3     0     31     0         Active


Shell> cpuconfig 1 off

CPU will be deconfigured on next boot.


Shell> cpuconfig

PROCESSOR INFORMATION

                    Proc              Arch   Processor
  CPU     Speed     Rev   Model Family Rev    State
  ---  ----------   ----  ----- ------ ----  -------------
    0   1000 MHz     B3     0     31     0         Active
    1   1000 MHz     B3     0     31     0   Sched Deconf


Shell> cpuconfig 1 on

CPU will be configured on next boot.


Shell> cpuconfig

PROCESSOR INFORMATION

                    Proc              Arch   Processor
  CPU     Speed     Rev   Model Family Rev    State
  ---  ----------   ----  ----- ------ ----  -------------
    0   1000 MHz     B3     0     31     0         Active
    1   1000 MHz     B3     0     31     0         Active


Shell>
```

You used **cpuconfig** to view the current CPU configuration showing that both processors are *Active*. Then you turned *off* processor *1* (**cpuconfig 1 off**). You then viewed the CPU configuration again to confirm that processor *1* had been turned off as indicated by the *Sched Deconf* (**cpuconfig**). After that, we turned processor *1 on* again (**cpuconfig 1 on**). Finally, we confirmed that both processors are again *Active* (**cpuconfig**).

As you can see, a lot of useful configuration information about your system is available using EFI. In addition to **cpuconfig**, you can also use **info** to get important system information. The following listing first shows the results of the **info** command. **info**, with no argument, lists all the differing information options available (such as **all, boot, cache,** and so on). After you see all the **info** options, you use **info all** to get a complete rundown on your system:

```
Shell> info

Usage: INFO [-b] [target]

target : all, boot, cache, chiprev, cpu,
         fw, io, mem, sys, warning


Shell> info all

SYSTEM INFORMATION

    Product Name: server rx2600
    Serial Number: US24758356
    UUID: B831CE57-19C2-11D7-A034-3483D23C4340

PROCESSOR INFORMATION

                     Proc            Arch  Processor
    CPU    Speed     Rev   Model  Family Rev   State
    ---  ----------  ----  -----  ------ ----  -------------
     0   1000 MHz    B3      0      31    0      Active
     1   1000 MHz    B3      0      31    0      Active


CACHE INFORMATON

           Instruction  Data         Unified
    CPU        L1         L1       L2         L3
    ---    ---------  ---------  ---------  ---------
     0       16 KB      16 KB     256 KB     3072 KB
     1       16 KB      16 KB     256 KB     3072 KB


MEMORY INFORMATION

           ---- DIMM A -----  ---- DIMM B -----
           DIMM   Current     DIMM   Current
    ---    ------ ----------  ------ ----------
     0     256MB    Active    256MB    Active
     1     256MB    Active    256MB    Active
     2     256MB    Active    256MB    Active
     3     256MB    Active    256MB    Active
     4     ----               ----
     5     ----               ----
```

```
        Active Memory     : 2048 MB
        Installed Memory  : 2048 MB


I/O INFORMATION

BOOTABLE DEVICES

   Order  Media Type  Path
   -----  ----------  ----------------------------------------
     1    HARDDRIVE   Acpi(HWP0002,100)/Pci(1|0)/Scsi(Pun0,Lun0)/
          HD(Part1,Sig8E89981A-0B97-11D7-9C4C-AF87605217DA)
     2    HARDDRIVE   Acpi(HWP0002,100)/Pci(1|0)/Scsi(Pun1,Lun0)/HD(Part1,Sig7C0F0000)




   Seg  Bus  Dev  Fnc  Vendor  Device  Slot
   #    #    #    #      ID      ID      #    Path
   ---  ---  ---  ---  ------  ------   ---   -----------
   00   00   01   00   0x1033  0x0035   XX    Acpi(HWP0002,0)/Pci(1|0)
   00   00   01   01   0x1033  0x0035   XX    Acpi(HWP0002,0)/Pci(1|1)
   00   00   01   02   0x1033  0x00E0   XX    Acpi(HWP0002,0)/Pci(1|2)
   00   00   02   00   0x1095  0x0649   XX    Acpi(HWP0002,0)/Pci(2|0)
   00   00   03   00   0x8086  0x1229   XX    Acpi(HWP0002,0)/Pci(3|0)
   00   20   01   00   0x1000  0x0030   XX    Acpi(HWP0002,100)/Pci(1|0)
   00   20   01   01   0x1000  0x0030   XX    Acpi(HWP0002,100)/Pci(1|1)
   00   20   02   00   0x14E4  0x1645   XX    Acpi(HWP0002,100)/Pci(2|0)
   00   40   01   00   0x1011  0x0019   03    Acpi(HWP0002,200)/Pci(1|0)
   00   80   01   00   0x1011  0x0019   01    Acpi(HWP0002,400)/Pci(1|0)
   00   E0   01   00   0x103C  0x1290   XX    Acpi(HWP0002,700)/Pci(1|0)
   00   E0   01   01   0x103C  0x1048   XX    Acpi(HWP0002,700)/Pci(1|1)
   00   E0   02   00   0x1002  0x5159   XX    Acpi(HWP0002,700)/Pci(2|0)



BOOT INFORMATION

   Monarch CPU:

   Current  Preferred
   Monarch  Monarch   Possible Warnings
   -------  ---------  -----------------
      0         0

   AutoBoot: ON - Timeout is : 10 sec

   Boottest:

   BOOTTEST Settings Default Variable

   OS is not speedy boot aware.

   Selftest    Setting
   ---------   --------------
   early_cpu   Skip this test
   late_cpu    Skip this test
   platform    Skip this test
   chipset     Skip this test
   io_hw       Skip this test
   mem_init    Skip this test
   mem_test    Skip this test

   LAN Address Information:

   LAN Address        Path
   -----------------  ----------------------------------------
   Mac(00306E39B724)  Acpi(HWP0002,0)/Pci(3|0)/Mac(00306E39B724))
  *Mac(00306E3927B0)  Acpi(HWP0002,100)/Pci(2|0)/Mac(00306E3927B0))



FIRMWARE INFORMATION
```

```
         Firmware Revision: 1.61 [4241]

         PAL A Revision: 7.31
         PAL B Revision: 7.36

         SAL Spec Revision: 0.20
         SAL A Revision: 2.00
         SAL B Revision: 1.60

         EFI Spec Revision: 1.10
         EFI Intel Drop Revision: 14.60
         EFI Build Revision: 1.22

         POSSE Revision: 0.10

         ACPI Revision: 7.00

         BMC Revision 1.30
         IPMI Revision: 1.00
         SMBIOS Revision: 2.3.2a
         Management Processor Revision: E.02.07

     WARNING AND STOP BOOT INFORMATION

     CHIP REVISION INFORMATION

         Chip                    Logical    Device    Chip
         Type                       ID         ID     Revision
         --------------------    -------    ------    --------
         Memory Controller          0        122b      0022
         Root Bridge                0        1229      0022
            Host Bridge           0000        122e      0032
            Host Bridge           0001        122e      0032
            Host Bridge           0002        122e      0032
            Host Bridge           0003        122e      0032
            Host Bridge           0004        122e      0032
            Host Bridge           0006        122e      0032
            Host Bridge           0007        122e      0032
            Other Bridge             0          0       0002
               Other Bridge          0          0       0007
                  Baseboard MC       0          0       0130

     Shell>
```

As you can see, **info all** produces a great overview of the system configuration. Note that two bootable devices are listed in the order in which they appear in the main EFI screen (see the "EFI Boot Administration Main Screen" on page 5).

In addition to selecting the *EFI Shell,* which we have been doing in our examples to this point, we also have other options. Selecting *Boot option maintenance menu* produces the selections shown here:

```
EFI Boot Maintenance Manager ver 1.10 [14.60]

Manage BootNext setting.  Select an Operation

    Red Hat Linux Advanced Server
    HP-UX Primary Boot: 0/1/1/0.1.0
    EFI Shell [Built-in]
    Reset BootNext Setting
    Save Settings to NVRAM
    Help
    Exit
```

You have some of the same selections that you had at the main menu level, including the two installed operating systems and the EFI shell, but you also have some new selections. If you were to select *Reset BootNext Setting,* the following selections would be produced:

```
EFI Boot Maintenance Manager ver 1.10 [14.60]

Main Menu. Select an Operation


        Boot from a File
        Add a Boot Option
        Delete Boot Option(s)
        Change Boot Order

        Manage BootNext setting
        Set Auto Boot TimeOut

        Select Active Console Output Devices
        Select Active Console Input Devices
        Select Active Standard Error Devices

        Cold Reset
             Exit
```

At this point, you could perform a variety of functions. On your system, for instance, we could use *Change Boot Order* to make the HP-UX partition the default boot selection instead of the Linux Advanced Server.

Although you are going to perform a console-only installation of Red Hat Advanced Server in Chapter 2, the rx2600 we're working on does indeed have a built-in VGA port and graphics display attached. If you wanted to enable the graphics display, we would select *Select Active Console Output Devices* from the menu above.

The *Select the Console Output Device(s)* menu appears listing all possible console devices. The first device with an * is the serial port that was selected by default. To enable the graphics as well, you must select the last console device. You know that this is the graphics device port because it does not contain *Uart* as part of the selection. Note that *Uart* devices are always serial devices. Also note that in the following example, the graphical device port is already selected (indicated by an * in front of it). We then select *Save Settings to NVRAM,* which saves the console device settings, and then exit:

```
EFI Boot Maintenance Manager ver 1.10 [14.60]

Select the Console Output Device(s)


    Acpi(PNP0501,0)/Uart(9600 N81)/VenMsg(PcAnsi)
    Acpi(PNP0501,0)/Uart(9600 N81)/VenMsg(Vt100)
    Acpi(PNP0501,0)/Uart(9600 N81)/VenMsg(Vt100+)
    Acpi(PNP0501,0)/Uart(9600 N81)/VenMsg(VtUtf8)
    Acpi(HWP0002,700)/Pci(1|1)/Uart(9600 N81)/VenMsg(PcAnsi)
    Acpi(HWP0002,700)/Pci(1|1)/Uart(9600 N81)/VenMsg(Vt100)
  * Acpi(HWP0002,700)/Pci(1|1)/Uart(9600 N81)/VenMsg(Vt100+)
```

```
    Acpi(HWP0002,700)/Pci(1|1)/Uart(9600 N81)/VenMsg(VtUtf8)
  * Acpi(HWP0002,700)/Pci(2|0)
  Save Settings to NVRAM
  Exit
```

This setting enables both the serial and graphics consoles. The early boot messages will go to the serial console. After the graphics server is started, the Advanced Server-related boot messages will display graphically. After the installation is complete, this would be true during the load of Advanced Server as well. The early selections would take place on the console and then the majority of the load selections would display graphically.

The first four entries with *PNP0501* in them are on the nine pin serial port. The next four entries with *HWP0002* in them are on the three cable device that fits into the 25 pin connector. Be sure to enable a serial console on only one of the two devices since the Linux kernel expects only one serial console to be enabled.

As you have seen, EFI is a useful and relatively easy to use tool. Of course, no one expects you to remember all you have seen here. If you need help, refer to "Commonly Used EFI Commands" on page 9 in Table 1-2. You can also type **help** at the *Shell>* prompt, or take a look at the tables summarizing EFI at the end of this chapter. Between them all, you'll be able to perform many useful functions using the EFI interface.

Configuring the Management Processor (MP)

There is a built-in processor on most HP systems, including Integrity servers, that can be used for either local or remote system administration functions called the Management Processor (MP). Occasionally, you may hear it referred to as the Service Processor (SP) or Guardian Service Processor (GSP), but MP is by far the most commonly used name. MP functionality gets enhanced on a regular basis so what you'll see in the upcoming examples may not be the same as the MP functionality you see on your system. Still, it should be very close. This section provides a quick overview of MP, including listing the overview supplied with the tool. Note that initial MP configuration is important because the first person to gain access to MP before it has been configured is a MP administrator by default.

You gain access to the MP with **^b** (ctrl b). If MP has not been configured, anyone who gets access to the console can type **^b** and gain access to the system. Because of this, perform MP configuration as soon as possible after installing your system.

After you issue **^b**, you see the *MP>* prompt. The following listing shows the output from the **he ov** (help overview) command:

```
------------------------------------------------------------------------

Service Processor login:
Service Processor password:



                     Hewlett-Packard Management Processor

    (c) Copyright Hewlett-Packard Company 1999-2002.  All Rights Reserved.

                        System Name: uninitialized



    **************************************************************************
                       MP ACCESS IS NOT SECURE
       No MP users are currently configured and remote access is enabled.
                   Set up a user with a password (see SO command)
                                     OR
           Disable all types of remote access (see EL and ER commands)
    **************************************************************************


    MP Host Name:  uninitialized
    MP> he

           Hardware Revision a1  Firmware Revision E.02.07 Aug  8 2002,23:00:38

                           MP Help System

        Enter a command at the help prompt:
                OVerview   : Launch the help overview
                LIst       : Show the list of MP commands
                <COMMAND>  : Enter the command name for help on individual command
                TOPics     : Show all MP Help topics and commands
                HElp       : Display this screen
                Q          : Quit help
    ====
    MP HELP: ov
    ov


    ==== MP Help Overview ===================================================

    The Management Processor (MP) is an independent support processor for
    the system console.  MP provides services that facilatate the management of
    the host system.  Its major features are:

      * Always-on capability: The MP is alive as long as the power cord is
        plugged in.
      * User/password access control:  Supports operator and administrator users
      * Multiple access methods:
        Local Port       - use terminal or laptop computer for direct connect
        Remote/modem Port - use dedicated modem RS-232 port and external modem
        LAN              - use telnet or web to access MP LAN
      * Mirrored console: the system console output stream is reflected to all
        of the connected console users, and any user can provide input.
      * Display and/or logging of:
        The system console, System event logs (chassis codes), Virtual
        Front Panel (VFP), and system power and configuration status
```

```
     * An independent, non-mirrored session:
       Available from local and modem ports for MP connection (CSP) or OS
       login (SE).
     * Power control, system reset, and TOC capabilities.

   MORE Help (Q to go back to main, <CR> for more):



   ==== MP Help =======================================================

                         HELP TOPICS

   The following topics can be entered for general information:

     * ADMINistrator          LIst of commands        PASSword resetting
     * CHASsis codes        * MODEM                  * PORT summary
     * COMmand summary      * MODES of the MP        * SESsion
     * CONSole              * OVERview               * TOPics
     * HPterm and VT100
                        (* topics which are included in the OVERview)

   The following commands can be entered for help on the command:

   AC  AR  CA  CL  CO  CSP DC  DF  DI  EL  ER  EX  HE  IT  LC  LS  MR
   MS  PC  PG  PS  RS  SDM SE  SL  SO  SR  SS  TC  TE  VFP WHO XD  XU

   MORE Help (Q to go back to main, <CR> for more):



   ==== MP Help Overview ==============================================
                          MP MODES

   THE MIRRORED MP SESSION:
     When first logging on, the user is part of the mirrored MP session.  The
     mirrored MP session has three modes:
       1) MP Command Mode   2) Console Mode      3) VFP or Alert Mode

     1.  You are in the MP Command Mode right now.  In this mode all the MP
         commands can be executed.  Typically this mode is entered by typing
         CTRL-B from console mode.
     2.  In Console Mode the user gets access to the Unix console.  This mode is
         entered from the MP Command Mode using the CO command.
     3.  In the VFP or Alert Mode the MP displays a representation of the front
         pannel leds, called the Virtual Front Panel (VFP).  This mode is entered
         from MP Command Mode using the VFP command.
     See the help on those commands for more information.

   LEAVING MIRRORED MP SESSION:
     From the local or remote/modem ports, it is also possible to leave the
     mirrored MP session and connect to either the OS (see the "SE" command)
     or to another MP on the network (see the "CSP" command).

   MORE Help (Q to go back to main, <CR> for more):



   ==== MP Help Overview ==============================================

                         MP COMMAND HELP

   The MP commands can be grouped into the following categories:
     * STATUS COMMANDS- Provide status on the server and the MP.
           CL, DF, LS, MS, PS, SL, SR, SS, VFP

     * SERVER CONTROL- Alter the state of the server
           MR, PC, RB, RS, TC

     * GENERAL MP CONFIGURATION
           AC, BP, CG, DC, IT, LOC, PR, SDM, SO, XD, XU

     * MP PORT CONFIGURATION- Configure LAN/WEB, remote/modem, and local ports
           CA, EL, ER, LC, PG
```

```
         * CONNECTIONS- Examine and make connections or change mode
                   CO, CSP, DI, EX, SE, TE, VFP, WHO
      MORE Help (Q to go back to main, <CR> for more):



      ==== MP Help Overview ======================================================
                          OPERATOR / ADMINISTRATOR HELP

      Administrators have more capabilities than Operators:
        Administrator-Only Commands:
        AR (Automatic system Restart), DC (Default Configuration), IT (Inactivity
        Timeout), LC (LAN Configuration), PG (PaGing), SO (Security Options)

      The MP Command interface permission/access level:
        The MP Command interface permission/access level is set by the first
        user that types CTRL-B to initiate it.  If that user is an operator-
        user, then the command interface runs at operator access level.  Even if an
        administrator-user logs in later or the operator-user disconnects, the
        access level stays the same.  The access level can be changed by leaving MP
        command mode and and typing CTRL-B again to return.

      MORE Help (Q to go back to main, <CR> for more):



      ==== MP Help Overview ======================================================
                              CONSOLE MODE HELP

      Typing "CO" from the MP Command interface provides a mirrored version of
      the OS console.  All mirrored users see the same output.  At any time, only
      one of the mirrored users has write access to the console.  To get write
      access to the console, type CTRL-e c f (not CTRL-e CTRL-c CTRL-f).

      SEE ALSO:  CO  (COnsole)


      MORE Help (Q to go back to main, <CR> for more):



      ==== MP Help Overview ======================================================
                              SESSION MODE HELP

      Typing "SE" from the MP Command interface provides a non-mirrored,
      normal OS login.  The session is not the console; it is a separate login to
      the OS, and the messages that the OS sends to the console will not be
      seen.

      RECOMMENDATION:

      Use the session for ASCII screen-oriented applications (SAM) or file
      transfer programs (ftp) from the local or modem ports.  To use these
      applications from the LAN, telnet directly to the system for a private
      login.

      SEE ALSO:  SE (SEssion)

      MORE Help (Q to go back to main, <CR> for more):



      ==== MP Help Overview ======================================================
                              CHASSIS CODES

      Chassis codes are encoded data that provide system information to the user.
      Some well-known names for similar data would be Event Logs or Post Codes.
      Chassis codes are produced by intelligent hardware modules, the O/S, and
      system firmware.  Use VFP to view the live chassis codes.  Use SL to view
      the chassis code log.

      The following severity (or alert) levels are defined:
```

```
0) Minor Forward Progress      4) Reserved
1) Major Forward Progress      5) Critical
2) Informational               6) Reserved
3) Warning                     7) Fatal
```

SEE ALSO: SL, VFP (Show Logs, Virtual Front Panel)

MORE Help (Q to go back to main, <CR> for more):

==== MP Help Overview ==

                              PORTS HELP

The local, remote/modem, and LAN ports are actual connections on the back of
the server. All ports can be used even when the server is non-functional.

   * Local port   : Provides serial port terminal access. To configure,
                        see the CA (Configure Asynchronous) command.
   * Remote/Modem port: Provides external modem access. Related commands
                        are ER, MS, and MR (Enable Remote/modem, Modem
                        Status, Modem Reset)
   * LAN port   : Provides telnet and web access into the MP. Related
                        commands are EL, LC, and LS (Enable LAN, LAN
                        Configuration, and LAN Status).

MORE Help (Q to go back to main, <CR> for more):

==== MP Help Overview ==

                         REMOTE/MODEM PORT HELP

The remote/modem port can be used for dial-in access to the MP or the OS,
and can be configured so that the OS or the MP can activate a pager.

The remote/modem port is configured via the CA command. The ER command
enables/disables the port and gives the modem control over to the MP or
the OS. See the help on those commands for more details.

SEE ALSO: CA, ER, DI, MR, MS, PG (Configure Asynchronous, Enable Remote,
          DIsconnect remote or LAN, Modem Reset, Modem Status, PaGing)

MORE Help (Q to go back to main, <CR> for more):

==== MP Help Overview ==
                           INTERNAL PORT HELP

The Internal Port has been obsoleted.
MORE Help (Q to go back to main, <CR> for more):

==== MP Help Overview ==

                         HPTERM & VT100 HELP

RECOMMENDATION: Do not mix HP and vt100 terminal types at the same time.

The MP mirrors the system console to the MP local, remote/modem, and
LAN ports. One console output stream is reflected to all of the connected
console users. If several different terminal types are used simultaneously
by the users, some users may see strange results.

HP-UX example:
Applications which care about the terminal type (install, SAM, vi, etc.)
running on HP-UX use three methods to determine the terminal type:
   1) The application takes the terminal information from the OS. This
      value is set in the CA command and takes effect for all MP ports.
   2) The $TERM shell environment variable

```
   3) The application directly queries the terminal (in this case, the
      write enabled terminal will establish the terminal type.)
Make sure that settings #1 and #2 agree with your terminal type.

====
(HE for main help, enter command name, or Q to quit)
MP HELP:

==== MP Help ==========================================(Administrator)---
      Hardware Revision a1  Firmware Revision E.02.07 Aug  8 2002,23:00:38

                          MP Help System

     Enter a command at the help prompt:
            OVerview  : Launch the help overview
            LIst      : Show the list of MP commands
            <COMMAND> : Enter the command name for help on individual command
            TOPics    : Show all MP Help topics and commands
            HElp      : Display this screen
            Q         : Quit help
====
MP HELP:
```

It is important to note that neither a login name or password were required to log in after the **^b** was issued. This is because at startup, no MP users have yet been configured. At this point, any user can get access to this menu by typing **^b** at the system console. Newer versions of the MP require a login name and password.

The MP overview provides a wealth of information. Although this was a long output, I included it because it describes many MP commands and functions. As previously mentioned, at startup any user can get access to the MP menu. Because you don't want unauthorized users to have access to many of theses commands, the first step we'll take is to set up security options using the Security Options command, **SO**. **SO** begins by summarizing its parameters after which it asks you a series of security related questions. I have listed them here. In the example, I answered *y* when asked if I wanted to modify the parameters so that we could see each one individually. I answered *n* when asked if I wanted to modify each individual parameter. Your answers should reflect your own security preferences:

```
MP> SO

This command allow you to modify the security options and access control.

MP wide parameters are:
    . Login Timeout: 1  minutes.
    . Number of Password Faults allowed: 3
    . Flow Control Timeout: 5  minutes.
    . SSL for Web Access: Disabled
    . Contact Information:
        ->contact person :
```

```
            ->contact phone number :
            ->contact email address :
            ->contact pager number :
     . Location Information:
            ->server location :
            ->server rack ID :
            ->server position :
Do you want to modify the MP wide parameters? (Y/[N]) y


     Current Login Timeout: 1  minutes.
     Do you want to modify it? (Y/[N]) n


     Current Number of Password Faults allowed: 3
     Do you want to modify it? (Y/[N]) n


     Current Flow Control Timeout: 5  minutes.
     Do you want to modify it? (Y/[N]) n


     Current SSL for Web Access: Disabled
     Do you want to modify it? (Y/[N]) n


     Do you want to modify the contact information? (Y/[N]) n


     Do you want to modify the location information? (Y/[N]) n


User number 1 parameters are:
     . User's Name:
     . User's Login:
     . Organization's Name:
     . Dial-back configuration: Disabled
     . Access Level: Operator
     . Mode: Single
     . User's state: Disabled

Do you want to modify the user number 1 parameters? (Y/[N]/Q to quit) q



MP Host Name:  uninitialized
MP>
```

You can see that there are many *Security Options*. Because you have
unlimited access to the system through the console, you will want to review
these to ensure that they meet your requirements. You can add users and perform other security-related tasks.

In addition to configuring users and security, there are many useful features of MP. I encourage you to experiment with it. One command I often
use is **cl**. I use **cl** to display a console history, as shown in the following listing for the rx2600 system used throughout the examples in this chapter:

```
MP> cl

EFI Boot Maintenance Manager ver 1.10 [14.60]

Select the Console Output Device(s)


      Acpi(PNP0501,0)/Uart(9600 N81)/VenMsg(PcAnsi)
      Acpi(PNP0501,0)/Uart(9600 N81)/VenMsg(Vt100)
      Acpi(PNP0501,0)/Uart(9600 N81)/VenMsg(Vt100+)
      Acpi(PNP0501,0)/Uart(9600 N81)/VenMsg(VtUtf8)
      Acpi(HWP0002,700)/Pci(1|1)/Uart(9600 N81)/VenMsg(PcAnsi)
      Acpi(HWP0002,700)/Pci(1|1)/Uart(9600 N81)/VenMsg(Vt100)
    * Acpi(HWP0002,700)/Pci(1|1)/Uart(9600 N81)/VenMsg(Vt100+)
      Acpi(HWP0002,700)/Pci(1|1)/Uart(9600 N81)/VenMsg(VtUtf8)
    * Acpi(HWP0002,700)/Pci(2|0)
      Save Settings to NVRAM
      Exit




EFI Boot Maintenance Manager ver 1.10 [14.60]

Select the Console Output Device(s)

Press Q/q to quit, Enter to continue:
```

This listing shows the last console task we completed, which was to enable the graphics console (the second entry with an * in front of it), which you did at the end of the last section.

You can also use MP to obtain the status of power modules with **ps**, as shown in the following listing:

```
MP> ps

PS
System Power state: On              Power Switch     : On
Temperature        : Low OverTemp   Selected fan state: Normal

           Power supplies      |  Fan
   #  State            Type    |  States
   ---------------------------------------------------------
   0  Normal           Type 0  |  Normal
   1  Not Installed    -       |  Normal
   2  -                -       |  Normal
   3  -                -       |  Normal
   4  -                -       |  Normal
   5  -                -       |  Normal
   6  -                -       |  Normal
   7  -                -       |  Normal


MP Host Name:  uninitialized
MP>
```

This shows output that you have one power supply and that our many fans are operating *Normal*. The second power supply is not installed.

You can view processor status with **ss**, as shown in the following listing:

```
MP> ss        (This command will not run on Integrity
               Superdome in the future)

SS

System Processor Status:

   Monarch Processor: 0

   Processor 0 is : Installed and Configured
   Processor 1 is : Installed and Configured


MP Host Name:  uninitialized
MP>
```

This listing shows that there are two processors installed and the *Monarch Processor* is *0*. This is the main controlling processor from the perspective of the operating system. This processor is designated as *CPU 0*. The Low Priority Machine Check (LPMC) monitor will not deactivate or replace a failing monarch processor.

Although they weren't shown in any examples, you can power on or off the system using the *PC* command, for Power Control.

After you complete your MP-related work you can return to console mode from the MP prompt simply by issuing **co**, as shown in the following listing:

```
MP> co
```

Anytime that you are on the console, you can issue ^**b** and get access to MP and then get back to console mode using **co**.

Table 1-3 contains a list of high-level MP commands available on Integrity servers at the time of this writing. The commands in this table include **co** to select the console and **vfp** to select the virtual front panel. These are high-level commands and descriptions only. A more detailed list of commands is included in later tables. Keep in mind the MP commands for your Integrity system may be somewhat different from those listed.

Table 1-3 Management Processor Commands

Command (Function)	Explanation
AC	Alert display configuration
CA	Configure asynchronous and modem parameters
CL	View console log
CO	Return to console mode
CSP	Connect to remote management processor
DC	Default configuration
DI	Disconnect remote or LAN console
EL	Enable or Disable LAN or Web access
ER	Enable remote or LAN console access
EX	Exit MP and disconnect
HE	Display help for menu or command
IT	Set inactivity timeout settings
LC	Configure LAN connected and PPP console
LOC	Locator LED control
LS	LAN status
MR	Modem reset
MS	Display the status of the modem
PC	Remote power control
PG	Configure paging
PR	Power restore policy configuration
PS	Display the status of the power
RB	Reset BMC through the toggle CPIO pin
RS	Request BMC to reset system through RST signal
SE	Activate a system session on local or remote port
SL	Display status logs
SO	Configure security options and access control
SS	Display the status of the system processors
TC	Request BMC to reset with a TOC
TE	Send a message to other terminals
VFP	Virtual Front Panel (VFP)
WHO	Display a list of connected MP users

Command (Function)	Explanation
XD	Diagnostics and/or reset of MP
XU	Upgrade the MP firmware

The following three tables (1-4 through 1-6) provide more detail about the commands that are issued at the *MP:CM>* prompt for specific users. Tables 1-7 through 1-9 provide detailed information about additional boot topics such as Cell Local Memory (CLM) and the HPUX boot loader.

Table 1-4   MP:CM> Commands for Single PD User-Commands Unique to User *Serv*

Command	Expansion	Description

BO - Boot Protection Domain: Ensures that all the cells assigned to the target partition have valid complex profiles and then releases Boot-Is-Blocked (BIB).

CP - Cells Assigned by Partition: Displays a table of cells assigned to partitions and arranged by cabinets.

DE - Display Entity Status: Displays the specified entity's status:
C-CLU, D-CIO, M-MP, P-PM, S-PDHC.

RP8400/7410: B-BPS, U-CLU, A-CIO, G-MP, P-PM, H-PDHC.

DF - Display FRUID: Displays the FRUID data of the specified FRU: A-ALL, B-CPB, C-CIO, D-DIMM, G-UGUY, H-SBCH, I-IOB M-PRM, O-IOPB, P-BPB, R-L(R)SB, S-SBC, T-PDH, W-CB, X-BPS, U-CPU (cpu only available on legacy pa-risc).

RP8400/7410: S-BACKPLANE, G-MP/CIO, P-PCI BACKPLANE, M-MASS STORAGE BACKPLANE, I-PCI POWER MODULE, B- BPS, C-CELL, D-DIMM, H-PDHC, U-CPU.

DU - Display USB Topology: A "*" indicates communication with Gsp bus (usb - superdome) or (I2C -RP8400/7410). Cells must past IODISC for a "*" to appear in the MP *Core IOs* or *IO Chassis* field.

HE - Display Available Commands: Lists all commands available to the user level: Admin, Oper or Serv - if defined.

ID - Configure System ID data: Configures system ID info: model number&string, serial # (see MP>he id). Use MP>CM:CC commad first.

LS - LAN Status: Displays all parameters and the current status of connections of the MP LAN ports (cu lan = sbch, priv lan = sbc).

MA - Return to Main menu: Returns the user from the command menu (MP>CM:) to their main menu (MP>).

PS - Power Status: Displays hardware status: B-CABINET*, C-CELL, G-MP, I-CIO. *8400/7410:* T-CABINET*, S-SYS-TEM BACKPLANE, G-MP/CIO, P-IO CHASSIS, C-CELL (*cabinet option shows present, availble, and power status of all entities.

RR - Reset Partition for Reconfiguration: Resets the specified partition, but does not automatically boot it. Sets BIB flag.

RS - Reset Partition: Shut down the OS before issuing this command. Execution of this command halts all system processing and I/O activity and restarts the partition. (Similar to a power cycle - a hard reset).

TC - Partition Reset through INIT or TOC: Same effect as MP>CM:RS command but the processors are signaled to dump state on way down. (Replaces legacy TOC button.)

SYSREV - System Revisions: Displays revisions of all firmware entities in the complex. devices. RP8400/74xx requires Admin access.

MP> SL (Show Event Logs): Displays event logs.

FPL - Forward progress log: Was activity log. Alerts 0 and up.

SEL - System event log: Was error log. Alerts 2 and up.

Note: (d)ump option is new. It cancels pager function and dumps from the current location to the end of the log. Use script or other logging command before using this.

 LIVE (U, K then P) Useful to determine partition heartbeat/status

TE - Broadcast a Message to all Users at GSP(MP):CM> Up to 80 characters can be typed in and the message is broadcast to the other users in the command menu. Users in the main menu are not shown the message.

WHO - Display GSP Connected Users: Displays the login name of the connected console client user and the port on which they are connected. For LAN console clients the remote IP address is displayed.

MR - Modem Reset: Sends an AT Z to the system modem connected to the remote port. Any modem connections will be lost.

MS - Modem Status: Displays the state of the modem lines connected to the remote/modem serial port. Status signals DCD, CTS, DSR, RI and the last state of DTR, RTS are displayed. (Use "q" to exit).

IO - IO Chassis Display: Shows Cell to I/O chassis relationship to determine physica location of I/O chassis. Read line vertically under Cell Slot. For example, Slot 0 is usually connected to cab 0, bay 1, chassis 3 -rear facing right.

Chassis Code format: *Cabinet,Cell,Cpu*

Table 1-5   MP:CM> Commands Unique to *Oper* (Includes *Serv* Commands)

Command Expansion	Description

CC - Complex Configuration: Used to create an single cell partition. "G" uses lowest cell slot # connected to a I/O chassis with CIO. Cell must be at BIB. "L" or restore option retieves last successfully downloaded profile.

DI - Disconnect Remote/Modem or LAN Console: Disconnects all remote/modem or LAN users from the MP. Caution!

IT - Inactivity Timeout Settings: Prevents a user from inadvertently keeping the MP command menu locked in a MP>:CM command Default is 3 minutes (3-1440). Useful if extra time needed for ID command.

PARPERM: Enables or Disables partition (Npar) reconfiguration.

PCIOLAD: Add/insert or remove/eject a pci card. Cab-Bay-Ch-Slot.

PD - Partition Number Default: Sets the default partition number used by commands, which require a partition number (e.g. RS). The user "serv" partition is default and cannot select other partitions.

PE - Power Entity: Allows the user to switch the power ON or OFF to a cabinet, cell or an I/O chassis. B-CABINET, C-CELL, I-HIOB.
 RP8400/7410: T-CABINET, C-CELL, D-DVD or TAPE, P-I/O CHASSIS
 (0 = Front Right, 1 = Front Left) **For I/O chassis always power cell off**

RE - Reset Entity: Resets the specified entity: C-CELL, I-HIOB, M-MAIN BACKPLANE. *RP8400/7410:* C-CELL, P-IO Chassis, S-SYSTEM BACKPLANE. Special use only; use RS or RR instead.

RL - Rekey Complex Profile Lock: Rekeys the complex profile lock. This command should only be used to recover from an error where the holder of the lock terminates before releasing the lock. Rarely used. A=Stable, B= Dynamic, C=Partition Config data.

XD - Diagnostics and/or Reset of MP: Diagnostics and/or Reset of GSP(MP). 1=Parameter Chksum, 2=Ping, R=Reset, *RP8400/7410:* 1 and 2 same as Superdome, 3=Soft Reset Master MP, 4=Soft Reset Slave MP. Note: bottom button on MP is reset. Holding button longer than five seconds resets LC and SO parameters.

ALERT LEVELS

0 = Minor fwd progress	**3** = Warning	**6** = Reserved
1 = Major fwd progress	**4** = Reserved	**7** = Fatal
2 = Informational	**5** = Critical	

Table 1-6   MP:CM> Commands Unique to *Admin*
(Includes *Serv* and *Oper* Commands)

Command	Expansion	Description

DATE - Change the MP Time and Date: Changes the value of the real time clock on the MP. This controls chassis log timestamps. Not DST aware so GMT time is used most.

CA - Configure Async local & remote parms: Changes the communications parameters of the local and remote RS232 ports.

DC - Reset Parameters to Default Configuration: Can reset all or a subset of the following parameters: CA, EL, ER, IT, LC, and SO.

SA - Display and set MP Remote Access
 T - Enable or disable telnet access
 M - Enable or disable modem access - e*nabled lights "secure light'*
 N - Enable or disable network diagnostics - *was GSP>CM:ND*
 D - Enable or disable DIAG menu - *Lockword needed to activate*
 I - Enable or disable IPMI lan access - *Enable for sms "ipmiacqd" and hpux "parstatus -g" option.*

EL - Enable LAN Console Access: Enables telnet access to MP LANs. Use ND to enable diag access over LANs also.

ER - Enable Remote Console Serial Port Access: Enables or disables remote console serial port access. Dome - Secure light on remote serial access denied. RP8400/7410 - Remote access is enabled.

IF - Network Interface Information: Displays information about the network interfaces on the MP. Brief or Verbose. SBC = priv lan = Lan 1, SBCH = customer lan = Lan 0.

LC- LAN Configurations: Modifies the LAN configuration for the MP LAN(s). The user can set the IP, host-name, mask and gateway.

ND - Enable/Disable Network Diagnostics: Enable to allow JUST/JET offline diags and FW(UU) to operate. *See MP>CM:SA also*

OSP - Onboard Scan Programming Utility: *RP8400/74xx only.*

PWRGRD - RP8400/74xx Pwr Grid: 1 = A0 + A1, 2 = B0 + B1, 3 = Both 1 & 2 *(74xx:4=A0+B0, 5=A1+B1)*
Rear View: B1 A0 B0 A0.

SO - Security Options and Access Control: Modifies security options and access control to the MP: 1=MP Wide Parameters; 2=User Edit, Add or Del Parameters;. 3=IPMI passwd. *sms "ipmiacqd" uses this.* Users Admin and Oper are by default. User "Serv" has to be added.

MP MAIN MENU:- Two options only accessible by user Admin:
   FW: Firmware Update (Connects to ftp server - usually SMS)
         Enter new server IP Address:
         Enter new firmware source directory:
         Ener new user name:
  DIAG: Diagnostic Menu (Wtec can grant lockword on needed basis.)
         DM: Diagnostic Message Viewer
         DE: Diagnostic event viewer
         DS: Diagnostic shell
         Q: Quit
MFG - Enter Manu. Level Command Mode: These commands are intended for HP internal use only. Need lockword to access.

Table 1-7   Filesystem, Memory, Shell, and Boot Commands

Filesystem Commands

Commands Requrired to Select a Volume First. i.e., fs0: fs1: fs2: or fs3

attrib - Display attributes of directories of fs0: - fs3: *Shell>attrib fs1:\efi*.*
cd - Change directory. Cd by itself shows current working directory .
comp file1 file2 - Compares two files.
cp [-r] [-q] src dst - Classic cp command (-r recursive, -q quiet).
edit - text based editor (Esc 3 to quit) .
eficompress [infile] [outfile] - Compresses "infile" to "outfile."
efidecompress [infile] [outfile] - Uncompresses "infile" to "outfile."
hexedit [[-f] [file | [-d diskname offset size] | [-m offset size]].
ls - list contents of directories (see "help ls" for options) S.
mkdir name [name] - Creates a directory.
mount blkdevice [sname] - Mounts a fs on a block device.
rm [-q] file | directory - Deletes a file or directory.
setsize newsize file - Changes the file size in bytes.
touch [-r] file | directory - Updates a file or directory. Must exist first.
type [-a | -u] file [file...] -b Similiar to **cat** command. Use **-b** to pause.
vol [filesystem] [label] - Display or change name of filesystem volume.

Memory Commands

default [clear] - Resets NVRAM to default settngs. Including boot options.
dmem [address] [size] [:MMIO] - Display memory contents.
dmpstore - Views all the EFI variables.
memmap - Shows how physical memory is mapped out.
mm - Memory Modify (see "help mm" for complete details).
pdt [cell] [clear] - Displays or clears the PDT table. Use "reset" afterwards.

Shell Commands

alias [-d | -v | -b] [sname] [value] - Displays/creates/del aliases.
cls [color #] Clears standard out and changes background color.
exit - Exits EFI shell and returns to EFI boot manager.
getmtc - Diplays monotonic counter (See "help getmtc" for info).
help [-a] [cmdclass] - Displays help (cmd /? also works).
set [-d | -v] [sname [value]] [-b] - Displays, changes, or deletes variables.
xchar [on | off] - Displays/sets extended char. feature. Default is on.

Boot Commands

autoboot [on|off] | [time [value]]
time = 2 - 65535 second. *Also "My computer -> Properties Advanced -> Startup & Recovery" System startup options.*
bcfg boot [dump [-v]] | [add # file "desc"] | [rm#] | [mv # #]
*"bcfg boot dump" then "bcfg boot mv **ori new**" | "bcfg boot add"*
*Easier to use "boot maintenance mgr." Type Shell> **exit***
Windows use fs#:\msutil\nvrboot.efi. Remember to change acpi.
boottest [on|off] | [[test] [on | off]
early_cpu, late_cpu, platform, chipset, io_hw, mem_init, mem_test
In hpux use "setboot -v" or setboot -T to change settings.
lanboot [select] Use "lanboot select" to search for LANs.
reconfigreset Same as MP>CM: RR *Use after cpu/cell config.*
reset Resets the partition and boots to EFI. Same as MP>CM:RS.
help [-a] [cmd | class] - Displays help. (cmd /? also works).
search <cells> [pcislot] | all *Useful to find scsi targets:*
cell = Cell number (0-15)
pcislot = pci slots (0-11) *Use "info io" to determine occupied slots*
 all : Load the drivers for all possible boot devices in the partition.

Table 1-8   Configuration Commands

<u>**Configuration Commands**</u>

acpiconfig [windows | default]
 default is for linux and hpux. *(Reset is required to take effect).*
cellconfig [cell] [on | off] *Note: MP>CM:mfg must be enabled*
 cell = Cell number (0-15)
 on|off : Specifes to configure or deconfgure a cell *(Reset required).*
cpuconfig [cell] [module] [on | off]
 cell = Cell number (0-15)d
 module : Specifies which cpu module to configure (0-3)
 on | off : Specifies to configure or deconfigure a cpu module.
date [mm/dd/[yy]yy] - Displays or sets the date.
dimmconfig [cell] [dimm] [on | off]
 dimm = XY where X = Echelon (0-15) Y = Side format (a-f)
 cell = Cell number (0-15).
err [errorlevel] - Display or set bitmask error reporting.
errdump <cell> | all <logtype> | clear | clear <logtype> [-n]
 cell = Cell number (0-15)
 all = Use **all** instead of **cell** # to retrieve/clear logs for all cells in pd.
 logtype = mca, init, cmc, drr or all. d*rr is deadlock recovery reset*
 -n = no interactive prompts.
fru [cell] [frutype]
 cell = Cell number (0-15) & frutype = only "mem" is available.
info [cell] [target] cell – Cell number (0-15)
 target – all, boot, cache, cell, chiprev, cpu, fabric, fw, io, mem, sys.
monarch [cell] [module] [cpu]
 cell = Cell number (0-15) & module = module number (0-3)
 cpu = which cpu on the module (0-1).
palproc - Make a PAL call (see help for additional info).
romdrivers - (see help) *shows vendor vs. hp partnumber.*
rootcell [clear] [[c0] [c1] [c2] [c3]] c = Cell number (0-15).
salproc - Sal procedure call (see help for additional info).
tftp [select] Use select option to select a LAN card.
time [hh:mm[:ss]] Displays or sets time *Accepts 24 hour format.*
variable <-s | -r > [filename] *Similar to nvrboot export/import.*
      ver - Displays EFI, Sal, Pal, and module version information.

Table 1-9   Cell Local Memory (CLM), HPUX Bootloader, and SAC> Commands

Cell Local Memory (CLM)

parstatus -V -p <par # > -g <ipmi passwd> -h <hostname of gsp lan0>

parmodify -p <par # > -m <Cell #>::::<# %> -g <ipmi passwd> -h <gsp hostname lan0>

HPUX> Bootloader Commands

boot [kernel] Boot hpux kernel. *hpux vmunix.prev is now "backup."*

help [-d] Show help. "-d" shows **debug** commands.

ls [-b] [dir] Lists directory of /stand.

ll [-b] [dir] Long listing of /stand directory.

mmap Displays current EFI memory map.

setauto [-d] [str] Sets autofile. *Same as Shell> type \efi\hpux\auto.*

showauto - Display contents of \efi\hpux\auto.

ver - Shows bootloader, hpux, efi, fw vendor, fw rev and cpu rev.

what - Shows vmunix details. *Use "what /stand/vmunix."*

exit - Exits back to Shell> or fs#.

hpux [-lm] [-vm] [-tm] [-lq] [-a [C|R|S|D] devicefile] [-fnumber] [-istring] [boot] [devicefile] *see "man*

hpux" lm **= LVM,** *vm* **= VXVM and** *tm* **= Tunable maintenance mode**

lq = Quorum override, C = console, R = root, S = swap and D = dump

SAC> Commands

ch - Lists all channels. *Use **cmd** first to create channel. See **ch -?**.*

cmd - Creates a command prompt channel. *"SAC> cmd" then ch -sn cmd0001."*

d - Dump the current kernel log.

f - Toggle detailed or abbreviated tlist info.

i | [<#> <ip> <subnet>] Displays or sets IP addr, subnet, and gw info.

id - Display computer identification info. *Shows version and uptime.*

k <pid> - Kills the given process.

l <pid> - Lowers the priority of a processs to the lowest possible.

lock - Locks access to the command prompt channels.

m <pid> <MB-allow> - Limits a process memory usage.

p - Toggle display paging. *Similar to "scroll on" in BCH.*

r <pid> - Raises the priority of a process by one.

s | [mm/dd/yyyy hh:mm] - Sets the time and date. *24-hour format.*

t - Thread list. *Nice! Sort of like hpux "ps -ef and swapinfo -tam" Also nice to use during headless install to view progress of "setup.exe" pid.*

restart - Restarts the system immediately.

shutdown - Shuts down the system immediately.

crashdump - "INIT" the system. You must have crashdump enabled.

Windows "shutdown /r" same as hpux "shutdown -R" ./s optionsets BIB

Tables 1-4 through 1-6 provide a lot of information about the commands that specific users can issue at the *MP:CM>* prompt. Although the commands issued in Tables 1-7 through 1-9 are beyond the scope of this book, I have found that these tables are an excellent reference for Integrity servers especially when running additional operating systems beyond Linux.

The next chapter discusses loading Linux on an Integrity server.

Chapter 2

Installing Linux, RPM, and LILO

This chapter covers two topics related to installing Red Hat Advanced Server. The first is installing Advanced Server on an Integrity server and the second is using the Red Hat Package Manager (RPM) to install additional software. You'll perform a console-only installation on an Integrity system since there is no guarantee that you'll have a VGA port or display for your Integrity system. RPM is covered because it is Red Hat's tool for adding additional software after your installation is complete. SUSE LINUX also uses packages to install software, but keep in mind that SUSE is not covered in this book.

At the time of this writing, the procedure used in this chapter for the console-only install of Red Hat Advanced Server works. However, you are dealing with a new technology. Because of this, keep in mind that this procedure may have been updated or refined.

The Integrity server used in this chapter has multiple internal disks. You'll install Advanced Server on one of these disks. The others have Windows 2003 Server and HP-UX installed on them. Loading the other two operating systems will not be covered. For simplicity, each of the three disks holds a separate operating system. This is not a requirement. Some of the operating systems can coexist on a single partitioned disk. On HP cell-based systems, you can run multiple operating systems simultaneously in Node Partitions (nPartitions), but this functionality won't be covered in this book.

The objective in this chapter is to cover the console-only installation of Red Hat's Advanced Server. I'll install RHEL 3 in the example, but the installation of 2.1 is very similar.

Installing Red Hat Advanced Server Using the Serial Console

This section covers installing Red Hat Advanced Server using the console-only. The console-only installation is focused on because many of the machines needing Advanced Server will not have a graphics display connected to them. Console-only installation has some nuances, so you should perform the steps outlined here. Please keep in mind that there may be modifications to the commands at any time, so your console installation might look slightly different. Graphical installation is straightforward and is documented in most Linux books. Even if you have a graphics display on your Integrity system you would still begin installing Advanced Server at the console. The graphical part of the Advanced Server install begins after the *Enablement Kit For Linux* is installed and the Advanced Server CD-ROM is booted. Control will be automatically switched to the graphical display if you have a VGA port on your server. The installation selections are the same whether you're using the graphical installation or console, so this chapter applies if you have graphics as well. Still, for the reasons mentioned, this chapter focuses only on the text-based console installation.

The first product that you'll install is the *HP Enablement Kit for Linux* (sometimes called LEK), which is a set of tools that provide a framework for installing, configuring, and recovering a Linux distribution on the Integrity server. The kit is completely distribution agnostic meaning that it is independent of a Linux distribution. You'll be installing *Red Hat Advanced Server* only in this book, but other Linux variants can be installed on some Integrity servers so the LEK needs to be independent of a specific Linux variant. The kit also provides a framework for delivering platform-specific drivers and updates. There is a workstation enablement kit and server enablement kit. You'll use the server LEK in the upcoming example. The **elilo** program used later to bootstrap our Integrity system was provided as part of the *HP Enablement Kit for Linux.*

To begin the installation process, boot the system and see the Extensible Firmware Interface (EFI) menu that was covered in Chapter 1 (see "Working with EFI" on page 5). This menu offers a variety of boot options as shown in Figure 2-1. We first want to install the *HP Enablement Kit for Linux,* which puts *boot* and *service* partitions on our destination disk. You'll install the Advanced Server software later.

Note that you may want to remove (or disable by disconnecting them from the power supply) any disks that already have other operating systems installed. That way, you don't run the risk of overwriting any of the other operating systems with the new installation. In the upcoming screen shots, examples of both scenarios are given. That is, you will see examples of what the installation would look like with and without all the disks installed.

To begin the installation, select *Boot option maintenance menu* from the EFI Boot Manager, as shown in Figure 2-1.

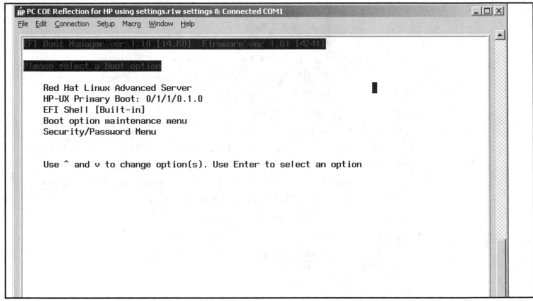

Figure 2-1   Select *Boot Option Maintenance Menu*

When the EFI Boot Maintenance Manager's *Main Menu* appears (Figure 2-2), select *Boot from a File*.

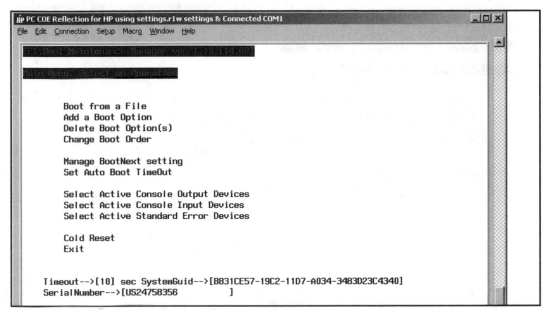

Figure 2-2   Select *Boot From a File*

After you select *Boot From a File,* you see one of the menus shown in Figure 2-3.

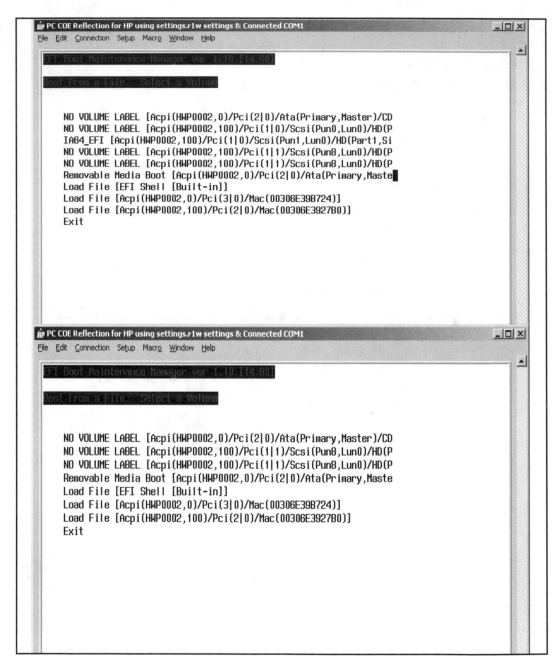

Figure 2-3   Select *Removable Media Boot*

Note that the top screen shot in Figure 2-3 shows more selections than the bottom screen shot. The top screen shot was produced with two additional disks in the system in addition to the target disk on which we want to install Advanced Server. The bottom screen shot was produced with only the target disk physically installed in the system.

In either case, when the *Boot From a File* menu appears, select *Removable Media Boot.* The menu displayed in Figure 2-4 is displayed.

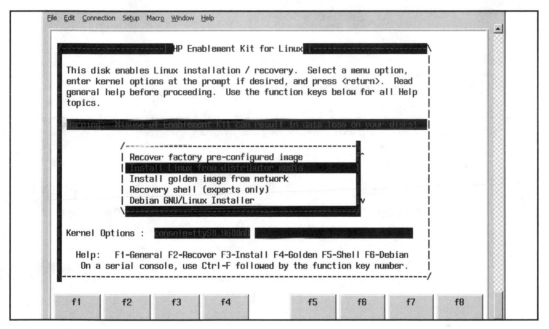

Figure 2-4   Loading the *Enablement Kit*

To install the *HP Enablement Kit for Linux,* select the second entry in the list (*Install Linux from distributor media*). You must also specify the console. To do so, at the *Boot:* prompt, enter the line *console=ttyS0,9600n8.* This specifies the *console* device, its speed and parity-related information. After you make this selection and enter the *console* line, press Enter. The *Prepare Boot and Service Partitions* screen displayed in Figure 2-5 appears.

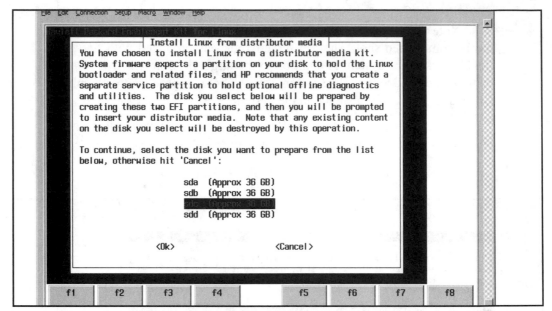

Figure 2-5   Loading *Boot and Service Partitions* from *Enablement Kit*

The *Prepare Boot and Service Partitions* screen prepares one of your hard disks to receive the Linux Advanced Server. Figure 2-5 shows a total of four disks on the system and I'll install RHEL 3 to *sdc,* which is selected in the figure.

After you select the installation drive, press *<Ok>*. The *Preparation Complete* screen displayed in Figure 2-6 appears.

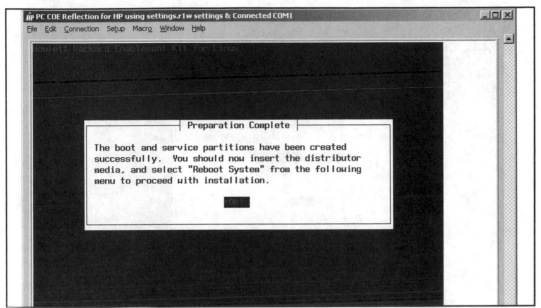

Figure 2-6   Load of *Boot and Service Partitions Complete* Message

This screen indicates that you have successfully installed the *boot* and *service* partitions, and that you are ready to move on. Press *<Ok>* and the *Options* screen appears (see Figure 2-7).

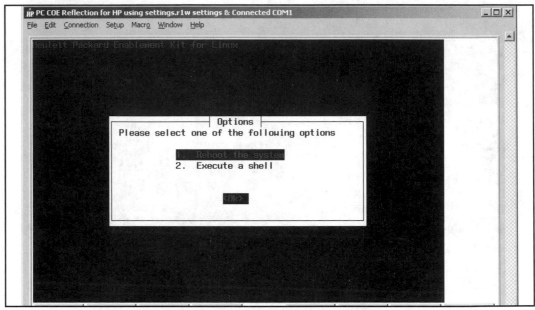

Figure 2-7   *Reboot* Message

The *Options screen* allows you to reboot or execute a command shell. Reboot the system and the boot option screen displayed in Figure 2-8 appears.

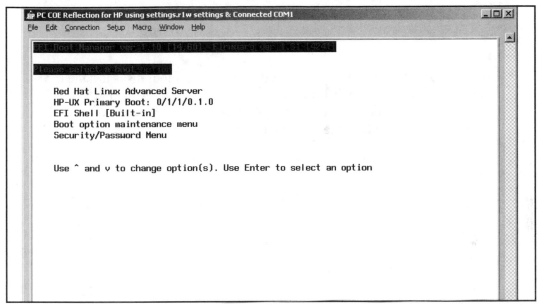

Figure 2-8   *Boot Manager* Screen After Reboot with Linux Media CD Loaded

This is the main *EFI Boot Manager* screen on which you may also see *Internal Bootable DVD*. This time, select *EFI Shell [Built-in]* and press Enter. The following listing of available devices is produced:

```
Loading.: EFI Shell [Built-in]
EFI Shell version 1.10 [14.61]
Device mapping table
   fs0  : Acpi(HWP0002,0)/Pci(2|0)/Scsi(Pun0,Lun0)/HD(Part1,Sig00000000)
   fs1  : Acpi(HWP0002,0)/Pci(2|0)/Scsi(Pun2,Lun0)/HD(Part1,SigA81750C2-1624-11D8-8002-D621
7B60E588)
   fs2  : Acpi(HWP0002,0)/Pci(2|0)/Scsi(Pun2,Lun0)/HD(Part3,SigA8175126-1624-11D8-8004-D621
7B60E588)
   fs3  : Acpi(HWP0002,0)/Pci(2|1)/Scsi(Pun3,Lun0)/CDROM(Entry0)
   fs4  : Acpi(HWP0002,100)/Pci(1|0)/Pci(1|1)/Scsi(Pun0,Lun0)/HD(Part1,Sig934FD5F8-1738-418
C-B579-CAC4A28A8F0E)
   fs5  : Acpi(HWP0002,100)/Pci(1|0)/Pci(1|1)/Scsi(Pun0,Lun0)/HD(Part2,Sig3A66A196-08B5-480
8-8D49-824292280DEC)
   blk0 : Acpi(HWP0002,0)/Pci(2|0)/Scsi(Pun0,Lun0)
   blk1 : Acpi(HWP0002,0)/Pci(2|0)/Scsi(Pun0,Lun0)/HD(Part1,Sig00000000)
   blk2 : Acpi(HWP0002,0)/Pci(2|0)/Scsi(Pun0,Lun0)/HD(Part2,Sig00000000)
   blk3 : Acpi(HWP0002,0)/Pci(2|0)/Scsi(Pun2,Lun0)
   blk4 : Acpi(HWP0002,0)/Pci(2|0)/Scsi(Pun2,Lun0)/HD(Part1,SigA81750C2-1624-11D8-8002-D621
7B60E588)
   blk5 : Acpi(HWP0002,0)/Pci(2|0)/Scsi(Pun2,Lun0)/HD(Part2,SigA81750F4-1624-11D8-8003-D621
7B60E588)
   blk6 : Acpi(HWP0002,0)/Pci(2|0)/Scsi(Pun2,Lun0)/HD(Part3,SigA8175126-1624-11D8-8004-D621
7B60E588)
   blk7 : Acpi(HWP0002,0)/Pci(2|1)/Scsi(Pun3,Lun0)
   blk8 : Acpi(HWP0002,0)/Pci(2|1)/Scsi(Pun3,Lun0)/CDROM(Entry0)
   blk9 : Acpi(HWP0002,100)/Pci(1|0)/Pci(1|1)/Scsi(Pun0,Lun0)
   blkA : Acpi(HWP0002,100)/Pci(1|0)/Pci(1|1)/Scsi(Pun0,Lun0)/HD(Part1,Sig934FD5F8-1738-418
C-B579-CAC4A28A8F0E)
   blkB : Acpi(HWP0002,100)/Pci(1|0)/Pci(1|1)/Scsi(Pun0,Lun0)/HD(Part2,Sig3A66A196-08B5-480
```

```
8-8D49-824292280DEC)
  blkC : Acpi(HWP0002,100)/Pci(1|0)/Pci(1|1)/Scsi(Pun2,Lun0)
  blkD : Acpi(HWP0002,100)/Pci(1|0)/Pci(1|1)/Scsi(Pun2,Lun0)/HD(Part1,Sig1690AF09-E88C-47D
7-B101-213ED9D1D1E3)
startup.nsh> echo -off

Shell>
```

This is the list of available boot devices with all four disks installed. At the *Shell>* prompt, enter *fs3:* as our boot device. Assuming you have already inserted the Advanced Server CD-ROM into the device, what you see the *fs3:* prompt, enter **dir** to see its contents:

```
fs3:\> dir
Directory of: fs3:\

    10/07/03  09:55p  <DIR>             2,048   EFI
    10/07/03  09:55p           351,822   bootia64.efi
    10/07/03  09:55p               130   elilo.conf
    10/07/03  09:55p           351,822   elilo.efi
    10/07/03  09:55p         3,890,655   initrd.img
    10/07/03  09:55p             3,091   syslinux-splash.png
    10/07/03  09:55p         2,636,729   vmlinuz
              6 File(s)    7,234,249 bytes
              1 Dir(s)

fs3:\>
```

A directory and a number of files are shown in this listing, including two *elilo* files and **vmlinuz**. Use *elilo* at the *fs3:\>* prompt to boot the system. At the same time, specify the console. To do so, enter the *elilo* command:

```
fs3:\> elilo linux console="ttyS0"
ELILO
Uncompressing Linux... done
Loading initrd initrd.img...done
Linux version 2.4.21-4.EL (bhcompile@rocky.devel.redhat.com) (gcc version 3.2.3
20030502 (
Red Hat Linux 3.2.3-20)) #1 SMP Fri Oct 3 17:29:39 EDT 2003
```

A series of messages fly by, not shown in the output above, and then you begin the console-only installation of Advanced Server. If you booted off of the Advanced Server CD-ROM directly instead of the console-only procedure, installation screens would have been automatically displayed using the graphics card.

Note that even using the console-only installation, you can enter graphics-related information on the type of graphics card. Integrity servers, such as the rx2600, commonly use ATI or NVIDIA graphics systems and a p930 display. You can also specify mouse information, such as the USB mouse. In addition, from the console you can also set up the default graphical environment such as GNOME or KDE.

Getting back to the console-only installation, you are asked if you'd like to test the CD media before the installation. Skip that step, as well as the one that asks whether you have an official version of RHEL Advanced Server. You are next asked what language you'd like; choose *English,* as shown in Figure 2-9.

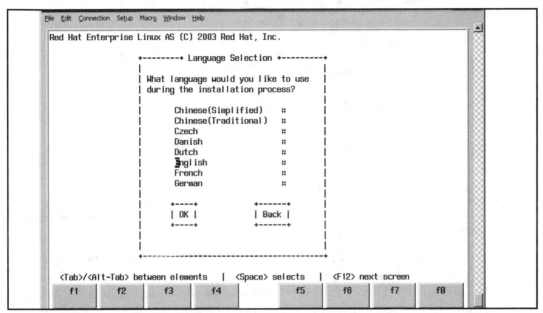

Figure 2-9   Select *Language*

Next, you are asked about *Disk Partitioning Setup,* as shown in Figure 2-10.

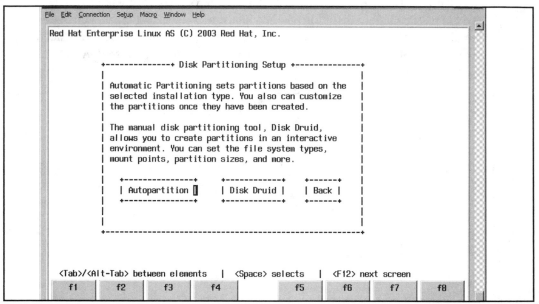

Figure 2-10   Partition Options

At this point, you can select from a variety of partition options. For simplicity, select *Autopartition*. If you have a preferred tool, such as *Disk Druid,* you can select it at this point. Although you'll use the defaults, the following is a list of custom partitions that I've used on Integrity Oracle 9i RAC systems:

```
# df
Filesystem          1k-blocks        Used Available Use% Mounted on
/dev/sda8             1007896      162484    794212  17% /
/dev/sda1              102166        6122     96044   6% /boot/efi
/dev/sda6            20158332       32828  19101504   1% /home
none                 2066160           0   2066160   0% /dev/shm
/dev/sda5             2015824       32868   1880556   2% /tmp
/dev/sda3             6047492     3302772   2437520  58% /usr
/dev/sda7             1007896      105840    850856  12% /var
#
```

These values are much different than the *Autopartition* will prepare on the system. The **/boot/efi** partition is a *vfat* partition used for boot. *vfat* is *FAT16* and **elilo** doesn't support *FAT32*.

After selecting *Autopartition,* the installation asks if you want to *Remove* or *Keep* existing partitions on the destination disk. Select *Remove,* and you see the *Automatic Partitioning* screen (see Figure 2-11).

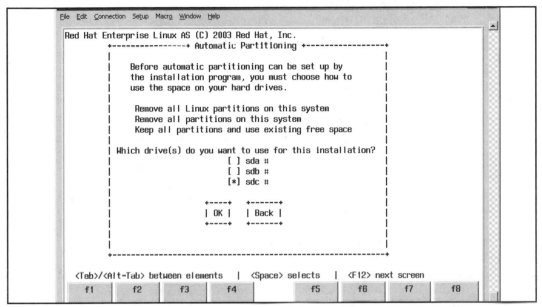

Figure 2-11   Removing Partitions for Advanced Server Installation

Select *Remove all Linux Partitions on the system* and then select the drive you want to use for the installation.

If you have to choose, make sure you choose the correct hard drive for the Linux installation. In the example, choose **[*] sdc #** and select OK. *sdd* scrolled off the screen so you have to unselect it as well. The installation creates the partitions and displays the results (see Figure 2-12).

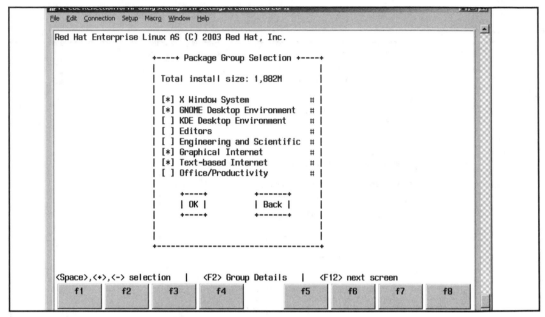

Figure 2-12   Partitions Automatically Created

After scrolling down so that *sdc* was visible, you could edit the partitions to change their size or make other modifications. After you're done, select OK. The installation then asks you for information on system-level configuration, including network-related information, hostname, firewall configuration, additional languages, time zone, root password, and so on.

As a side note: If you should need to boot in single-user mode for any reason, you would interrupt the boot process of Linux with *^Ecf* and then at the *ELILO boot:* prompt, issue **linux single** as shown below:

```
ELILO boot: linux single
```

Linux package information is then read from the CD-ROM and the installation displays the *Package Group Selection* screen (see Figure 2-13).

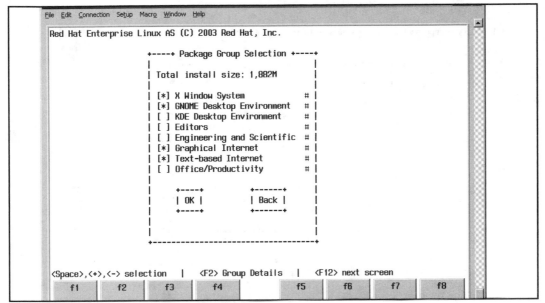

Figure 2-13   Selecting Package Groups

Review and select individual software package groups (each consists of multiple packages) on this screen. After you select the software you want to install, press *OK*. The *Package Installation* screen appears and regular updates on the install procedure are produced, as shown in Figure 2-14.

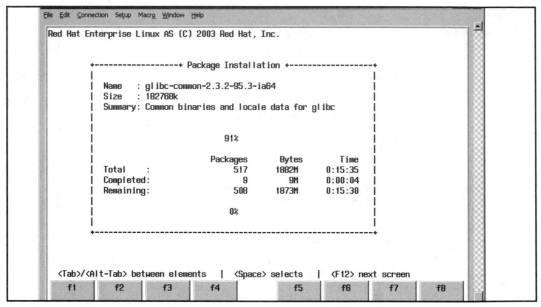

Figure 2-14   Software Load Update Screen

Depending on the packages that you select, you may be asked to put in the second, third, and fourth Advanced Server CD-ROMs. During package installation, you are asked a couple of more installation-related questions and the installation completes.

Since this is a console-only installation, your only access to the system is through the console. However, if you have a graphical display, the graphics would have been activated early in the process of installing Advanced Server. If the graphical display is installed and activated, when the system reboots after the install is complete, you would be able to use the graphical display to login.

After the installation is complete, if you have disconnected or removed the other two hard drives make sure you reinstall or reconnnect them. After they are reinstalled, when you boot your system, the *Boot Option* menu displays all the operating systems, including the Advanced Server installation that you just completed. Figure 2-15 shows the *Boot Option* menu with Microsoft Windows .NET Server, Red Hat Linux Advanced Server, and HP-UX as installed bootable operating systems on a system.

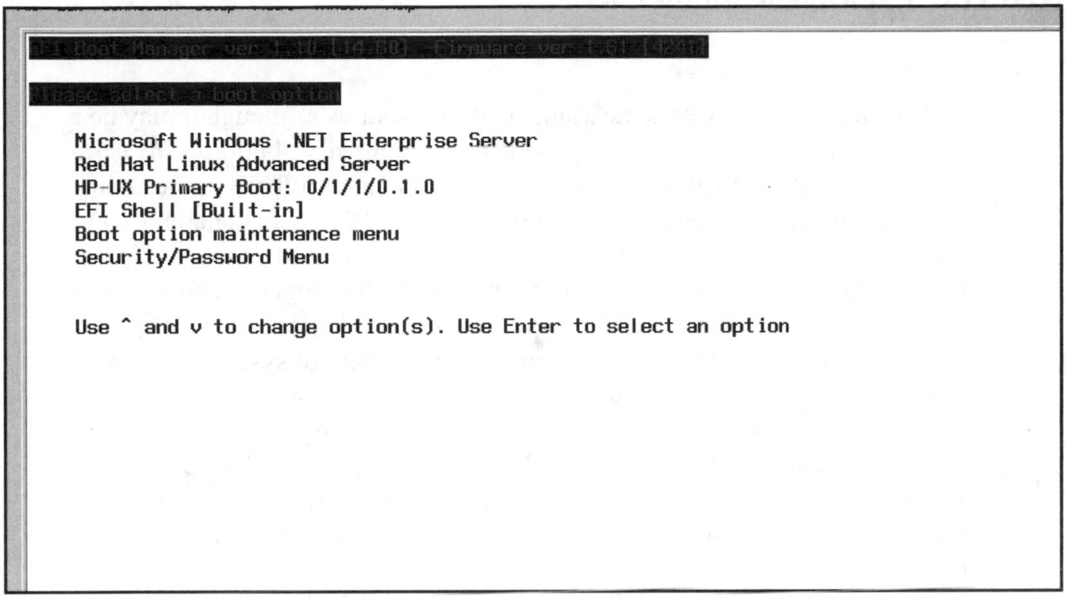

```
EFI Boot Manager ver 1.10 [14.60]  Firmware ver 1.61 [4241]

Please select a boot option

    Microsoft Windows .NET Enterprise Server
    Red Hat Linux Advanced Server
    HP-UX Primary Boot: 0/1/1/0.1.0
    EFI Shell [Built-in]
    Boot option maintenance menu
    Security/Password Menu


    Use ^ and v to change option(s). Use Enter to select an option
```

Figure 2-15   Three Operating Systems Installed

The system on which you've performed this example does not support multiple bootable partitions, so you can only boot one of these operating systems at a time. On Integrity servers, all these operating systems are bootable, not just the Advanced Server that you installed earlier.

Red Hat Package Manager RPM

Although the Red Hat Package Manger (RPM) sounds as though it may be a
Red Hat-only product, it is used in many other Linux distributions. The command line RPM functionality is easy to understand. What's more, many
graphical tools have been built around it as well. RPM files contain a lot of
important information related to software installation such as the version of
the program, installation scripts, a description of the program, and so on. If
you need more information about RPM, you can get it at *www.rpm.org*.

The examples in this chapter come from a variety of systems, including
the Integrity server that you just installed and an IA-32 system. RPM works
the same on all systems, even though you'll be running 64-bit applications
on your Integrity server and 32-bit applications on your IA-32 systems.
Because different versions of RPM exist (versions 3 and 4 are available at
the time of this writing), you need to know which version you are running in
order to avoid incompatibility.

Let's start by running RPM at the command line. The command **rpm -
-help** is issued in the following listing to give a run down on all the commonly used RPM options:

```
# rpm --help

Usage: rpm [OPTION...]

Query options (with -q or --query):
  -c, --configfiles            list all configuration files
  -d, --docfiles               list all documentation files
  --dump                       dump basic file information
  -l, --list                   list files in package
  --queryformat=QUERYFORMAT    use the following query format
  -s, --state                  display the states of the listed files
  -v, --verbose                display a verbose file listing
  -a, --all                    query/verify all packages
  -f, --file                   query/verify package(s) owning file
  -g, --group                  query/verify package(s) in group
  -p, --package                query/verify a package file (i.e. a binary
                               *.rpm file)
  --querytags                  display known query tags
  --specfile                   query a spec file
  --whatrequires               query/verify the package(s) which require a
                               dependency
  --whatprovides               query/verify the package(s) which provide a
                               dependency

Verify options (with -V or --verify):
  --nomd5[|=0x1]               don't verify MD5 digest of files
  --nofiles[|=0x10000]         don't verify files in package
  --nodeps[|=0x20000]          don't verify package dependencies
  --noscript[|=0x40000]        don't execute %verifyscript (if any)
  -a, --all                    query/verify all packages
  -f, --file                   query/verify package(s) owning file
  -g, --group                  query/verify package(s) in group
  -p, --package                query/verify a package file (i.e. a binary
                               *.rpm file)
  --querytags                  display known query tags
```

```
  --specfile                          query a spec file
  --whatrequires                      query/verify the package(s) which require a
                                      dependency
  --whatprovides                      query/verify the package(s) which provide a
                                      dependency

Signature options:
  --addsign                           add a signature to a package
  --resign                            sign a package (discard current signature)
  -K, --checksig                      verify package signature
  --nogpg[&=~0x4]                     skip any GPG signatures
  --nomd5[&=~0x2]                     do not verify file md5 checksums

Database options:
  --initdb                            initialize database
  --rebuilddb                         rebuild database inverted lists from
                                      installed package headers

Install/Upgrade/Erase options:
  --allfiles[|=0x40]                  install all files, even configurations
                                      which might otherwise be skipped
  --allmatches[|=0x2]                 remove all packages which match <package>
                                      (normally an error is generated if
                                      <package> specified multiple packages)
  --badreloc[|=0x8]                   relocate files in non-relocateable package
  -e, --erase=<package>+              erase (uninstall) package
  --excludedocs[|=0x20]               do not install documentation
  --excludepath=<path>                skip files with leading component <path>
  --force[|=0x74]                     short hand for --replacepkgs --replacefiles
  -F, --freshen=<packagefile>+        upgrade package(s) if already installed
  -h, --hash[|=0x2]                   print hash marks as package installs (good
                                      with -v)
  --ignorearch[|=0x2]                 don't verify package architecture
  --ignoreos[|=0x1]                   don't verify package operating system
  --ignoresize[|=0x180]               don't check disk space before installing
  --includedocs                       install documentation
  --install=<packagefile>+            install package
  --justdb[|=0x8]                     update the database, but do not modify the
                                      filesystem
  --nodeps                            do not verify package dependencies
  --noorder[|=0x8]                    do not reorder package installation to
                                      satisfy dependencies
  --noscripts[|=0xff0000]             do not execute package scriptlet(s)
  --notriggers[|=0x990000]            do not execute any scriptlet(s) triggered
                                      by this package
  --oldpackage[|=0x40]                upgrade to an old version of the package
                                      (--force on upgrades does this
                                      automatically)
  --percent[|=0x1]                    print percentages as package installs
  --prefix=<dir>                      relocate the package to <dir>, if
                                      relocatable
  --relocate=<old>=<new>              relocate files from path <old> to <new>
  --repackage[|=0x400]                save erased package files by repackaging
  --replacefiles[|=0x30]              install even if the package replaces
                                      installed files
  --replacepkgs[|=0x4]                reinstall if the package is already present
  --test[|=0x1]                       don't install, but tell if it would work or
                                      not
  -U, --upgrade=<packagefile>+        upgrade package(s)

Common options for all rpm modes:
  --version                           print the version of rpm being used
  --quiet                             provide less detailed output
  -v, --verbose                       provide more detailed output
  --define='<name> <body>'            define macro <name> with value <body>
  --eval=<expr>+                      print macro expansion of <expr>+
  -r, --root=<dir>                    use <dir> as the top level directory
                                      (default: "/")
  --macros=<file:...>                 read <file:...> instead of default macro
                                      file(s)
  --rcfile=<file:...>                 read <file:...> instead of default rpmrc
                                      file(s)
  --showrc                            display final rpmrc and macro configuration

Options implemented via popt alias/exec:
```

```
    --scripts                           list install/erase scriptlets from
                                        package(s)
    --setperms                          set permissions of files in a package
    --setugids                          set user/group ownership of files in a
                                        package
    --conflicts                         list capabilities this package conflicts
                                        with
    --obsoletes                         list other packages removed by installing
                                        this package
    --provides                          list capabilities that this package provides
    --requires                          list capabilities required by package(s)
    --info                              list descriptive information from package(s)
    --changelog                         list change logs for this package
    --triggers                          list trigger scriptlets from package(s)
    --last                              list package(s) by install time, most
                                        recent first
    --filesbypkg                        list all files from each package
    --redhatprovides                    find package name that contains a provided
                                        capability (needs rpmdb-redhat package
                                        installed)
    --redhatrequires                    find package name that contains a required
                                        capability (needs rpmdb-redhat package
                                        installed)
    --buildpolicy=<policy>              set buildroot <policy> (e.g. compress man
                                        pages)
    --with=<option>                     enable configure <option> for build
    --without=<option>                  disable configure <option> for build

Help options:
  -?, --help                            Show this help message
    --usage                             Display brief usage message
#
```

rpm --help provides a good summary of **rpm** functionality. To get the details on all **rpm** options, see the **rpm** man page.

In this example, you want to know if the telnet java package is installed on my IA-32 system. To do so, combine the *q* option for query and the *a* option for all to find all the installed gcc packages (**rpc -qa | grep gcc**).

```
# cd /mnt/cdrom/RedHat/RPMS
# rpm -qa | grep gcc
gcc-objc-2.96-110
gcc-g77-2.96-110
gcc-2.96-110
gcc-c++-2.96-110

#
```

This output shows that there are several gcc-related packages installed, but not the java package you'd like to use. So, install the correct package from the CD-ROM. After mounting the CD-ROM at */mnt/cdrom,* we can traverse its hierarchy to look for software. (Note that the following examples all assume we have mounted the CD-ROM at */mnt/cdrom.*) The CD-ROM in this example is part of the Red Hat distribution. The CD-ROM may have to be mounted before you can load the software:

```
# cd /mnt/cdrom/RedHat/RPMS
# ls | grep gcc
gcc-2.96-110.i386.rpm
gcc-c++-2.96-110.i386.rpm
gcc-chill-2.96-110.i386.rpm
gcc-g77-2.96-110.i386.rpm
gcc-java-2.96-110.i386.rpm
gcc-objc-2.96-110.i386.rpm

# rpm -i gcc-java*
error: failed dependencies:
                libgcj >= 2.96 is needed by gcc-java-2.96-110
                libgcj-devel >= 2.96 is needed by gcc-java-2.96-110
#
```

Installation fails because the dependencies listed by the **rpm** command are not installed. You want to have these dependencies installed in order for the install of the gcc java package to succeed.

You can also use wildcards when installing with **rpm**. In the following example, the system has no apache-related software installed. To install all of it, use **rpm** and specify *apache** so that all apache-related software on the CD-ROM will be installed. After you're done installing the software, query the system to confirm that all apache-related software was installed. After all that, use **rpm** to remove one of the packages:

```
# cd /mnt/cdrom/RedHat/RPMS
# rpm -iv apache*
Preparing packages for installation...
apache-1.3.23-11
apacheconf-0.8.2-2
apache-devel-1.3.23-11
apache-manual-1.3.23-11

# rpm -qa | grep apache
apache-1.3.23-11
apache-devel-1.3.23-11
apache-manual-1.3.23-11
apacheconf-0.8.2-2

# rpm -ev apache-manual-1.3.23.-11
# rpm -qa | grep apache
apache-1.3.23-11
apache-devel-1.3.23-11
apacheconf-0.8.2-2
#
```

This example shows installing all apache software (**rpm -iv apache***), querying to see that it was installed (**rpm -qa | grep apache**), removing a select package (**rpm -ev apache-manual-1.3.23.-11**), and then re-querying to ensure that the select package was removed (**rpm -qa | grep apache**).

The previous examples were performed on an IA-32 system. Now, take a look at the gcc-related files installed on the Integrity server. You will start again with the query all option (**rpm -qa | grep gcc**).

```
# rpm -qa | grep gcc
gcc3-g77-3.0.4-1
gcc-objc-2.96-112.7.2
gcc-2.96-112.7.2
libgcc-3.0.4-1
gcc-g77-2.96-112.7.2
gcc-chill-2.96-112.7.2
gcc3-objc-3.0.4-1
gcc3-c++-3.0.4-1
gcc-c++-2.96-112.7.2
gcc3-3.0.4-1
gcc3-java-3.0.4-1
#
```

gcc-related tools are essential to many of the software development work done on Integrity servers, so the packages listed are vital to this work.

As you can see, working with **rpm** on IA-32 systems and Integrity servers is nearly identical, although the progams that run on the two platforms are different in that applications must be ported from IA-32 to Itanium. In RHEL 3, there are IA-32 packages installed on Integrity servers, so don't be surprised when you see this.

A variety of graphical tools use **rpm**. One of the most commonly used is **gnorpm**, which runs on the Integrity server and IA-32 systems. **gnorpm** is invoked from the command line with the **gnorpm** command, or from the *Programs* menu. Pick *Programs-System-GnoRPM* in Advanced Server. This tool runs on both GNOME and KDE desktops. Figure 2-16 shows the **gnorpm** interface from the Integrity server running Advanced Server.

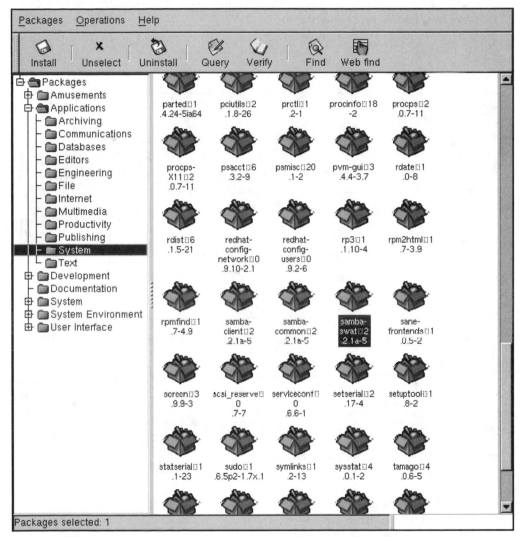

Figure 2-16   **gnorpm** Interface with *samba-swat* Selected

gnorpm organizes the packages in a hierarchical fashion and displays the information graphically. Figure 2-16 shows that *samba-swat* is selected (one of the packages you use in the Samba chapter), which is under *Packages-Applications-System.*

You can perform a variety of tasks from the **gnorpm** window using the toolbar at the top of the **gnorpm** window. For example, assuming samba-swat-2.2.1a-5 is selected (as shown in Figure 2-16), clicking the *Query* tool produces the window shown in Figure 2-17.

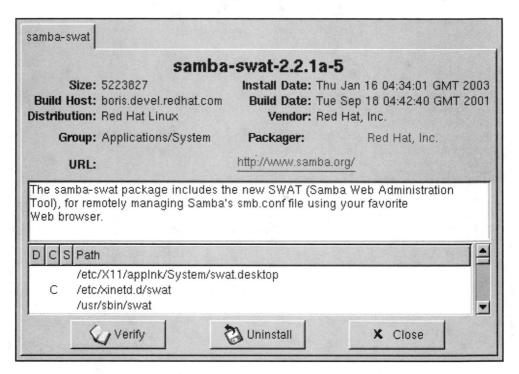

Figure 2-17   *Query* of *samba-swat*

Query provides a lot of useful information. From this window, you can *Verify* or *Uninstall* the package.

Clicking *Web find* in the main **gnorpm** window causes **gnorpm** to search the Web for your software. The *Preferences* button allows you to specify the Internet servers which **gnorpm** uses to find Web information. The *Preferences* button also allows you to select a variety of setup options for **gnorpm**, such as *Behaviour, Package Listing, Install Window, Network, Rpmfind,* and *Distributions*.

As with most GUIs, you need to work through a few screens to get the feel for **gnorpm**. At its core, however, **gnorpm** is using **rpm** commands to accomplish its work with packages. Thus, if you become comfortable with **rpm** at the command line, you probably won't be using the GUI too much.

On the other hand, if you're only going to be loading software occasionally, **gnorpm** will probably be your preferred method for loading packages.

Red Hat 8.0 (to be replaced by Fedora), which was for IA-32 systems only, has another great graphical tool called *Package Management*. You can invoke it by selecting *System Settings - Packages* from the GNOME menu. From this tool, you can select any packages or packages you would like to install. We use this tool later to install *OpenOffice*. This was done by opening *Package Management* and then selecting *Applications => Office/Productivity => Details => OpenOffice*.

Chapter 3

GNOME and KDE

GNOME and KDE are Graphical User Interfaces (GUIs) that are available for Linux. Most Linux variants bundle both of these GUIs so you have your choice of which to use. Both are based on the X Window System (X Windows) and provide a fully functional graphical user environment. Both GNOME and KDE are independent of the core Linux operating system, including the kernel. You can customize and even crash either of these GUIs and Linux keeps running.

This chapter does not spend a lot of time explaining these environments and showing a lot of screen shots for each. Everyone has used a graphical environment and the best way to customize one is by experimenting and finding what best suits your needs. Thus, this chapter provides an overview of each with most customization preferences left to the reader. This chapter also touches on the free office software package, *OpenOffice.org,* available from *www.openoffice.org.*

This chapter covers the following.

- Overview of GNOME and KDE

- Obtaining and installing *OpenOffice.org*

GNOME

GNOME (GNU Network Object Model Environment) is a full graphical desktop environment and application framework for Linux and other Linux like systems. GNOME includes a panel for starting applications, a graphical desktop, and a set of standard desktop tools and applications. If you want a newer version of GNOME, want it for another platform, or want any information related to GNOME, you can find it at *www.gnome.org*. GNOME is part of the GNU project, which means it is open-source software.

GNOME is not a window manager itself. Instead, it uses a variety of window managers from which you can select (*Sawfish* being the default window manager). GNOME provides development libraries and session management. Applications that use these features are tightly integrated with GNOME. Since GNOME is based on X Windows, X-based applications work great with GNOME.

GNOME is included with Red Hat Advanced Server for your Integrity server and also comes with all Red Hat distributions. After logging in using GNOME, I had a fully functional GNOME windowing environment, as shown in Figure 3-1. Note that the windows displayed in Figure 3-1 are not the default. My session opens with the applications open from my last session. GNOME remembers these and my other preferences automatically. By default, when you logout, GNOME also asks you if you would like to save your current session settings. If you do, whatever you were doing last will be started when you login again. GNOME also lets you configure your session using the Session advanced preference tool (*Main (or Start) Menu ⇒ Preferences ⇒ More Preferences ⇒ Sessions*).

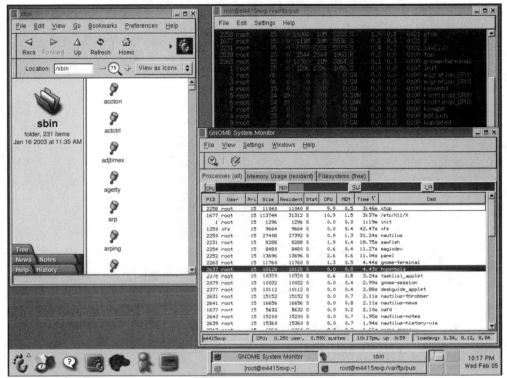

Figure 3-1   Full-Screen GNOME Screen Shot

As you can see, when you login, several windows are already open. At the bottom of the desktop is the main tool bar. Starting at the left are the GNOME icons for the *Start Menu* (footprint), *Start Here*, *Documentation*, *Terminal, Web Browser, Gaim* (instant messenger), and *GNOME System Monitor*.

In the middle of the main toolbar is a task list that lists the programs currently running. Just to the right of the task list on the bottom is the *Workspace Switcher*. The *Workspace Switcher* allows you to choose any one of four workspaces by default.

In the current workspace, you see several programs open, including a file manager window on the right, a terminal window on the top right, and *GNOME System Monitor* on the bottom right.

To open other programs, click the *Main Menu* on the lower left, as shown in Figure 3-2.

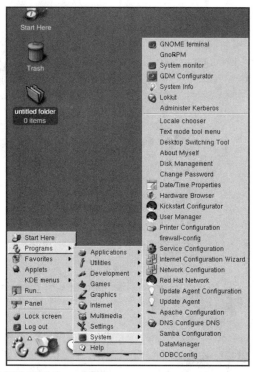

Figure 3-2   GNOME Menu Pick

Figure 3-2 hows the default organization of programs on the menu. Selecting *Start ⇒ Programs ⇒ System,* which brings up various system programs we can run. We'll invoke some of these shortly. For now, you can see that on the Integrity Advanced Server system, we can invoke many system-related programs.

Open the *System Monitor.* When it appears, it looks like the window shown in Figure 3-3.

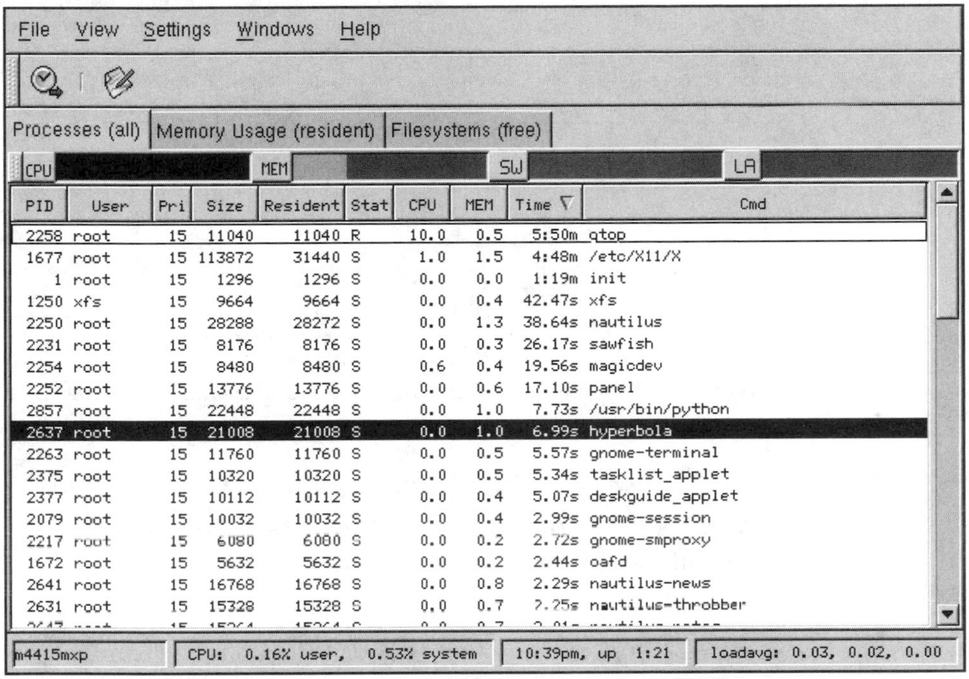

Figure 3-3   GNOME System Monitor

GNOME System Monitor is similar to *top* in that it provides useful information about processes and overall system utilization (shown along the bottom of the window) including the system *loadavg.*

If you select *Start ⇒ Programs ⇒ System ⇒ Network Configuration,* the *Network Configuration* program appears, as shown in Figure 3-4.

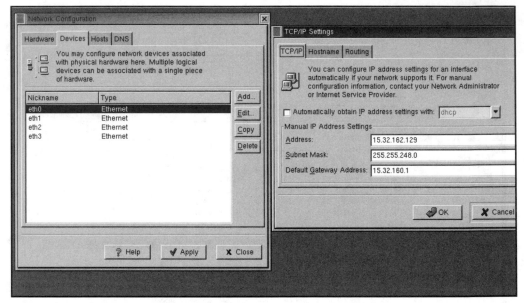

Figure 3-4   Network Configuration

This *Network Configuration* tool is covered extensively in Chapter 8. You can see that this tool lists the four network cards in the rx2600 Integrity server, which allows us to edit information related to each of the interfaces.

Figure 3-5 shows the *Gnome Red Hat Package Manager (RPM)* tool, which is used to manage software packages on Linux systems.

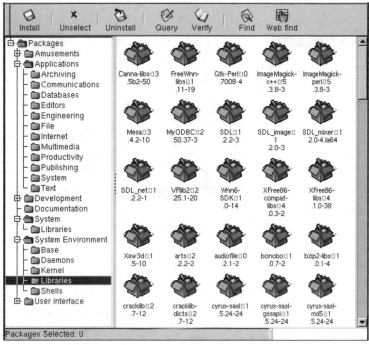

Figure 3-5   *Gnome RPM* Package Management

Using this tool, you could load, remove, and perform other package-related work. Working with Linux software packages is covered in Chapter 2.

The last system-related tool that this chapter covers is the *Hardware Browser*. Figure 3-6 shows two different *Hardware Browser* windows.

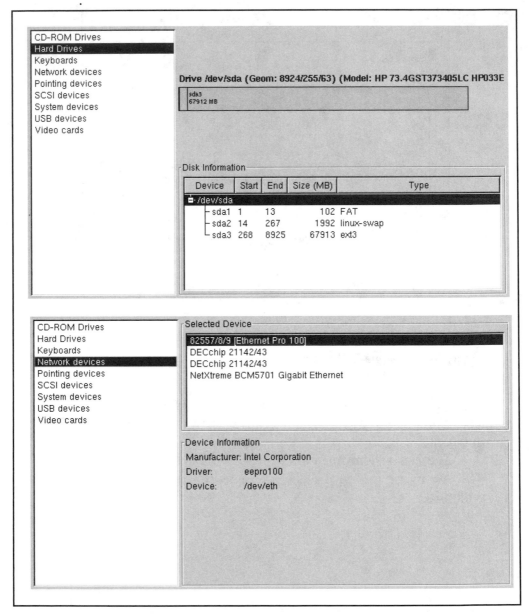

Figure 3-6   *Hardware Browser* Showing *Hard Drives* and *Networking devices*

The top window of Figure 3-6 shows the three internal hard drive partitions on our rx2600 that are all part of **/dev/sda**, and the bottom window shows the four network devices (although the DEC-chip cards shown are not supported in Linux, at the time of this writing, but the four-port cards are supported). The Hardware Browser can be a useful tool if you have forgotten what's installed in your system.

When you want to logout, select *Logout* from the *Start* menu. GNOME asks you if you want to save the current configuration. If you do, check the *Save the Current Configuration* checkbox, and click *OK*. The next time you log in, you will see the same windows you were working with when you logged off.

If you like GNOME and you're an HP-UX user, you can get GNOME for HP-UX from the GNOME project at *www.gnome.org*. Check out the Web site listed earlier. You can download and work with the latest version of ximian GNOME on HP-UX. Be sure to read the requirements for your system and other related information when you visit the Web site.

KDE

The K Desktop Environment (KDE) is an enhanced window manager. KDE not only describes the interface of the window environment, it also includes a set of libraries that allow applications to take advantage of special KDE features. This means that applications designed specifically for KDE may have to be ported to other window managers in order to work.

If you've selected KDE as the default for your window environment, it starts automatically when you login. If GNOME is your default and you want to use KDE, select *Session* at the bottom of your login screen. When the session dialog appears, select KDE. When you login, you may be asked again if you want to use KDE as your default window manager. If you do, select *yes*. If you only want to use KDE for the current session, select *no*. You can also a **switchdesk** command to switch desktops.

After logging in, you see a fully functional KDE environment. The one shown in Figure 3-7 is different than what you will see because KDE, like GNOME, is configured to remember your last session and to start all the applications you had open when you last logged out.

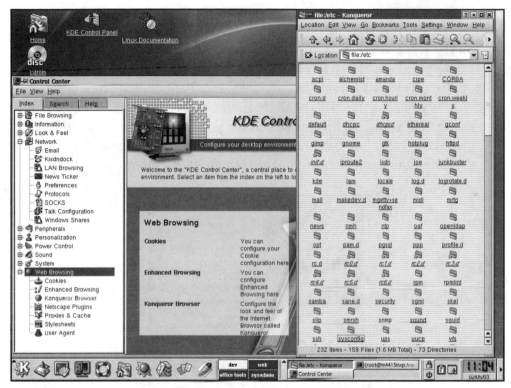

Figure 3-7   Full KDE Screen Shot

As you can see, because KDE remembers your last session, when you login, several application windows are already open. But, let's start at the bottom of the desktop with KDE's main toolbar. Starting at the left is the KDE icon for *Start Applications* (the "K") followed by the icons for *Show Desktop, Control Center, Help* (a life preserver), *Home Directory, Konqueror Web Browser, Email, KOffice* (office productivity tool), and finally *Kate* (a KDE editor).

Immediately to *Kate*'s right are the four *Desktop* names (GNOME calls them *Workspaces*). In this case, they are named *dev, web, office tools,* and *sysadmin,* but by default, they are called *Desktop 1, Desktop 2,* and so on. To the right of the Desktops, on the bottom, are the programs currently running. In this case, *Konqueror, Control Center,* and a terminal window for root are open and running.

To the right of the open applications, there are miscellaneous icons, such as the lock and time.

In Figure 3-7, the visible open windows are the *Control Center* on the left and the *Konqueror* file manager on the right. The *Control Center* is particularly interesting because from it, you can perform almost all system administration tasks, but more on that later.

If you click the "K" (or *Start Applications*) menu at the bottom of the screen, you see a menu from which you can select most of the programs available through the KDE window manager. Figure 3-8 shows the default organization of the *Start Applications* menu.

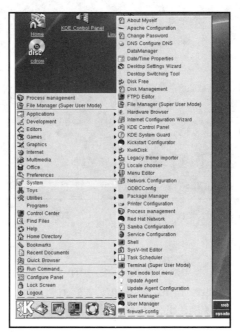

Figure 3-8   KDE Menu Pick

From the main menu, you select the *System* sub-menu to illustrate the number and variety of system administration tools available.

If you select the *KDE Control Center* either by finding and clicking it on the *Start Applications* menu or clicking the *Control Center* icon on the toolbar (fourth icon from the left in Figure 3-7), you can control almost any aspect of your system. Along the left side of the KDE *Control Center* window are menus that allow you to configure any aspect of your KDE environment. Figure 3-9 shows the *Control*

Center open to the *Web Browsing* controls. If you look closely, you can see the many *Web Browser* options that you can configure using this selection.

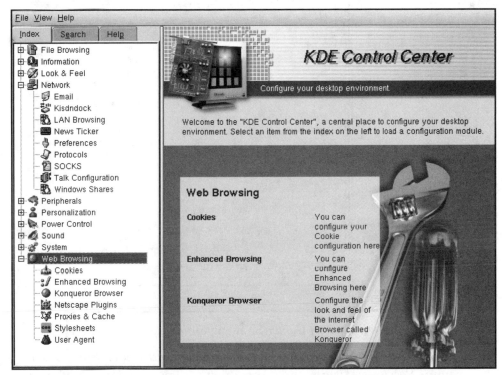

Figure 3-9 *KDE Control Center* Showing *Web Browsing*

If you click *System* and then *Login Manager* in the *KDE Control Center,* you can customize almost every aspect of your environment, as shown in Figure 3-10.

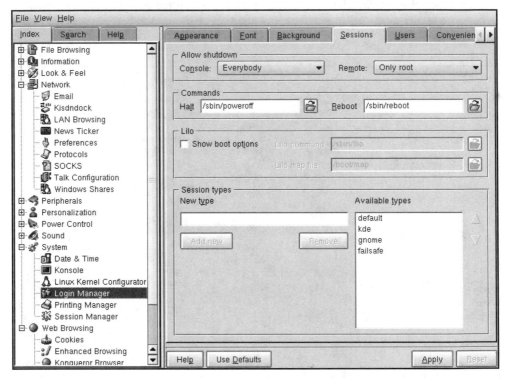

Figure 3-10   *KDE Control Center* Showing *System-Login Manager*

In this window, you can manipulate *Appearance, Font, Background, Sessions, Users,* and *Convenience.* The *Sessions* window is open, which includes additional *Session types* that you can choose. The *gnome* and *kde* types are included by default.

Window environments and managers are purely a matter of preference. In the case of Linux, you have GNOME and KDE as widely used window managers and you can download many others.

You can customize your GNOME or KDE desktop environments in an almost unlimited number of ways. In this section, we've only scratched the surface of what you can do. For more information about these window managers, look at the help included with the distribution.

To log out from either desktop environment, select *Logout* from the *Start* menu.

OpenOffice.org

OpenOffice.org is a suite of office software. It comes with many Linux distributions or you can download it from *www.openoffice.org*. This software provides your Linux (or other operating system) with a complete set of office software for free. You can download many other great products to your Linux system, but I included *OpenOffice* in this introductory desktop chapter because it demonstrates the power of the Open Source community. The software is easy to download and configure and provides a word processor, spreadsheet, drawing, and presentation program...all for free. At the time of this writing, the software is not available for Integrity servers, so the examples in this chapter are from a Red Hat 8.x system but plans are for it to be available in RHEL 3. Because the Integrity servers are new, there is still some software yet to be fully certified on the platform. I included the next section because the tools will be available at some point in the near future. As a sidenote, the "retail" versions of Red Hat, such as 8.x used in this section, have been replaced by Fedora. Fedora Project is a Red Hat-sponsored and community-supported open source project. Fedora Core 2 is available at the time of this writing.

I'm not going to describe the download and setup of *OpenOffice.org* in detail. I am only going to show you enough to get you started. The Web site provides all the information that you will need. Instead, I'll show a few screen shots of *OpenOffice.org* so you can see how powerful it is. The screenshots should also indicate how similar it is to *Microsoft Office,* thus illustrating that you won't have to learn a new way of working with office software. Lets start with the download. Figure 3-11 shows how easy it is to download *OpenOffice.org* from the *Open Office* Web site.

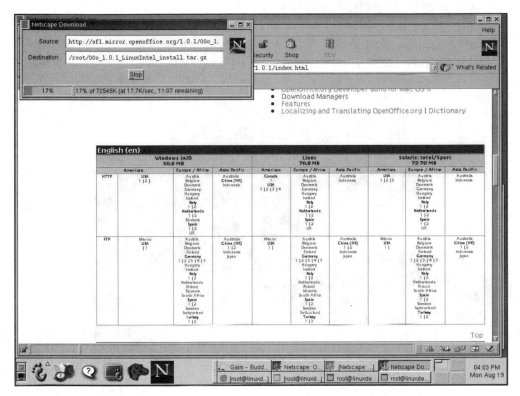

Figure 3-11   *OpenOffice.org* Download

After selecting the language for *OpenOffice.org* that you want to download, you simply select the destination for the software (as shown in the upper-left corner of the figure) and download. Notice that *OpenOffice.org* is available not only for Linux, but for other operating systems as well. After the download is complete, you simply run the setup program. The complete instructions for the download and setup are on the Web site.

If downloading is a problem, *OpenOffice* is available with the Red Hat 8 or 9 CD-ROMs. If you didn't install *OpenOffice.org* when you installed your Red Hat product, select *System Settings* ⇒ *Packages* (or *System Settings* ⇒ *Add/Remove Applications*) from the GNOME menu. When the *Package Management* tool opens, find the *Applications* section and check *Office/Productivity* and then click *Details*. When the *Office Productivity Details* window opens, check the box next to *OpenOffice,* then click *Close* to close the details window. When the *Package Mangagment* window reappears, click *Update* to install the suite.

After the download (or CD-ROM install) and setup of *OpenOffice.org* are complete, your user environment is enhanced to allow you to use the *OpenOffice.org* programs. Figure 3-12 shows the *OpenOffice.org* menu structure together with all the great tools available in the suite.

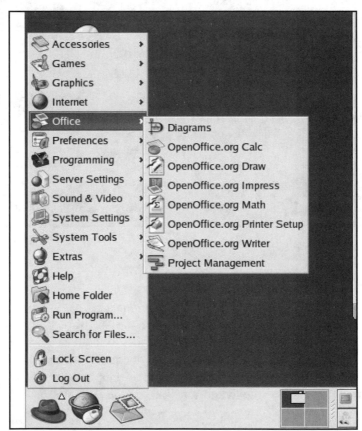

Figure 3-12   *OpenOffice* Menu Picks

You create new *OpenOffice* files in much the same way you would create them using the tools included with *Microsoft Office*. Additionally, if you already have *Microsoft Office* files, many can be read and modified using the tools supplied with *OpenOffice.org*. Figure 3-13 shows an file created with *Microsoft PowerPoint* file open for editing in *OpenOffice.org*.

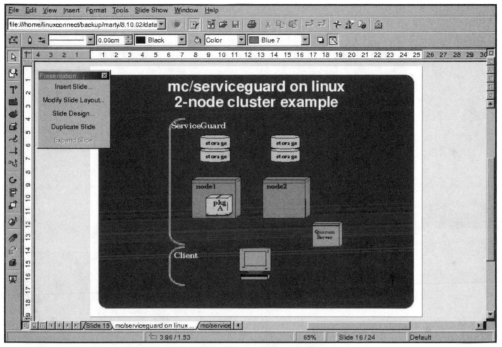

Figure 3-13   Existing File Read into *OpenOffice.org*

I have found that *OpenOffice.org* can create new (or modify) old files created in *Microsoft Office* easily and efficiently. I believe it will only get better. With the open-source community working on this application, you can only expect better things. I am using version *1.0.1* at the time of this writing, and it works great. I'm sure that future releases will include even more functionality.

Of all the almost unlimited number of applications of all types available for download and use on your Linux system, I've found that this is one of the best. It really enhances your Linux user environment and office tools.

Chapter 4

Disk and File System Topics

In keeping with the "how to" format of this book, this chapter presents disk and file system-related topics primarily by working with examples. First, you add a hard disk to an Integrity (Itanium-based) server with SCSI disks and then you add one to an IA-32 system with IDE drives. After that, you take a look at some of the filesystem tools and utilities just as a comparison. Along the way, the following topics are covered. Note that you must be logged on as root to perform most of these tasks:

- Adding and partitioning a disk and all related topics, such as **parted** (on Integrity), **fdisk** (on IA-32), and **mke2fs**.

- File system checking with **e2fsck** and related topics.

- **fstab**, **mount**, **e2label**, and **umount**

- Linux log files

- Smart Array Configuration

Adding and Partitioning a SCSI Disk on an Integrity Server

A commonly run procedure on Linux systems is to add a new disk and partition it. In Chapter 2, you installed Linux on a SCSI disk on the Integrity server and now you want to expand our system to include an additional disk.

Linux automatically detects new SCSI and IDE disks if you already have one such disk in your system. In the example in this section, you add a SCSI disk to the existing system that already has an SCSI drive in it. I'll walk through all the steps required to add the disk. In this section, you perform disk-related procedures on an Integrity server with SCSI disks. Later in this chapter, you perform the same procedures on an IA-32 system with IDE disks.

As with the installation of Linux, you'll employ partitions when you set up your new disk. In the example, we'll have only one partition that will contain the entire capacity of the disk.

The Integrity system on which I'll install the new disk has four disks internal to it. Linux was loaded in on **/dev/sdc** (**sdc** for SCSI disk C). **/dev/sda** and **/dev/sdb** (for SCSI disk A and B respectively) have other operating systems on them. The unused disk of **/dev/sdd** will be used in this example to create one large partition and mount it.

Our existing disk is already partitioned into **/dev/sdc1** for partition Á */boot/efi*, **/dev/sdc3** for partition */,* and a *none* partition for **/dev/shm**. Our new disk will be **/dev/sdd** and we will create one partition on it that will be named **/dev/sdd1**.

After physically adding the disk drive and booting the system, invoke **parted** to partition the disk. **parted** has many options. The following listing shows what happens when you invoke **parted** for the new SCSI disk and then view the available command options with **help**:

```
[root@linux1 root]# parted /dev/sdd
GNU Parted 1.6.3
Copyright (C) 1998, 1999, 2000, 2001, 2002 Free Software Foundation, Inc.
This program is free software, covered by the GNU General Public License.

This program is distributed in the hope that it will be useful, but WITHOUT
ANY
WARRANTY; without even the implied warranty of MERCHANTABILITY or FITNESS FOR
A
PARTICULAR PURPOSE.  See the GNU General Public License for more details.

Using /dev/sdd
(parted) help
  check MINOR                       do a simple check on the filesystem
    cp [FROM-DEVICE] FROM-MINOR TO-MINOR        copy filesystem to another par-
tition
```

```
help [COMMAND]                      prints general help, or help on COMMAND
mklabel LABEL-TYPE                  create a new disklabel (partition table)
mkfs MINOR FS-TYPE              make a filesystem FS-TYPE on partititon MINOR
mkpart PART-TYPE [FS-TYPE] START END       make a partition
mkpartfs PART-TYPE FS-TYPE START END    make a partition with a filesystem
move MINOR START END                move partition MINOR
name MINOR NAME                     name partition MINOR NAME
print [MINOR]                       display the partition table, or a partition
quit                                exit program
rescue START END                    rescue a lost partition near START and END
resize MINOR START END              resize filesystem on partition MINOR
rm MINOR                            delete partition MINOR
select DEVICE                       choose the device to edit
set MINOR FLAG STATE                change a flag on partition MINOR

(parted)
```

Because your new disk might have been obtained from another system, it's important to delete any existing partitions. Consequently, the next step you perform is to delete the existing partition on the disk with **rm**, and then view the partition table to confirm the partitions have been removed with **p**:

```
(parted) rm
Partition number? 1
(parted) p
Disk geometry for /dev/sdd: 0.000-34732.890 megabytes
Disk label type: gpt
Minor    Start        End      Filesystem  Name                 Flags

(parted)
```

You successfully deleted the partition and can now proceed to add your new partition which will consist of the entire contents of the disk. To do so, issue **mkpart** for adding a new partition, make it primary with *default*, select file system type *ext3*, and then specify as size of a start of *0* and an end of *34732* (the whole disk). Finally, use **p** to view the partition table:

```
(parted) mkpart
Partition type?   [primary]?
File system type?   [ext2]? ext3
Start? 0
End? 34732

(parted) p
Disk geometry for /dev/sdd: 0.000-34732.890 megabytes
Disk label type: gpt
Minor    Start        End      Filesystem  Name                 Flags
1        0.017   34732.874
(parted)
```

Note that when you viewed the partition, it consumed the total capacity of the disk because you selected *0-34732* for the range. This partition looks just the way we want it with the entire disk in a single partition.

Now that you have the disk partitioned, you'll need to create and mount a file system on the partition we created. Use **mke2fs** to make it and **mount** to mount it to a directory called **/backup**. After you're done, you'll take a look at all the partitions with **df**:

```
[root@linux1 root]# mke2fs -j /dev/sdd1
mke2fs 1.32 (09-Nov-2002)
Filesystem label=
OS type: Linux
Block size=4096 (log=2)
Fragment size=4096 (log=2)
4447744 inodes, 8891611 blocks
444580 blocks (5.00%) reserved for the super user
First data block=0
272 block groups
32768 blocks per group, 32768 fragments per group
16352 inodes per group
Superblock backups stored on blocks:
     32768, 98304, 163840, 229376, 294912, 819200, 884736, 1605632, 2654208,
        4096000, 7962624

Writing inode tables: done
Creating journal (8192 blocks): done
Writing superblocks and filesystem accounting information:
done

This filesystem will be automatically checked every 37 mounts or
180 days, whichever comes first.  Use tune2fs -c or -i to override.

[root@linux1 root]# mkdir /backup
[root@linux1 root]# mount /dev/sdd1 /backup
[root@linux1 root]# df
Filesystem           1K-blocks      Used Available Use% Mounted on
/dev/sdc3             32891620   1915540  29305280   7% /
/dev/sdc1               102182      4532     97650   5% /boot/efi
none                   2072832         0   2072832   0% /dev/shm
/dev/sdd1             35008108     32828  33196960   1% /backup
[root@linux1 root]#
```

df shows you that **/dev/sdd1** is now mounted as **/backup**. You can now use it for whatever purpose we want. If you want the filesystem mounted at boot time, we can add an entry to **/etc/fstab**. You'll look at that in the **fstab** section later in this chapter.

parted gives you the option to create many different types of file systems. For example, if you wanted to use this partition for swap, you would have created a swap partition with **parted** and then used **mkswap** to create a swap file system on it.

Many other Linux commands support many different types of file systems. When you issue the **mount** command, for instance, you can use the *-t* option to specify the type of file system you want to mount. The man page for the **mount** command lists many types of file systems that can be used with the *-t* option.

For example, one common file system I often mount on Linux IA-32 systems is a DOS floppy disk. You probably won't be doing this on an Integrity server, but it's good to know anyway. To use a DOS floppy disk, use the following commands to mount a DOS floppy, copy a file to it, and unmount it on an IA-32 system. (Note that in most cases, you must be logged on as root to mount filesystems.)

```
# mount -t msdos /dev/fd0 /mnt/floppy
# cp * /mnt/floppy
# ls /mnt/floppy
file1               file2      file3      file4
# umount /dev/fd0
```

This sequence of commands first mounts **/dev/fd0**, which is the floppy disk device file. At the mount point **/mnt/floppy**, **/dev/fd0** is mounted as type *msdos,* as specified by the *-t msdos*. I next copy all files in the current directory to the floppy. All the files on the floppy are then listed with **ls**, producing the list of four files shown. I then unmount the floppy disk with the **umount** command so that I can take the floppy to a DOS system and read the files. Because the floppy was mounted as type *msdos,* the files were written to the floppy in DOS format.

Similarly, to mount a CD-ROM on a Linux system, you would issue the following **mount** command, unless it's mounted at boot. This CD-ROM is, of course, a read-only device, as the message from **mount** indicates:

```
[root@localhost root]# mount /dev/cdrom /mnt/cdrom
mount: block device /dev/cdrom is write-protected, mounting read-only
[root@localhost root]# df
Filesystem           1k-blocks       Used Available Use% Mounted on
/dev/sda3             68450624    1419592  63553900   3% /
/dev/sda1               104184       6120     98064   6% /boot/efi
none                   1024560          0   1024560   0% /dev/shm
/dev/sdb1             35001508      32828  33190688   1% /backup
/dev/cdrom              658016     658016         0 100% /mnt/cdrom
[root@localhost root]#
```

Adding an IDE Disk to an IA-32 System Using fdisk

As a comparison only to the Integrity procedure, look at the installation of a second IDE disk, this time on your IA-32 system. Keep in mind though that most IA-32 systems, like Proliants, have SCSI disks. It's really not that different from installing a second SCSI disk, but it's worth going over again. Linux automatically detects new SCSI and IDE disks if you already have one such disk in your system. In the example in this section, we'll add an IDE disk to the existing system that already has an IDE drive in it. In keeping with the "how to" format of this book, I'll walk through all the steps required to add the disk.

Just like when you installed Linux on the first IDE drive, you'll employ partitions when you set up our new disk. In the following example, you'll have only one partition that will contain the entire capacity of the disk.

The existing disk on the system is **/dev/hda**. Our new disk will be **/dev/hdb**, which are the names that Linux selects for IDE disks. Our existing disk is partitioned into **/dev/hda1** for partition number one, **/dev/hda2** for partition number two, and so on. If you want to see the partitions on your first disk, before you start adding the new disk, log on as root and issue the command **fdisk -l /dev/hda**. You will see all the partitions on your existing disk. Because this is the second IDE hard disk, our new disk will be **/dev/hdb.** Because there will be only one partition on it, the partition will be **/dev/hdb1**. If you read the earlier section, "Adding and Partitioning a SCSI Disk on an Integrity Server," you already know that the naming convention for SCSI disks is similar with **/dev/sda** being the first SCSI disk and **/dev/sdb** being the second disk.

In the example, you add an IDE drive that already has two partitions on it. Keep in mind that if you have a brand new drive, it may not have any partitions on it, and you can skip the sections where we delete the existing partitions.

After physically adding the disk drive and booting the system, log on as root to invoke **fdisk** in order to partition the disk. After fdisk starts, select *m* to view all the available **fdisk** options.

```
# fdisk /dev/hdb

Command (m for help): m
Command action
   a   toggle a bootable flag
   b   edit bsd disklabel
   c   toggle the dos compatibility flag
   d   delete a partition
   l   list known partition types
   m   print this menu
   n   add a new partition
   o   create a new empty DOS partition table
   p   print the partition table
   q   quit without saving changes
   s   create a new empty Sun disklabel
   t   change a partition's system id
   u   change display/entry units
   v   verify the partition table
   w   write table to disk and exit
   x   extra functionality (experts only)
```

Now that you can see the **fdisk** options, we'll print the disk's partition table with **p**, delete the two existing partitions on the disk with **d**, and then confirm the partitions have been removed by printing the partition table again with **p**:

```
Command (m for help): p

Disk /dev/hdb: 255 heads, 63 sectors, 488 cylinders
Units = cylinders of 16065 * 512 bytes

   Device Boot    Start       End    Blocks   Id  System
/dev/hdb1   *         1       128   1028128+   83  Linux
Partition 1 has different physical/logical endings:
     phys=(135, 239, 63) logical=(127, 254, 63)
Partition 1 does not end on cylinder boundary:
     phys=(135, 239, 63) should be (135, 254, 63)
/dev/hdb2           129       137     68040   82  Linux swap
Partition 2 has different physical/logical beginnings (non-Linux?):
     phys=(136, 0, 1) logical=(128, 0, 1)
Partition 2 has different physical/logical endings:
     phys=(144, 239, 63) logical=(136, 119, 63)
Partition 2 does not end on cylinder boundary:
     phys=(144, 239, 63) should be (144, 254, 63)

Command (m for help): d
Partition number (1-4): 1

Command (m for help): d
Partition number (1-4): 2

Command (m for help): p

Disk /dev/hdb: 255 heads, 63 sectors, 488 cylinders
Units = cylinders of 16065 * 512 bytes

   Device Boot    Start       End    Blocks   Id  System
```

As you can see, the second **p** command reports that you have successfully deleted both of the existing disk partitions and can now proceed to add our partition that will consist of the entire contents of the disk. As you can see in the next listing, we issue **n** to add a new partition, then make it primary with **p**. After that, set the partition number to *1* and accept the defaults for the first cylinder (*1*) and the last cylinder (*488*). This creates a partition that uses the entire disk. Lastly, use **p** to print the partition table:

```
Command (m for help): n
Command action
   e   extended
   p   primary partition (1-4)
p
Partition number (1-4): 1
First cylinder (1-488, default 1):
Using default value 1
Last cylinder or +size or +sizeM or +sizeK (1-488, default 488):
Using default value 488

Command (m for help): p

Disk /dev/hdb: 255 heads, 63 sectors, 488 cylinders
Units = cylinders of 16065 * 512 bytes

   Device Boot    Start       End    Blocks   Id  System
/dev/hdb1              1       488  3919828+   83  Linux
```

When you viewed the partition, it was nearly four GB, which is the total capacity of the disk because we selected the defaults for the beginning and end of the partition. This partition looks just the way we want it with the entire disk in this single partition. Next, you'll change the type of partition with **t**, and then specify a type *Linux* with *83*:

```
Command (m for help): t
Partition number (1-4): 1
Hex code (type L to list codes): l

   0  Empty           1c  Hidden Win95 FA 65  Novell Netware  bb  Boot Wizard hid
   1  FAT12           1e  Hidden Win95 FA 70  DiskSecure Mult c1  DRDOS/sec (FAT-
   2  XENIX root      24  NEC DOS         75  PC/IX           c4  DRDOS/sec (FAT-
   3  XENIX usr       39  Plan 9          80  Old Minix       c6  DRDOS/sec (FAT-
   4  FAT16 <32M      3c  PartitionMagic  81  Minix / old Lin c7  Syrinx
   5  Extended        40  Venix 80286     82  Linux swap      da  Non-FS data
   6  FAT16           41  PPC PReP Boot   83  Linux           db  CP/M / CTOS / .
   7  HPFS/NTFS       42  SFS             84  OS/2 hidden C:  de  Dell Utility
   8  AIX             4d  QNX4.x          85  Linux extended  df  BootIt
   9  AIX bootable    4e  QNX4.x 2nd part 86  NTFS volume set e1  DOS access
   a  OS/2 Boot Manag 4f  QNX4.x 3rd part 87  NTFS volume set e3  DOS R/O
   b  Win95 FAT32     50  OnTrack DM      8e  Linux LVM       e4  SpeedStor
   c  Win95 FAT32 (LB 51  OnTrack DM6 Aux 93  Amoeba          eb  BeOS fs
   e  Win95 FAT16 (LB 52  CP/M            94  Amoeba BBT      ee  EFI GPT
   f  Win95 Ext'd (LB 53  OnTrack DM6 Aux 9f  BSD/OS          ef  EFI (FAT-12/16/
  10  OPUS            54  OnTrackDM6      a0  IBM Thinkpad hi f0  Linux/PA-RISC b
  11  Hidden FAT12    55  EZ-Drive        a5  FreeBSD         f1  SpeedStor
  12  Compaq diagnost 56  Golden Bow      a6  OpenBSD         f4  SpeedStor
  14  Hidden FAT16 <3 5c  Priam Edisk     a7  NeXTSTEP        f2  DOS secondary
  16  Hidden FAT16    61  SpeedStor       a9  NetBSD          fd  Linux raid auto
  17  Hidden HPFS/NTF 63  GNU HURD or Sys b7  BSDI fs         fe  LANstep
  18  AST SmartSleep  64  Novell Netware  b8  BSDI swap       ff  BBT
  1b  Hidden Win95 FA
Hex code (type L to list codes): 83

Command (m for help): p

Disk /dev/hdb: 255 heads, 63 sectors, 488 cylinders
Units = cylinders of 16065 * 512 bytes

   Device Boot    Start       End    Blocks   Id  System
/dev/hdb1              1       488  3919828+   83  Linux
```

When you entered partition *l*, **fdisk** listed many types of partitions, including *Linux*, *Linux swap*, *Linux extended*, and *Linux LVM*. You selected *Linux,* but we could have selected any partition type. **fdisk** is a versatile program that can be used to create many types of partitions and the list is growing all the time.

Now that you're done partitioning the hard disk, it's time to write changes to the disk with *w*:

```
Command (m for help): w
The partition table has been altered!

Calling ioctl() to re-read partition table.
Syncing disks.

#
```

The partition is now ready for a file system. You'll use **mke2fs** to create one. Just like it did for our SCSI disk earlier, **mke2fs** puts a *Linux second extended file system* on the partition. When you specify the j option with **mke2fs**, an *ext3* journal is placed on the partition. This is a little confusing because using the *ext2* command of **mke2fs**, but specifying an option for the *ext3* journaling. Note that if this partition were to be used for swap, you would create a swap file system on it with **mkswap** instead **mke2fs**:

```
# mke2fs -j /dev/hdb1
mke2fs 1.27 (8-Mar-2002)
Filesystem label=
OS type: Linux
Block size=4096 (log=2)
Fragment size=4096 (log=2)
490560 inodes, 979957 blocks
48997 blocks (5.00%) reserved for the super user
First data block=0
30 block groups
32768 blocks per group, 32768 fragments per group
16352 inodes per group
Superblock backups stored on blocks:
            32768, 98304, 163840, 229376, 294912, 819200, 884736

Writing inode tables:  0/30
Creating journal (8192 blocks): done
Writing superblocks and filesystem accounting information: done

This filesystem will be automatically checked every 28 mounts or
180 days, whichever comes first.  Use tune2fs -c or -i to override.
```

Now, mount it with **mount** and view all of the partitions with **df**:

```
# mount /dev/hdb1 /backup
# df


Filesystem          1k-blocks      Used Available Use% Mounted on
/dev/hda5              381139      75222    286239  21% /
/dev/hda1               46636       8646     35582  20% /boot
/dev/hda3             1423096      48216   1302588   4% /home
none                    47160          0     47160   0% /dev/shm
/dev/hda2             3889924    1661608   2030720  46% /usr
/dev/hda6              256667      44297    199118  19% /var
/dev/hdb1             3858204      32828   3629388   1% /backup

#
```

As you can see, **/dev/hdb1** is mounted on **/backup**. Now that it's mounted, you can use it for whatever purpose you want. Just as you did with Á **/dev/sdb1** earlier, if you want the filesystem mounted at boot time, you can add an entry to **/etc/fstab**. That's discussed that in the **fstab** section later in this chapter.

As you have seen, **fdisk** allows us to create many different types of file systems. Similarly, many other commands used in Linux support many different types of file systems. When you issue the **mount** command, for instance, you can use the **-t** option to specify the type of file system you want to mount. The man page for the **mount** command lists many types of file systems that can be used with the **-t** option. To see how to use **mount** to mount a DOS floppy disk or a CD-ROM drive, see page 87.

File System Maintenance with fsck and e2fsck, inodes, and Superblock

This section looks at maintaining file systems. Most examples will refer to the Integrity server with SCSI that you worked on earlier in this chapter. Even so, the tools and utilities work the same way on the IA-32 system with IDE drives. Again, remember that to use almost all of these tools, you must be logged on as root.

fsck and e2fsck

fsck (file system check) is a program used for file system maintenance on Linux and UNIX systems. **fsck** checks file system consistency and can make many "life-saving" repairs to a corrupt file system. **fsck** can be run with several options. The program used for *ext2* file systems checking is **e2fsck**. If you try running **fsck** on an *ext2* or *ext3* file system, you'll see that **fsck** automatically calls **e2fsck**. The following are some of the more commonly used options with **e2fsck**:

-b superblock	Normally, **e2fsck** uses block 1 to find partition-related information. If, however, block 1 id is corrupted, you can specify a block number that usually exists every 8192 blocks. You'd specify 8193, 16385, and so on as alternates. You can also find backup superblocks by noting them when the files system is created (as shown in the earlier listing), or by using the mke2fs program using the -n option to print out where the superblocks were created. The -b option to mke2fs, which specifies blocksize of the filesystem must be specified in order for the superblock locations that are printed out to be accurate. See the man pages for **e2fsck** and **mke2fs** for more information.
-c	Runs the *badblocks* program to find bad blocks on the file system and adds them to the bad block inode.
-f	Forces checking of the file system even if it is thought to be clean.
-y	Responds *yes* to all questions so that **e2fsck** can be run non-interactively.
-v	Runs in *verbose* mode.

To run **e2fsck** on partition **/dev/sdb1** with the *-y* and *-v* options, you would do the following:

```
[root@localhost root]# umount /backup
[root@localhost root]# e2fsck
Usage: e2fsck [-panyrcdfvstFSV] [-b superblock] [-B blocksize]
              [-I inode_buffer_blocks] [-P process_inode_size]
              [-l|-L bad_blocks_file] [-C fd] [-j ext-journal] device

Emergency help:
 -p                     Automatic repair (no questions)
 -n                     Make no changes to the filesystem
 -y                     Assume "yes" to all questions
 -c                     Check for bad blocks
 -f                     Force checking even if filesystem is marked clean
 -v                     Be verbose
 -b superblock          Use alternative superblock
 -B blocksize           Force blocksize when looking for superblock
 -j external-journal    Set location of the external journal
 -l bad_blocks_file     Add to badblocks list
 -L bad_blocks_file     Set badblocks list
[root@localhost root]# e2fsck /dev/sdb1 -y -v
e2fsck 1.26 (3-Feb-2002)
/dev/sdb1: clean, 11/4447744 files, 147791/8889961 blocks
[root@localhost root]#
```

Before you ran **e2fsck**, you first unmounted the */backup* file system (**umount /backup**). Before you can check any filesystem, you must first be sure to unmount it. After you unmounted **/backup**, you then intentionally typed **e2fsck** without any options to see a summary of the command.

Since boot time, your system runs **e2fsck** on any file systems that were not marked as clean at the time you shut down the system, you can rest assured that when your system boots, any disks that were not properly shut down will be checked. Still, it is a good idea to unmount your file systems and run **e2fsck** interactively on a periodic basis just so you can see firsthand that all of your file systems are in good working order.

Should **e2fsck** find a problem with a directory or file, it would place these in the **lost+found** directory, which is at the top level of each file system. If a file or directory appears in **lost+found,** you may be able to identify the file or directory by examining it and moving it back to its original location. You can use the **file**, **what**, and **strings** commands on a file to obtain more information about it to help identify its origin.

How are file system problems created? The most common cause of a file system problem is improper shutdown of the system. The information written to file systems is first written to a buffer cache in memory. It is later written to the disk with the **sync** command by unmounting the disk, or through the normal use of filling the buffer and writing it to the disk. If you walk up to a system and shut off the power, you will likely end up with a file system problem. Data in the buffer that was not synchronized to the disk will be lost, the file system will not be marked as properly shut down, and **e2fsck** will run when the system boots. A sudden loss of power can also cause an improper system shutdown.

Proper shutdown of the system is described with the **shutdown** command. Although **e2fsck** is a useful utility that has been known to work miracles on occasion, you don't want to take any unnecessary risks with your file systems. So, be sure to properly shut down your system.

Inodes

You may see messages that include references to *inodes* when running **e2fsck**. Inodes are control mechanisms in Linux and UNIX that point to data blocks or other inodes on your storage subsystem. The inode contains the inode number, the length of the file, the file's creation date, the time the file was last accessed, the time the file was last changed, the time the inode was last changed, the owner of the file and group, the size of the file, the access rights, direct and indirect pointers to blocks of data, device numbers for special files, and a variety of other information. In the case of a directory, which is a simply a special type of file in Linux, the inode points to data blocks that contain important information about the files in the directory. Because the inode contains important information and pointer information, it is vital to the existence of a healthy file system.

In addition to inodes, you may also see information related to the *superblock*. The superblock contains important information about the disk on which it resides, such as the location of the first inode, the amount of available space, and so on.

/etc/fstab, e2label, and mount

/etc/fstab

The **/etc/fstab** file mentioned earlier is used by **e2fsck** to determine the sequence of the file system check if it is required at the time of boot. The sequence of entries in **/etc/fstab** is important if a "pass number" for any of the entries does not exist. Here is an example of the **/etc/fstab** file from the Integrity server with SCSI:

```
LABEL=/              /                 ext3      defaults           1        1
/dev/sda1            /boot/efi         vfat      defaults           0        0
none                 /dev/pts          devpts    gid=5,mode=620     0        0
none                 /proc             proc      defaults           0        0
none                 /dev/shm          tmpfs     defaults           0        0
/dev/sda2            swap              swap      defaults           0        0
/dev/cdrom           /mnt/cdrom        iso9660   noauto,owner,      0        0
                                                   kudzu, ro

     |                    |                 |          |            |        |

     V                    V                 V          V            V        V
```

/dev/device or label	directory	fstype	options	dump frequency	pass #

Table 4-1   Description /etc/fstab fields

Field	Description
/dev/device or label the device special file (if any)	The partition to be mounted, such as **/dev/sda1**. The device does not have to be given explicitly. You can use *LABEL* instead of the device by mapping the device to a label with the following: # **/sbin/e2label /dev/***sdbx* */mountpoint* # **/sbin/e2label /dev/sdb1 /backup** The entry for **/backup** can then be added to the **/etc/fstab** file with the *LABEL* as described shortly. You have to be careful using the *LABEL* because in some cases, it is not supported.
directory	The name of the directory under which the device special file is mounted such as **/backup**.

Field	Description
fstype	Can be one of several types, includingÁ *ext2* local file system version 2,Á *ext3* local file system version 3,Á *msdos* local MS-DOS partition,Á *nfs* remotely mounted NFS,Á *swap* partition used for swapping, or *iso9660* local CD-ROM file system
options	Options associated with the file system type. These are *-o* options.
dump frequency	Used by **dump** command to determine which file systems need to be dumped.
pass #	Specifies the order in which file systems are to be checked by **e2fsck** at reboot time.
Comments	Anything you want, as long as it's preceded by a # (pound sign or cross-hatch).

As you can see, in the **/etc/fstab** example, the *cdrom* has several options, including *ro* for read only. Swap, or virtual memory, is on **/dev/sda2**. **/proc** has a *none* associated with it because it is an interface to kernel parameters and not a file system like the others. **/dev/pts** also has a *none* associated with it because it is a way for remote system access with programs, such as **telnet** and **rlogin**, to get access to your system.

You could easily add entries to **/etc/fstab** so that the system will mount **/backup** when it boots. Because you want to mount **/dev/sdb1** using its label (**/backupB**), first use the command **e2label** to create a label. After you do that, run the **e2label** command again to display the results:

```
[root@localhost root]# /sbin/e2label /dev/sdb1 /backup
[root@localhost root]# /sbin/e2label /dev/sdb1
/backup
[root@localhost root]#
```

As you can see, we performed the desired labeling. Now, in order to automatically mount the new partition at boot time, add the following line to the **/etc/fstab** file:

```
LABEL=/backup    /backup   ext3    defaults  1 2
```

Then, save the file. If you want to check if the partition will be mounted in the correct place at boot time, reboot and log on again, or issue the following commands.

```
[root@localhost root]# mount -a
[root@localhost root]# df
Filesystem          1k-blocks     Used Available Use% Mounted on
/dev/sda3           68450624   1419368  63554124  3% /
/dev/sda1             104184      6120     98064  6% /boot/efi
none                1024560         0   1024560  0% /dev/shm
/dev/sdb1           35001508     32828  33190688  1% /backup
[root@localhost root]#
```

mount -a reads **/etc/fstab** and mounts all unmounted file systems listed in the file. **df** asks the system to report on all the free disk on the system. It reports that **/dev/sbd1** is mounted on **/backup**, and that it is only 1% full.

The **mount** command has been used a lot in this chapter and hasn't really been covered yet. That's because most of the work you do with **mount** is basic. Still, there are a lot of options to the command that you can see on the man page. However, the basic form of the **mount** command is as follows:

```
mount   [options]   device   dir
```

You've already used some of the **mount** options in the examples. The following lists of some of the more commonly used options:

-a	Mounts all filesystems in **/etc/fstab**. This was used in the earlier example.
-t *fstype*	Specifies the type of file system being mounted, but **mount** usually senses this on its own, so you don't normally need this option.
-o *options*	When using **-o**, you can specify many options, such as *ro* for read only, *rw* for read write, *noauto* for disabling automatic mount when *-a* is specified.

Now that you can mount a file system, you should know how to unmount it. Linux uses the **umount** (note that its **umount**, not unmount) command to unmount a file system:

```
umount [-f] directory
```

Provided that the file system is not in use, it will be unmounted immediately. Being in use includes simply being in the directory or a process of having a file open that resides on the mounted file system. Consequently, you may have to change directories if you are in a directory on the file system to be unmounted, or you may have to use **kill** to stop the process attached to the file system. Similarly, if you have a file open on the file system you want to unmount, you'll have to close it. You may have to use **umount -f** to force the filesystem to be unmounted, or go into what Linux calls "single user mode."

Linux Log Files

The most important activities that take place on your Linux system are recorded in log files. There are many log files on your Linux system. One of the most important is *syslog*, which is the system event logger used by many programs to perform logging.

syslog supports message sorting that allows a given message to be sorted by its importance and source and then sent to the appropriate destination. *syslog* consists of the **syslogd** (the logging daemon), **openlog**, which is a series of library routines the submit messages to **syslogd**, and **logger**, a user-level command that submits log entries from the shell. **syslogd** is started at boot time. If you want to see it running on your system, use the **ps** command to display all the processes running on your system.

To specify the file in which specific log entries will be placed, use **/etc/syslog.conf**. The general format of this file is to have a *selector* field and an *action* field. Both fields have several sub-levels. For instance, the *selector* field can have levels that go from informational (*info*) all the way to emergencies (*emerg*). The *action* field can go from the file to which messages are written (*filename*) to writing messages to the screen of all users (*), if there is an important message to send.

The following is the **/etc/syslog.conf** file from our Integrity server:

```
# Log all kernel messages to the console.
# Logging much else clutters up the screen.
#kern.*                                                  /dev/console

# Log anything (except mail) of level info or higher.
# Don't log private authentication messages!
*.info;mail.none;news.none;authpriv.none;cron.none                 /var/log/messages

# The authpriv file has restricted access.
authpriv.*                                               /var/log/secure

# Log all the mail messages in one place.
mail.*                                                   /var/log/maillog

# Log cron stuff
cron.*                                                   /var/log/cron

# Everybody gets emergency messages
*.emerg                                                  *

# Save news errors of level crit and higher in a special file.
uucp,news.crit                                           /var/log/spooler

# Save boot messages also to boot.log
local7.*                                                 /var/log/boot.log

#
# INN
#
news.=crit                                        /var/log/news/news.crit
news.=err                                         /var/log/news/news.err
news.notice                                       /var/log/news/news.notice
```

You can see from this file that kernel-related messages are sent to the console, mail-related messages are sent to **/var/log/maillog**, cron-related messages are sent to **/var/log/cron**, and so on.

In the previous listing, you can see that all the log files on the system are in **/var/log**, which is the most common location for log files. The following is a long listing of the **/var/log** directory of the Integrity server:

```
# ls -l /var/log
total 3664
-rw-r-----   1 root       root         1425 Jan 28 20:08 acpid
-rw-------   1 root       root         9222 Jan 28 20:09 boot.log
-rw-------   1 root       root         8667 Jan 24 22:15 boot.log.1
-rw-------   1 root       root        12593 Jan 24 16:58 boot.log.2
-rw-------   1 root       root       750359 Jan 29 17:00 cron
-rw-------   1 root       root       305847 Jan 26 04:02 cron.1
-rw-------   1 root       root       207252 Jan 24 17:03 cron.2
-rw-r--r--   1 root       root        12034 Jan 28 20:08 dmesg
drwxr-xr-x   2 root       root         4096 Jun 24  2001 fax
drwxr-xr-x   2 root       root         4096 Jan 16 16:41 gdm
drwxr-xr-x   2 root       root         4096 Jun 24  2002 httpd
drwx------   2 root       root         4096 Feb 22  2002 iptraf
-rw-r--r--   1 root       root          442 Jan 28 20:08 iscsi.log
drwxr-xr--   2 junkbust   junkbust     4096 Jul  7  2001 junkbuster
-rw-r--r--   1 root       root        79506 Jan 28 20:08 ksyms.0
-rw-r--r--   1 root       root        79506 Jan 28 19:41 ksyms.1
-rw-r--r--   1 root       root        79506 Jan 28 19:20 ksyms.2
-rw-r--r--   1 root       root        79506 Jan 28 19:06 ksyms.3
-rw-r--r--   1 root       root        79506 Jan 24 22:15 ksyms.4
```

```
-rw-r--r--    1 root     root         79506 Jan 24 20:07 ksyms.5
-rw-r--r--    1 root     root         79506 Jan 24 18:38 ksyms.6
-rw-r--r--    1 root     root      19398360 Jan 29 01:05 lastlog
-rw-------    1 root     root          7665 Jan 29 16:08 maillog
-rw-------    1 root     root          3104 Jan 26 04:02 maillog.1
-rw-------    1 root     root          1716 Jan 24 16:58 maillog.2
drwxrwsr-x    2 root     mailman       4096 Jan 26 04:02 mailman
-rw-------    1 root     root        263224 Jan 29 04:03 messages
-rw-------    1 root     root        123647 Jan 25 04:03 messages.1
-rw-------    1 root     root        173869 Jan 24 16:58 messages.2
-rw-r-----    1 mysql    mysql            0 Jan 26 04:02 mysqld.log
-rw-r-----    1 mysql    mysql            0 Jan 24 17:03 mysqld.log.1
-rw-r--r--    1 root     root             0 Jan 16 11:32 mysqld.log.2
drwxr-xr-x    3 news     news          4096 Jan 16 10:54 news
-rw-------    1 root     root        177984 Jan 29 17:00 pacct
-rw-------    1 root     root         95922 Jan 29 04:02 pacct.1.gz
-rw-------    1 root     root         29079 Jan 28 04:02 pacct.2.gz
-rw-------    1 root     root         50909 Jan 27 04:02 pacct.3.gz
-rw-------    1 root     root         29069 Jan 26 04:02 pacct.4.gz
-rw-------    1 root     root         91306 Jan 25 04:02 pacct.5.gz
-rw-------    1 root     root         50800 Jan 24 17:03 pacct.6.gz
-rw-------    1 root     root         89431 Jan 17 04:02 pacct.7.gz
-rwx------    1 postgres postgres         0 Jan 16 10:54 pgsql
drwxrwxr-x    2 piranha  root          4096 Jan 16 11:26 piranha
-rw-r--r--    1 root     root         28991 Jan 29 04:02 rpmpkgs
-rw-r--r--    1 root     root         28991 Jan 25 04:02 rpmpkgs.1
-rw-r--r--    1 root     root         28991 Jan 17 04:02 rpmpkgs.2
drwxr-xr-x    2 root     root          4096 Jan 29 04:03 sa
drwx------    2 root     root          4096 Sep 18  2001 samba
-rw-------    1 root     root             0 Sep  6  2001 savacct
-rw-------    1 root     root          1473 Jan 29 01:05 secure
-rw-------    1 root     root          1857 Jan 24 22:15 secure.1
-rw-------    1 root     root          1393 Jan 24 16:58 secure.2
-rw-------    1 root     root             0 Jan 26 04:02 spooler
-rw-------    1 root     root             0 Jan 24 17:03 spooler.1
-rw-------    1 root     root             0 Jan 16 10:42 spooler.2
drwxr-x---    2 squid    squid         4096 Jun 27  2002 squid
-rw-------    1 root     root             0 Sep  6  2001 usracct
drwxr-xr-x    2 uucp     uucp          4096 Jan 16 11:35 uucp
drwxr-xr-x    2 root     root          4096 May 21  2002 vbox
-rw-rw-r--    1 root     utmp        206400 Jan 29 01:05 wtmp
-rw-------    1 root     root             0 Jan 26 04:02 xferlog
-rw-------    1 root     root             0 Jan 24 17:03 xferlog.1
-rw-------    1 root     root             0 Jan 16 10:54 xferlog.2
-rw-r--r--    1 root     root        112525 Jan 28 21:34 XFree86.0.log
drwxr-x---    2 root     root          4096 Aug  2 14:24 zebra
#
```

Most of the log files in this directory are ASCII files that can be viewed or edited as text files. Because **wtmp** contains a list of logins and logouts for users and is a binary file, you must use a command that can interpret it. In the following example, **last -20** shows the last 20 lines in the file. As you can see, the **last** command decodes the information in this file:

```
# last -20
root     pts/0        pal2nai168208.ns Wed Jan 29 01:05   still logged in
rootroot pts/1        atl2nai162053.ss Tue Jan 28 21:19 - 21:23  (00:04)
root     pts/2        :0               Tue Jan 28 21:11 - 21:34  (00:23)
root     pts/0        :0               Tue Jan 28 20:09 - 21:34  (01:24)
root     :0                            Tue Jan 28 20:09 - 21:34  (01:25)
root     :0                            Tue Jan 28 20:09 - 20:09  (00:00)
reboot   system boot  2.4.18-e.12smp   Tue Jan 28 20:08          (20:54)
root     pts/0        :0               Tue Jan 28 19:43 - down   (00:23)
root     :0                            Tue Jan 28 19:42 - down   (00:23)
```

```
reboot    system boot  2.4.18-e.12smp    Tue Jan 28 19:41          (00:24)
root    pts/0          :0               Tue Jan 28 19:21 - down  (00:18)
root    :0                              Tue Jan 28 19:21 - down  (00:18)
reboot    system boot  2.4.18-e.12smp    Tue Jan 28 19:20          (00:19)
root    pts/0          :0               Tue Jan 28 19:08 - down  (00:10)
root    :0                              Tue Jan 28 19:07 - down  (00:10)
reboot    system boot  2.4.18-e.12smp    Tue Jan 28 19:06          (00:11)
root    pts/1          :0               Tue Jan 28 16:44 - 19:04 (02:20)
root    pts/0          :0               Tue Jan 28 16:19 - 19:04 (02:44)
root    :0                              Tue Jan 28 16:18 - down  (02:46)
reboot    system boot  2.4.18-e.12smp    Fri Jan 24 22:15          (3+20:49)

wtmp begins Thu Jan 16 16:40:37 2003
#
```

This example shows the last 20 entries in **wtmp** including reboots.

Most of the files are automatically "rotated" meaning that the newest files have an extension of *1* and the oldest files have an extension with a higher number.

Notice in the long listing of **/var/log** that some subdirectories for some applications such as *samba.* Many log files that are in the **/var/log/samba** directory on the IA-32 system are used in the Samba chapter, as shown in the following long listing:

```
# ll /var/log/samba

total 53
-rw-r--r--    1 root     root            0 Jun 15 11:15 f4412bfg.log
-rw-r--r--    1 root     root            0 Aug 17 04:03 f4457mxp.log
-rw-r--r--    1 root     root          118 Aug 17 04:03 f4457mxp.log.1
-rw-r--r--    1 root     root          235 Jul 22 04:03 f4457mxp.log.
-rw-r--r--    1 root     root          664 Jun 23 04:03 f4457mxp.log.3
-rw-r--r--    1 root     root            0 Jun 21 12:22 linuxdev.log
-rw-r--r--    1 root     root        25738 Aug 17 04:03 log.nmbd
-rw-r--r--    1 root     root         5069 Aug 16 08:36 log.smbd
-rw-r--r--    1 root     root          411 Aug 15 17:40 nmbd.log
-rw-r--r--    1 root     root          209 Aug 11 04:03 nmbd.log.1
-rw-r--r--    1 root     root          460 Aug 10 10:30 nmbd.log.2
-rw-r--r--    1 root     root          158 Jul 28 04:03 nmbd.log.3
-rw-r--r--    1 root     root           79 Jul 21 04:03 nmbd.log.4
-rw-r--r--    1 root     root          130 Aug 17 04:03 smbd.log
-rw-r--r--    1 root     root           65 Aug 11 04:03 smbd.log.1
-rw-r--r--    1 root     root          130 Aug 10 10:30 smbd.log.2
-rw-r--r--    1 root     root          130 Jul 28 04:03 smbd.log.3
-rw-r--r--    1 root     root           65 Jul 21 04:03 smbd.log.4
-rw-r--r--    1 root     root            0 Aug 10 10:30 smbmount.log
-rw-r--r--    1 root     root         1224 Aug 10 10:30 smbmount.log.1
-rw-r--r--    1 root     root          135 Jul 29 04:03 smbmount.log.2
-rw-r--r--    1 root     root          402 Jul 21 04:03 smbmount.log.3
-rw-r--r--    1 root     root         3405 Jun 30 04:03 smbmount.log.4
```

If all these files were to be placed in the **/var/log** directory, it would become too crowded, so the subdirectory is produced for *samba*.

A large number of log files are in **/var/log**. You may want to take a look at some of these. For example, the **boot.log** file contains a history of the significant commands that you've issued and **dmesg** provides a dump of the kernel message buffer. Many others can give you insight into your system operation.

Sometimes, log files can be very long. When they are, it is a good idea to try searching (**grep**) for what you need. In the following example, you copy the output of **dmesg** to the screen (**cat dmesg**). This is a long file, so before it displays, you have used **grep** to search for the three-letter string, *CPU,* in the output:

```
# cat dmesg | grep CPU
CPU   0:   mapping   PAL   code   [0x3ff40000-0x3ff80000)   into   [0xe00000003f000000-
0xe000000040000000)
CPU 0: 61 virtual and 50 physical address bits
CPU 0 (0x0000) enabled (BSP)
CPU 1 (0x0100) enabled
2 CPUs available, 2 CPUs total
CPU 0: base freq=200.000MHz, ITC ratio=10/2, ITC freq=1000.000MHz
CPU   1:   mapping   PAL   code   [0x3ff40000-0x3ff80000)   into   [0xe00000003f000000-
0xe000000040000000)
CPU 1: 61 virtual and 50 physical address bits
CPU 1: synchronized ITC with CPU 0 (last diff 0 cycles, maxerr 451 cycles)
CPU 1: base freq=200.000MHz, ITC ratio=10/2, ITC freq=1000.000MHz
CPU1: CPU has booted.
#
```

The two CPUs and information associated with them are shown in the output, including the 1 GHz frequency. Next, use **grep** to look for *hpzx1* in the output:

```
# cat dmesg | grep hpzx1
booting generic kernel on platform hpzx1
hpzx1: HWP0001 SBA at 0xfed00000; pci dev 00:1e.0
hpzx1: HWP0001 IOC at 0xfed01000; pci dev 00:1d.0
hpzx1: HWP0002 PCI LBA _BBN 0x00 at 0xfed20000; pci dev 00:1c.0
hpzx1: HWP0002 PCI LBA _BBN 0x20 at 0xfed22000; pci dev 20:1e.0
hpzx1: HWP0002 PCI LBA _BBN 0x40 at 0xfed24000; pci dev 40:1e.0
hpzx1: HWP0002 PCI LBA _BBN 0x60 at 0xfed26000; pci dev 60:1e.0
hpzx1: HWP0002 PCI LBA _BBN 0x80 at 0xfed28000; pci dev 80:1e.0
hpzx1: HWP0002 PCI LBA _BBN 0xc0 at 0xfed2c000; pci dev c0:1e.0
hpzx1: HWP0002 PCI LBA _BBN 0xe0 at 0xfed2e000; pci dev e0:1e.0
#
```

This output shows information related to the *hpzx1 chipset*. This chipset provides high bandwidth and low latency solution for one to four-way workstations and servers such as the two-way rx2600 used in the example.

I check log files on an as-needed basis, but many system administrators review the log files frequently to look for potential problems in an effort to be proactive.

Linux File System Layout

The Linux file system layout is hierarchical. Files are contained in directories, and directories can have any number of subdirectories. Most operating systems are arranged this way, including UNIX. The following are descriptions of some of the more important directories found on a Linux system:

/   The root directory, which is the base of the file system's hierarchical tree structure. A directory is logically viewed as being part of /. Regardless of the disk on which a directory or logical volume is stored, it is logically viewed as a part of the root hierarchy.

/bin   Contains commonly used commands that you issue at the command line all the time.

/boot   The kernel files and those related to the kernel are in this directory.

/dev   Contains host-specific device files.

/etc   Contains host-specific system and application configuration files. The information in this directory is important to the system's operation and is of a permanent nature. There are also additional configuration directories below **/etc**.

/home   Users' home directories are recommended to be located here. Because the data stored in users' home directories will be modified often and much will be added over time, you can expect this directory to grow in size.

/initrd   An initrd image is needed for loading your SCSI module at boot time or if you are compiling the kernel with ext3 support as a module.

/lib   Libraries and parts of the C compiler are found in this directory.

/lost+found   The lost files directory. Here, you find files that are in use, but are not associated with a directory. These files typically become "lost" as a result of a system crash that caused the link between the physical information on the disk and the logical directory to be severed. The program **fsck**, which is run at the time of boot, finds these files and places them in the **lost+found** directory. You will typically see one of these for every disk that you have mounted.

/misc   A directory that is in place to contain miscellaneous information.

/mnt   Directory for mounting, especially temporary mounts, such as floppies and DVD-ROMs.

/opt   The directory under which applications are installed. As a rule, application vendors never specify a particular location for their applications to be installed. Now, with **/opt**, there is a standard directory under which applications should be installed. This is an organizational improvement for system administrators because they can now expect applications to be loaded under /**opt** and the application name.

/proc   Images of all running processes are shown here.

/root   Home directory for the user *root*.

/sbin   Contains commands and scripts used to boot, shut down, and
                  fix file system mounting problems.

/tmp   A free-for-all directory, where any user can temporarily store
                  files. Because of the loose nature of this directory, it should not
                  be used to store anything important, and users should know
                  that whatever they have stored in **/tmp** can be deleted without
                  notice. Application working files should go in **/var/tmp** or /
                  var/opt/appname, not in **/tmp**.

/usr   Most of the UNIX operating system is contained in **/usr**.
                  Included in this directory are commands, libraries, and docu-
                  mentation. A limited number of subdirectories can appear in /
                  usr.

/var   Holds files that are primarily temporary. Files such as log files,
                  which are frequently deleted and modified, are stored here.
                  Think of this as a directory of "variable" size. Files that an
                  application or command create, at runtime should be placed in
                  this directory, including logfile and spool files. However, some
                  applications, including **init** scripts, may store state information
                  in **/var**.

The following is a long listing of the root (/) directory of the Integrity
server used throughout this book:

```
# ls -l /
total 244
drwxr-xr-x    2 root     root         4096 Jan 16 11:37 bin
drwxr-xr-x    3 root     root         4096 Jan 16 16:40 boot
drwxr-xr-x   18 root     root        86016 Jan 28 20:08 dev
drwxr-xr-x   66 root     root         8192 Jan 28 20:08 etc
drwxr-xr-x    3 root     root         4096 Jan 16 11:37 home
drwxr-xr-x    2 root     root         4096 Jun 21  2001 initrd
drwxr-xr-x    6 root     root         4096 Jan 16 11:32 lib
drwx------    2 root     root        16384 Jan 16 10:39 lost+found
drwxr-xr-x    2 root     root         4096 Aug 29  2001 misc
drwxr-xr-x    3 root     root         4096 Jan 16 16:40 mnt
drwxr-xr-x    2 root     root         4096 Aug 23  1999 opt
dr-xr-xr-x   59 root     root            0 Jan 28 15:07 proc
drwxr-x---   13 root     root         4096 Jan 28 21:34 root
drwxr-xr-x    2 root     root         8192 Jan 16 11:35 sbin
```

```
drwxrwxrwt   10 root      root         77824 Jan 29 04:02 tmp
drwxr-xr-x   17 root      root          4096 Jan 16 11:26 usr
drwxr-xr-x   26 root      root          4096 Jan 16 11:35 var
#
```

You'll be working extensively in some of these directories in upcoming chapters. You'll become familiar with the contents of some of these directories in upcoming chapters, such as **/boot** and **/proc** in the kernel chapter.

The previous sections of this chapter covered some of the most important aspects of working with a Linux system, such as adding and partitioning a disk, mounting the disk, the layout of the file system, and log files. This working knowledge of the file system is important Linux knowledge. The next section covers configuration of the Smart Array controller.

Smart Array Configuration

The Smart Array controller provides data protection with RAID, mirroring, on-board cache, and a variety of other high availability features. In this section I'll cover the basics of Smart Array setup including many screen shots to give you an idea of the setup process. Figure 4-1 shows the results of an EFI scan.

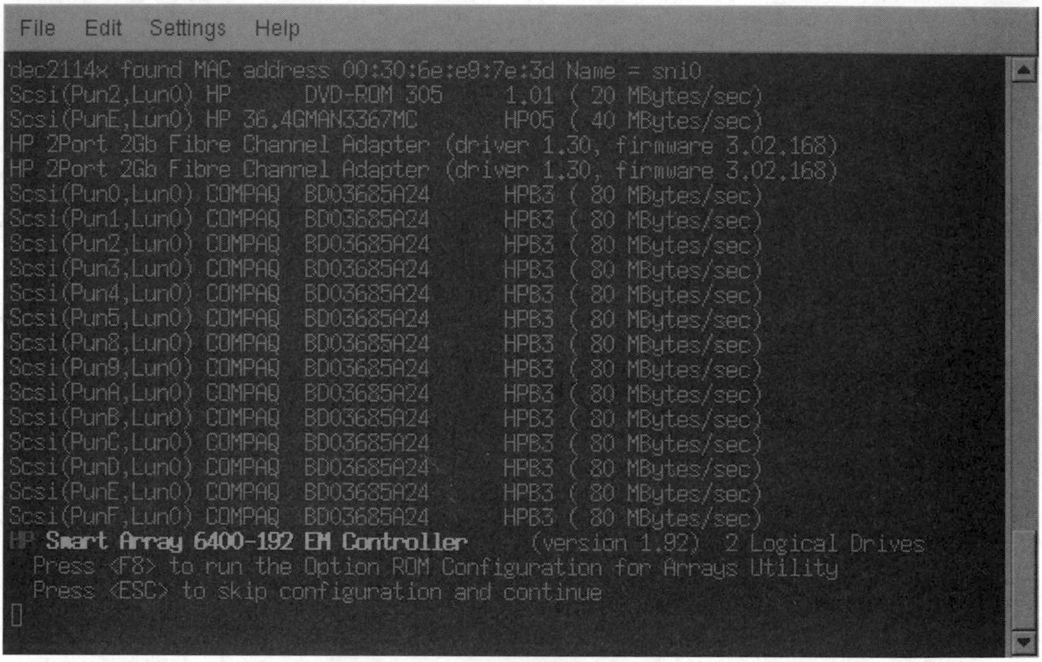

Figure 4-1   EFI Scan Showing Smart Array Controller

At this point, you would select *Esc F8* (on a serial console) in order to proceed with the configuration. Figure 4-2 shows the Smart Array main menu.

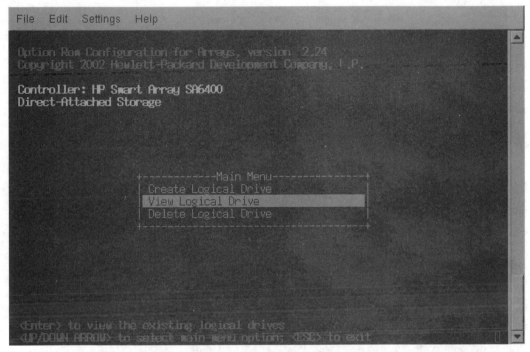

Figure 4-2   Smart Array Main Menu with *View Logical Drive* Selected

This is the main menu with *View Logical Drive* selected. Figure 4-3 shows viewing the available logical drives.

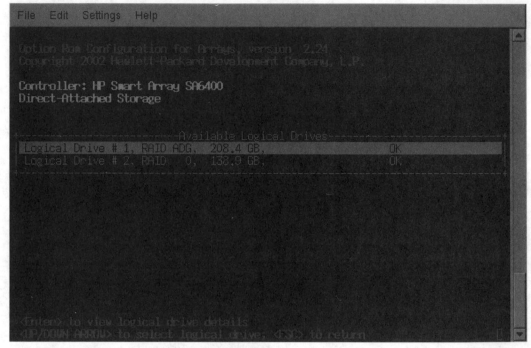

Figure 4-3   Available Logical Drives

From this figure, you can see that there are two logical drives. Figure 4-4 shows the results of viewing the *ADG* drive.

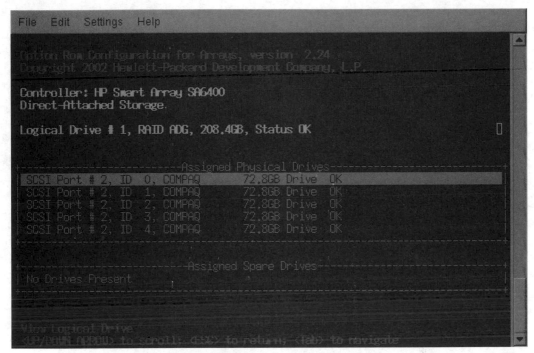

Figure 4-4   Viewing *ADG* Drive

This figure shows the details of *ADG* drive including the size, port, and status of the logical drive and the five disks of which it is comprised.

In the subsequent steps, this logical drive will be deleted and then recreated in order to show the steps involved in working with the Smart Array.

Figure 4-5 shows going back to the main menu to delete a logical drive.

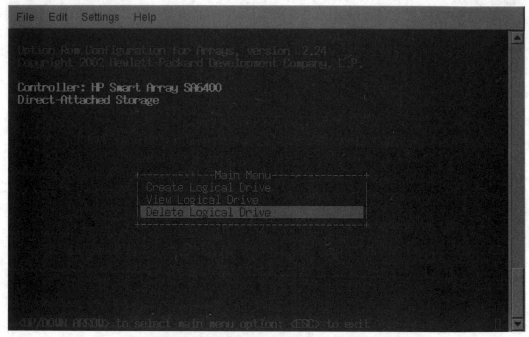

Figure 4-5   Smart Array Main Menu with Delete Selected

We'll now select *Delete Logical Drive* and the menu in Figure 4-6 appears.

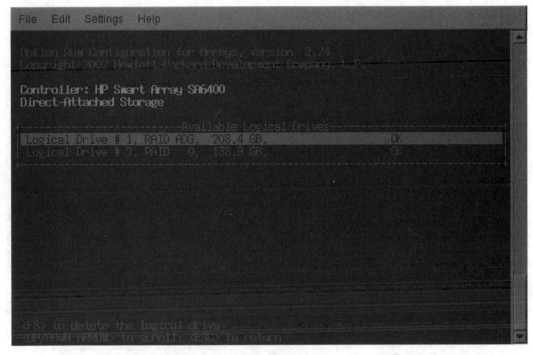

Figure 4-6   Drive *ADG* is Selected for Deletion

In this figure, I've again selected the *ADG* drive, this time to delete it. After selecting this drive for deletion, the information in Figure 4-7 appears.

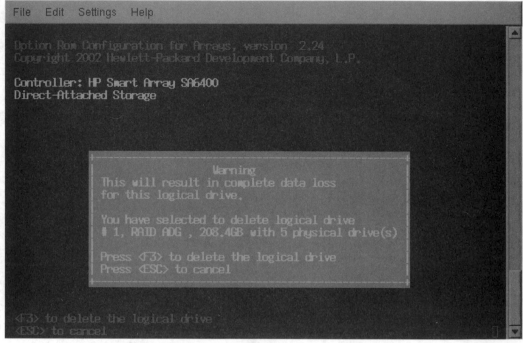

File   Edit   Settings   Help

Option Rom Configuration for Arrays, version 2.24
Copyright 2002 Hewlett-Packard Development Company, L.P.

Controller: HP Smart Array SA6400
Direct-Attached Storage

Warning
This will result in complete data loss
for this logical drive.

You have selected to delete logical drive
1, RAID ADG , 208.4GB with 5 physical drive(s)

Press <F3> to delete the logical drive
Press <ESC> to cancel

<F3> to delete the logical drive
<ESC> to cancel

Figure 4-7   Warning Messages When Deleting *ADG*

This warning message makes clear that deleting this drive will result in data loss for the drive. After deleting the drive, windows appear that indicate that the configuration has been saved.

At this point, you could go to the main screen, select the *ADG* drive, and view it to confirm that it has been deleted. Now we'll construct a new logical drive with the available disks, as shown in Figure 4-8.

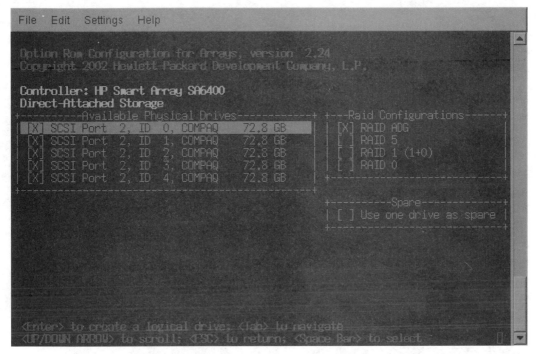

Figure 4-8   Create a Drive

This figure shows selecting the components of the logical drive, including the five disks of which the logical drive is comprised. After all selections are made, you receive messages indicating that the drive has been created and saved.

In this exercise, the same ADG drive was created as originally existed when we started this section.

Chapter 5

Working with the Linux Kernel

Because the Linux kernel plays such a critical role in the operation of your Linux system, it is important to know how to obtain and build a new kernel. You'll also want to know how to make adjustments to your existing kernel. When your system is installed, you get a kernel that is for general purpose use. You may want to completely update your kernel to a newer version or modify your existing kernel to meet special needs.

In this chapter, I'll cover installing a new kernel and then talk about modifying your existing kernel. We'll start by looking at kernel building on IA-32 systems running Red Hat 8.x, and then look at some of the options available for Integrity servers running Advanced Server. The Advanced Server, for example, has a different processor type (IA-64), EFI support, and other advanced settings. The process for building a kernel is the same in the two releases, so the basic procedure applies to either type of system. As a side note, the "retail" versions of Red Hat, such as 8.x, used in this section, has been replaced by Fedora. Fedora Project is a Red Hat-sponsored and community-supported open source project. Fedora Core 2 is available at the time of this writing.

Please keep in mind that new kernels are not usually supported on Integrity servers, and other systems for that matter, so if there is any way that you can avoid building a new kernel, you'll want to consider it. Having said that, the following procedure provides some of the fundamentals of building a new kernel.

Steps to Creating a Linux Kernel

It is common to completely update your Linux kernel when a new version becomes available. There may be features introduced into the new kernel that you want, or you may just want to remain current. Another common reason to create a new kernel is for security patches. In the upcoming sections, you'll install a new kernel. Updating the kernel can result in an unsupported configuration, so always check on this before creating a new kernel. Figure 5-1 shows the steps you'll cover in the next few sections for obtaining and working with our new kernel.

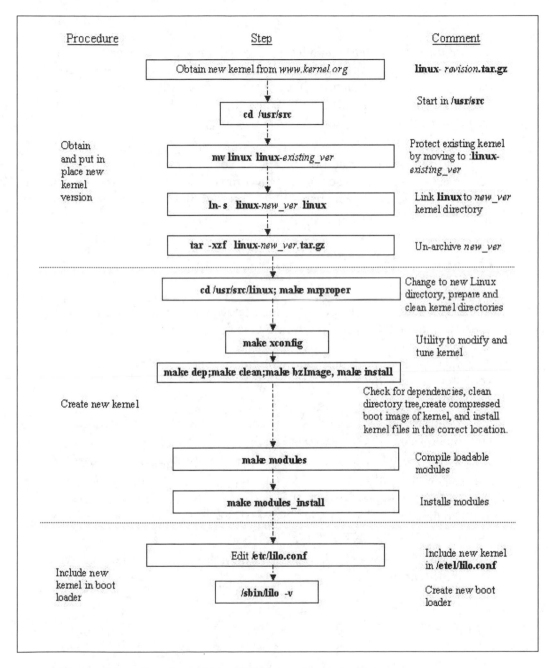

Figure 5-1   Creating a Linux Kernel on Integrity Servers

make compressed would be replaced with **make bzImage** on an x86-based system at the time of this writing. In addition, the **make xconfig** command was not yet certified on Integrity, at the time of this writing, so you may have to use **make oldconfig**; however, as you'll see in an upcoming example, I did indeed use **make xconfig** on Integrity.

As you can see, there are many steps to updating or creating your new kernel. After you go through the procedure yourself, you'll see that the procedure is rewarding because it gives you complete control over how this critical part of your system operates. Please keep in mind that, in some cases, running a new kernel is unsupported.

Obtaining Linux Kernel Source Code

In the upcoming example, you're going to download the latest kernel source code available at the time of this writing for an IA-32 system. After you have the source, you are going to perform the entire process of building a new kernel. In the later examples, you will modify our 64-bit Advanced Server kernel on the Integrity server.

www.kernel.org has many versions of Linux kernel source code including the latest versions. You can also select one of the mirror sites from which you can download the source code.

Kernels with even numbers, such as *2.4* (full number is *2.4.18-3*) on our system, are fully tested production kernels. Those with odd numbers, such as the *2.5.25* kernel we use in our upcoming example, are experimental. You should assume the odd number kernels are not stable and are therefore not suitable for your production systems.

Figure 5-2 shows the *www.kernel.org* Web site and the kernels available at the time of this writing.

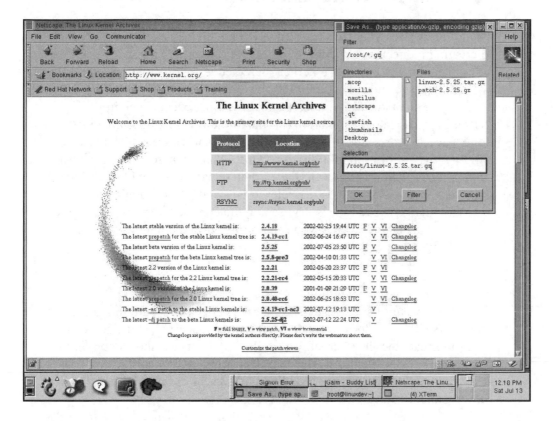

Figure 5-2   Obtaining a Linux Kernel from *www.kernel.org*

You can see from Figure 5-2 that you have selected the very latest available kernel at the time of this writing, which is *2.5.25*. This is, of course, an experimental kernel, but that is part of the fun of Linux. You can load and experiment with this kernel knowing that you can boot your current stable kernel and resume the uninterrupted operation anytime.

Selecting the *F* provides a full version, which means that you get all the kernel-related files to compile and work with this kernel.

The compressed file that you have chosen to download has a file name of **linux-2.5.25.tar.gz**, and you asked for it to be downloaded to **/root**. Because the file is relatively small, it did not take long to download (1.5 hours on a 56K modem). You'll work with it in the upcoming sections.

Setting Up Directories and Files for the Linux Kernel

The first few steps you must perform to work with the new kernel are related to creating a directory structure that will house the old and new kernel versions. That is, you may have kernel source code for an existing kernel that you need to save and the code for the new kernel you want to work with.

If you don't know if you have existing kernel code, check inÁ **/usr/src** for a directory called **linux**. If the **linux** directory does not exist, you don't have to worry about saving the existing source tree. If it does exist, simply move it from **linux** to **linux-***releaseNumber*, where *releaseNumber* is something like **linux-2.4.18-3** (the kernel release on the IA-32 system). Once that is done, your existing release is saved. If you don't know what your existing kernel release is, try issuing the command **uname -r**. The following is what happens when you run **uname -r** on the Integrity Server running RHEL Advanced Server:

```
# uname -r
2.4.18-e.12.smp
#
```

If you were to save the existing kernel code, you would move the current **linux** directory to **linux-2.4.18-e.12.smp**. Once you did that, you are ready to create the new kernel. The following example shows copying the newly compressed kernel to the **/usr/src** directory, changing directory to **/usr/src**, making a directory called **linux-2.5.25** for our new kernel, and performing another long listing of **/usr/src**:

```
# cp /root/linux-2.5.25.tar.gz /usr/src
#
# cd /usr/src
#
# ls -l
total 34144
-rw-r--r--    1 root      root      34918191 Jul 13 12:21 linux-2.5.25.tar.gz
drwxr-xr-x    7 root      root          4096 Jun 11 05:38 redhat
#
# mkdir linux-2.5.25
#
# ls -l
total 34148
drwxr-xr-x    2 root      root          4096 Jul 13 12:25 linux-2.5.25
-rw-r--r--    1 root      root      34918191 Jul 13 12:21 linux-2.5.25.tar.gz
drwxr-xr-x    7 root      root          4096 Jun 11 05:38 redhat
#
```

The long listings in the previous example indicate that we did not have an existing **linux** directory. Thus, we don't have to save it by renaming it **linux-***releaseNumber*.

Next, create a symbolic link from the new kernel directory name to **linux**, unpack the gunziped *tar* file you downloaded into **/usr/src/linux-**

2.5.25, change directories into **/usr/src/linux** and run **make mrproper** to clean up kernel configuration directories, as shown in the following example:

```
# ln -s linux linux-2.5.25 linux
#
# ls -l
total 34148
lrwxrwxrwx   1 root     root           12 Jul 13 12:26 linux -> linux-2.5.25
drwxr-xr-x   2 root     root         4096 Jul 13 12:26 linux-2.5.25
-rw-r--r--   1 root     root     34918191 Jul 13 12:21 linux-2.5.25.tar.gz
drwxr-xr-x   7 root     root         4096 Jun 11 05:38 redhat
# tar -xzf linux-2.5.25.tar.gz
#
# ls -l linux-2.5.25
total 268
drwxrwxr-x  19 1046     101          4096 Jul  5 19:42 arch
-rw-r--r--   1 1046     101         18691 Jul  5 19:42 COPYING
-rw-r--r--   1 1046     101         79460 Jul  5 19:42 CREDITS
drwxrwxr-x  32 1046     101          4096 Jul  5 19:42 Documentation
drwxrwxr-x  39 1046     101          4096 Jul  5 19:42 driver
drwxrwxr-x  47 1046     101          4096 Jul  5 19:42 fs
drwxrwxr-x  27 1046     101          4096 Jul  5 19:42 include
drwxrwxr-x   2 1046     101          4096 Jul  5 19:42 init
drwxrwxr-x   2 1046     101          4096 Jul  5 19:42 ipc
drwxrwxr-x   2 1046     101          4096 Jul  5 19:42 kernel
drwxrwxr-x   4 1046     101          4096 Jul  5 19:42 lib
lrwxrwxrwx   1 root     root            5 Jul 13 12:26 linux -> linux
-rw-r--r--   1 1046     101         41881 Jul  5 19:42 MAINTAINERS
-rw-r--r--   1 1046     101         25218 Jul  5 19:42 Makefile
drwxrwxr-x   2 1046     101          4096 Jul  5 19:42 mm
drwxrwxr-x  29 1046     101          4096 Jul  5 19:42 net
-rw-r--r--   1 1046     101         14402 Jul  5 19:42 README
-rw-r--r--   1 1046     101          2815 Jul  5 19:42 REPORTING-BUGS
-rw-r--r--   1 1046     101         18139 Jul  5 19:42 Rules.make
drwxrwxr-x   4 1046     101          4096 Jul  5 19:42 scripts
drwxrwxr-x  11 1046     101          4096 Jul  5 19:42 sound
#
# cd /usr/src/linux
# make mrproper
#
```

Because of the symbolic link, the **linux** directory is actually the directory, **linux-2.5.25**. In the example, you used **tar** to unpack the downloaded file **linux-2.5.25.tar.gz**. This is not an *RPM* file like those you worked with earlier in this book. **tar** *-x* specifies that you'll extract the files from the archive, *-f* allows us to specify the file on which we'll work, and *-z* specifies that we'll use *gzip* to unzip it. After the files are extracted, **ls -l** shows us that we end up with the man files and directories under our new linux directory **linux-2.5.25**.

make xconfig

At the time of this writing, **make xconfig** hasn't yet been certified on Integrity servers; however, there are examples of **make xconfig** on Integrity in this section. The **make oldconfig** command is tested on Integrity. The **make xconfig** command uses the **make** utility to compile and invoke a kernel configuration tool. When **make xconfig** is run, the kernel configuration tool is X Windows-based. If you wanted to run the same tool in a character-based environment, run **make menuconfig**. I have used this command on both IA-32 and Integrity servers, but I have received reports that there are sometimes unusual results on Integrity servers, so please use it with caution.

After issuing the **make xconfig** command, a lot of *gcc*-related (compiler) messages appear and the top-level kernel configuration window opens. The top-level **make xconfig** window for our IA-32 system running Red Hat 8.x is shown in Figure 5-3.

Code maturity level options	Telephony Support	Multimedia devices
General setup	ATA/IDE/MFM/RLL support	File systems
Loadable module support	SCSI support	Console drivers
Processor type and features	Fusion MPT device support	Sound
Power management options (ACPI, APM)	IEEE 1394 (FireWire) support (EXPERIMENTAL)	USB support
Bus options (PCI, PCMCIA, EISA, MCA, ISA)	I2O device support	Bluetooth support
Executable file formats	Network device support	Kernel hacking
Memory Technology Devices (MTD)	Amateur Radio support	Library routines
Parallel port support	IrDA (infrared) support	
Plug and Play configuration	ISDN subsystem	Save and Exit
Block devices	Old CD-ROM drivers (not SCSI, not IDE)	Quit Without Saving
Multi-device support (RAID and LVM)	Input device support	Load Configuration from File
Networking options	Character devices	Store Configuration to File

Figure 5-3   Top-Level **make xconfig** for IA-32 System Running Red Hat 8.x

There are default settings for each of the buttons, shown in Figure 5-3. You can select any of the areas to see the default settings that apply in that area and change them.

The top level of **make xconfig** on Integrity running Advanced Server has different options, as shown in Figure 5-4.

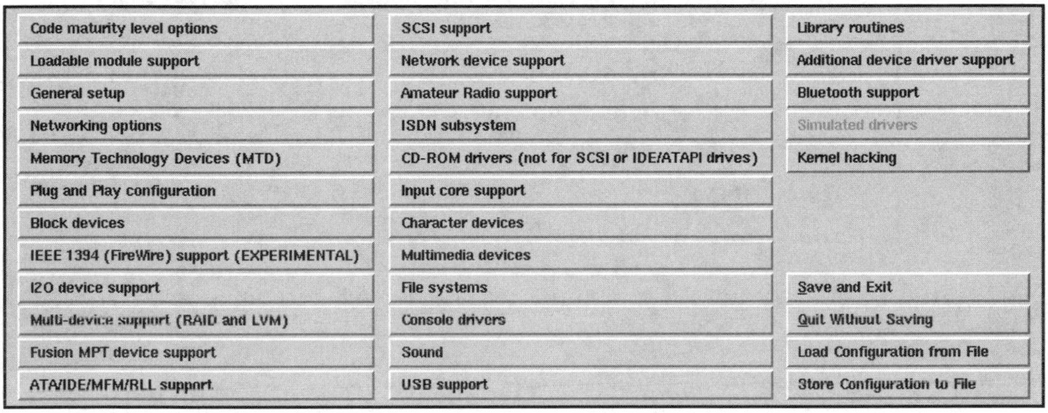

Code maturity level options	SCSI support	Library routines
Loadable module support	Network device support	Additional device driver support
General setup	Amateur Radio support	Bluetooth support
Networking options	ISDN subsystem	Simulated drivers
Memory Technology Devices (MTD)	CD-ROM drivers (not for SCSI or IDE/ATAPI drives)	Kernel hacking
Plug and Play configuration	Input core support	
Block devices	Character devices	
IEEE 1394 (FireWire) support (EXPERIMENTAL)	Multimedia devices	
I2O device support	File systems	Save and Exit
Multi-device support (RAID and LVM)	Console drivers	Quit Without Saving
Fusion MPT device support	Sound	Load Configuration from File
ATA/IDE/MFM/RLL support	USB support	Store Configuration to File

Figure 5-4 Top-Level **make xconfig** for Integrity Server

In either case, from the top-level **make xconfig** window, you would typically select *General setup* to check the defaults. Figure 5-5 shows the *General setup* defaults for the IA-32 system running Red Hat 8.x.

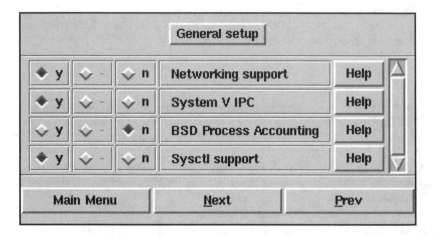

Figure 5-5   *General Setup* in **make xconfig** for IA-32 Running Red Hat 8.x

The *General Setup* **make xconfig** window is a model for all the other windows. In the three left-most columns, you can select *y* for yes, *m* for module (although no *m* is present in the figure) or *n* for no. This means that you can select *y* to build functionality into the kernel or *n* to not build-in the functionality. If you select *m* for module, the functionality will be dynamically loaded into the kernel when it is needed, but won't be a permanent part of the kernel. This results in a smaller, more efficient kernel that won't take up as much memory. The bottom three buttons allow you to go back to the *Main Menu, Next*, or *Previous* area in the **make xconfig** interface.

An Integrity server running Advanced Server *General setup* has many additional selections, some of which are shown in Figure 5-6:

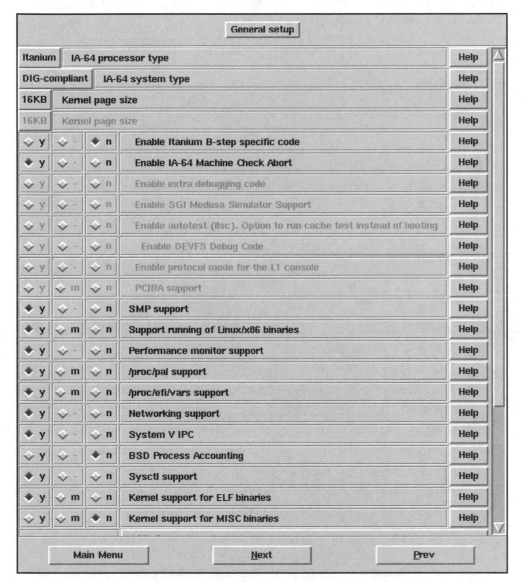

Figure 5-6   **make xconfig** *General setup* for an Integrity Server

In this figure, *Itanium* is the processor type. As you can see, *General setup* on Integrity servers has many additional selections, including */proc/efi/*

vars support. This parameter allows EFI variable information to be set in **/proc/efi/vars**. The following is a listing of **/proc/efi/vars**, which shows variable information. Among the variables shown are *Boot-Order* and *Time-out.* These are Itanium-specific variables:

```
# cd /proc/efi/vars
# ls
Boot0000-8be4df61-93ca-11d2-aa0d-00e098032b8c
Boot0001-8be4df61-93ca-11d2-aa0d-00e098032b8c
Boot0002-8be4df61-93ca-11d2-aa0d-00e098032b8c
Boot0003-8be4df61-93ca-11d2-aa0d-00e098032b8c
BootCurrent-8be4df61-93ca-11d2-aa0d-00e098032b8c
BootOrder-8be4df61-93ca-11d2-aa0d-00e098032b8c
CellularPlatform-8be4df61-93ca-11d2-aa0d-00e098032b8c
ConIn-8be4df61-93ca-11d2-aa0d-00e098032b8c
ConInDev-8be4df61-93ca-11d2-aa0d-00e098032b8c
ConOut-8be4df61-93ca-11d2-aa0d-00e098032b8c
ConOutDev-8be4df61-93ca-11d2-aa0d-00e098032b8c
Driver0000-8be4df61-93ca-11d2-aa0d-00e098032b8c
DriverOrder-8be4df61-93ca-11d2-aa0d-00e098032b8c
EDD30-964e5b21-6459-11d2-8e39-00a0c969723b
ErrOut-8be4df61-93ca-11d2-aa0d-00e098032b8c
ErrOutDev-8be4df61-93ca-11d2-aa0d-00e098032b8c
fibre_pri_path-8be4df61-93ca-11d2-aa0d-00e098032b8c
Lang-8be4df61-93ca-11d2-aa0d-00e098032b8c
MTC-eb704011-1402-11d3-8e77-00a0c969723b
Timeout-8be4df61-93ca-11d2-aa0d-00e098032b8c
```

Moving back to the IA-32 system running Red Hat 8.x, Figure 5-7 shows *make xconfig ... File systems* menu. Note that this menu displays several possible *m* selections.

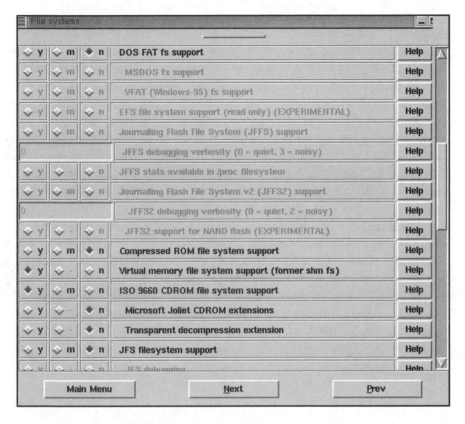

Figure 5-7 *Filesystems* in **make xconfig**

The *Filesystems* menu window provides the option to select many common file systems, such as *DOS FAT* and *JFS.* You can work your way through all the areas of **make xconfig** to craft a kernel that meets your specific needs. You can select the functionality you want to be built directly into the kernel (**y**); the functionality you want selected as a module (used infrequently **m**); and the functionality you don't need at all can be excluded from the kernel altogether (**n**).

The ability to build a kernel to meet your specific needs is one of the most powerful and desirable features of working with Linux.

Compiling the New Kernel

After you configure the new kernel with **make xconfig**, you can begin the process of compiling or making it. In this section, you run a few **make** commands to perform a variety of tasks. Note that all these commands will be run in the directory where the new kernel will be built. In the following example, we'll change directory to **/usr/src/linux** before we begin. Remember that earlier, you linked (symbolic link) **linux** to **linux-2.5.25**, so all the work you perform the **linux** directory is actually done in **linux-2.5.25**. Also note that you are building an odd-number release. This means that it is an experimental kernel. Although that might be perfect for purposes here, I recommend using the fully tested even number kernel releases for production systems.

The **make dep** command is run first to make a dependency tree. This command checks for any dependencies of one module upon another module. The **make clean** command prepares a new directory tree for the kernel we are about to build. The **make bzImage** (replaced by **make compressed** on Integrity) command creates a compressed boot image of the kernel. This command takes a long time. The **make install** command installs the kernel files in the correct location:

```
# cd /usr/src/linux
# make dep; make clean; make bzImage; make install

make[1]: Entering directory `/usr/src/linux-2.5.25'
make[2]: Entering directory `/usr/src/linux-2.5.25/scripts'
  gcc -Wp,-MD,./.split-include.d -Wall -Wstrict-prototypes -O2
        -fomit-frame-pointer   -o split-include split-include.c
make[2]: Leaving directory `/usr/src/linux-2.5.25/scripts'
  Generating include/linux/version.h (updated)
  Making asm->asm-i386 symlink
  SPLIT   include/linux/autoconf.h -> include/config/*
  Starting the build. KBUILD_BUILTIN=1 KBUILD_MODULES=
make[2]: Entering directory `/usr/src/linux-2.5.25'
make[3]: Entering directory `/usr/src/linux-2.5.25/init'
make[3]: Leaving directory `/usr/src/linux-2.5.25/init'
make[3]: Entering directory `/usr/src/linux-2.5.25/kernel'
                 .
                 .
                 .
```

You can see that I removed the vast majority of output from commands. The **make bzImage** produces a ton of output that I couldn't include in this book. There were, however, no errors from having run these commands. Note that I usually use output redirection with the **make** command to store standard output and standard error in files for later review.

In the next listing, you'll run **make modules** to compile the loadable modules in the kernel. Then you'll run **make modules_install** to install the modules into the correct directory for the new kernel:

```
# make modules
make[1]: Entering directory `/usr/src/linux-2.5.25/scripts'
make[1]: Leaving directory `/usr/src/linux-2.5.25/scripts'
  Starting the build. KBUILD_BUILTIN= KBUILD_MODULES=1
make[1]: Entering directory `/usr/src/linux-2.5.25/init'
make[1]: Leaving directory `/usr/src/linux-2.5.25/init'
make[1]: Entering directory `/usr/src/linux-2.5.25/kernel'
make[1]: Leaving directory `/usr/src/linux-2.5.25/kernel'
make[1]: Entering directory `/usr/src/linux-2.5.25/mm'



#
# modules_install
make[1]: Entering directory `/usr/src/linux-2.5.25/init'
make[1]: Leaving directory `/usr/src/linux-2.5.25/init'
make[1]: Entering directory `/usr/src/linux-2.5.25/kernel'
make[1]: Leaving directory `/usr/src/linux-2.5.25/kernel'
make[1]: Entering directory `/usr/src/linux-2.5.25/mm'
make[1]: Leaving directory `/usr/src/linux-2.5.25/mm'
make[1]: Entering directory `/usr/src/linux-2.5.25/fs'
make[2]: Entering directory `/usr/src/linux-2.5.25/fs/autofs4'
make[2]: Leaving directory `/usr/src/linux-2.5.25/fs/autofs4'
make[2]: Entering directory `/usr/src/linux-2.5.25/fs/devpts'
make[2]: Leaving directory `/usr/src/linux-2.5.25/fs/devpts'
make[2]: Entering directory `/usr/src/linux-2.5.25/fs/driverfs'
make[2]: Leaving directory `/usr/src/linux-2.5.25/fs/driverfs'
make[2]: Entering directory `/usr/src/linux-2.5.25/fs/exportfs'
make[2]: Leaving directory `/usr/src/linux-2.5.25/fs/exportfs'
make[2]: Entering directory `/usr/src/linux-2.5.25/fs/ext2'
make[2]: Leaving directory `/usr/src/linux-2.5.25/fs/ext2'
make[2]: Entering directory `/usr/src/linux-2.5.25/fs/fat'
make[2]: Leaving directory `/usr/src/linux-2.5.25/fs/fat'


```

Now, the loadable modules have been compiled and installed in the correct directories. Loadable modules are included (by being linked) or removed from the kernel while it is running. This means that the kernel binary does not have to be changed to include or exclude the module. In addition, the kernel is smaller because the drivers are not loaded unless they're needed. Modules are loaded into the kernel with **insmod** and removed with **rmmod**.

Loadable kernel modules are usually located under **/lib/modules/***version*. You can view the currently loaded modules on our IA-32 Red Hat 8.x system with the **lsmod** command, as shown in the following listing:

```
# lsmod
Module                      Size  Used by     Not tainted
ad1848                     25696  0  (autoclean) (unused)
sound                      72012  0  (autoclean) [ad1848]
soundcore                   6692  2  (autoclean) [sound]
autofs                     12164  0  (autoclean) (unused)
3c59x                      28520  1
ide-cd                     30272  0  (autoclean)
cdrom                      32192  0  (autoclean) [ide-cd]
usb-uhci                   24484  0  (unused)
usbcore                    73152  1  [usb-uhci]
ext3                       67136  6
jbd                        49400  6  [ext3]
```

This output shows that several modules are used on the system. Note that every kernel is different based on installed peripherals and programs, so your output could be slightly different.

The following listing shows the modules installed on the Integrity server running RHEL Advanced Server:

```
# lsmod
Module                      Size  Used by     Not tainted
smbfs                     103080  0  (autoclean)
ide-cd                     74600  0  (autoclean)
soundcore                  14368  0  (autoclean)
iscsi                     208384  0
button                      8808  0  (unused)
autofs                     31056  0  (autoclean) (unused)
tulip                      96672  0  (unused)
tg3                       105616  0  (unused)
eepro100                   53408  1
nls_iso8859-1               6048  1  (autoclean)
nls_cp437                   7728  1  (autoclean)
vfat                       31096  1  (autoclean)
fat                        88216  0  (autoclean) [vfat]
mousedev                   14544  1
keybdev                     6080  0  (unused)
hid                        52888  0  (unused)
input                      13648  0  [mousedev keybdev hid]
usb-ohci                   57712  0  (unused)
usbcore                   176472  1  [hid usb-ohci]
ext3                      166536  1
jbd                       126016  1  [ext3]
mptscsih                   89760  3
mptbase                    97944  3  [mptscsih]
#
```

Next, you'll update the boot file to allow you to boot either the new kernel or the existing stable kernel that you had been using.

Update Boot Program

Now that you have our new kernel in place, you want to be able to boot both the original rock-solid kernel and the new experimental one. I'll use the *LILO* boot loader. Many boot loaders exist, including *GRUB* (GRand Unified Bootloader), that work in a similar fashion. *LILO* is simple and easy to understand, so it will be ideal for this example.

Update the **/etc/lilo.conf** file to include the new kernel in addition to the existing kernel, and make the default the new experimental kernel, as shown in the following IA-32 system **/etc/lilo.conf** file:

```
prompt
timeout=50
default=linux-2.5.25
boot=/dev/hda
map=/boot/map
install=/boot/boot.b
message=/boot/message
linear

image=/boot/vmlinuz-2.5.25
            label=linux-2.5.25
            initrd=/boot/initrd-2.5.25.img
            read-only
            root=/dev/hda5

image=/boot/vmlinuz-2.4.18-3
            label=linux
            initrd=/boot/initrd-2.4.18-3.img
            read-only
            root=/dev/hda5
```

There are two kernel entries in this file, and you'd add one for each kernel you want to boot. The *default* simply specifies the default; however, all the kernels will be displayed for you when the system boots and you can select the one you want to boot.

You run the **/sbin/lilo** command to install the boot loader and activate the changes you made to the **/etc/lilo.conf** file. If you use the *-v* option, you get a lot of informative messages related to your update. The following listing shows running **/sbin/lilo -v**:

```
# /sbin/lilo -v

LILO version 21.4-4, Copyright (C) 1992-1998 Werner Almesberger
'lba32' extensions Copyright (C) 1999,2000 John Coffman

Reading boot sector from /dev/hda
Merging with /boot/boot.b
Mapping message file /boot/message
Boot image: /boot/vmlinuz-2.5.25
Mapping RAM disk /boot/initrd-2.5.25.img
Added linux-2.5.25 *
Boot image: /boot/vmlinuz-2.4.18-3
Mapping RAM disk /boot/initrd-2.4.18-3.img
Added linux
/boot/boot.0300 exists - no backup copy made.
Writing boot sector.
#
```

You can see from this output that our new boot image of **/boot/ vmlinuz-2.5.25** exists and will be used as the default. The other boot image of **/boot/vmlinuz-2.4.18-3** also exists and can be selected when the system boots.

You went through all the steps required to download and create a new kernel. Keep in mind that you may perform additional steps when creating your kernel, including working with new drivers. You may install a driver in the **/usr/src/linux** directory and edit its source file before running **make modules** and **make modules_install**. Even though we didn't cover every possible type of change you'd make to the kernel, you now know the fundamental steps to kernel creation and can download and load a new kernel on your system.

On the Integrity server, the boot file is in **/boot/efi/efi/redhat/ elilo.conf**, which you can see here:

```
prompt
timeout=50
default=linux

image=vmlinuz-2.4.18-e.12smp
        label=linux
        initrd=initrd-2.4.18-e.12smp.img
        read-only
        root=/dev/sda3

image=vmlinuz-2.4.18-e.12
        label=linux-up
        initrd=initrd-2.4.18-e.12.img
        read-only
        root=/dev/sda3
```

The *default image* is specified early in the file. It is the one that you observed running the system when you checked earlier in this chapter using **uname -r**. Note that the location of the **elio.conf** file is different on Integrity servers. On IA-32 systems, it is located in **/etc**. On Advanced Server systems, it is located in **/boot/efi/efi/redhat**. Keep in mind that IA-32 uses *lilo* and Integrity servers uses *elilo*.

Tuning Your Existing Linux Kernel

In the previous section, you downloaded and installed a completely new kernel. We made various selections regarding the functionality of our new kernel in the **make xconfig** step. You were, however, limited in the amount of customization we could perform to the kernel during installation. Now look at some additional customization that you can perform to the kernel after it's installed.

The first area to investigate is the **/proc** file system.

/proc File System

An interesting component of the Linux operating system is the **/proc** file system. **/proc** doesn't really exist in the sense that it is on the disk like other file systems. The 'files' in **/proc** are a function of the kernel and/or variables in the kernel. **/proc** provides a mechanism by which you can view and set parameters in the kernel.

/proc gives us a lot of useful information about the kernel. For instance, you can see a complete rundown of the processor in your system by issuing **cat /proc/cpuinfo**, as shown in the following example first on our two-processor Integrity server and then on our IA-32 system:

```
# cat /proc/cpuinfo                        (On Integrity dual processor)
processor   : 0
vendor      : GenuineIntel
arch        : IA-64
family      : Itanium 2
model       : 0
revision    : 7
archrev     : 0
features    : branchlong
cpu number  : 0
cpu regs    : 4
cpu MHz     : 1000.000000
```

```
itc MHz       : 1000.000000
BogoMIPS      : 1497.36

processor     : 1
vendor        : GenuineIntel
arch          : IA-64
family        : Itanium 2
model         : 0
revision      : 7
archrev       : 0
features      : branchlong
cpu number    : 0
cpu regs      : 4
cpu MHz       : 1000.000000
itc MHz       : 1000.000000
BogoMIPS      : 1497.36
```

```
# cat /proc/cpuinfo                              (On IA-32)
processor       : 0
vendor_id       : GenuineIntel
cpu family      : 6
model           : 3
model name      : Pentium II (Klamath)
stepping        : 3
cpu MHz         : 232.675
cache size      : 512 KB
fdiv_bug        : no
hlt_bug         : no
f00f_bug        : no
coma_bug        : no
fpu             : yes
fpu_exception   : yes
cpuid level     : 2
wp              : yes
flags           : fpu vme de pse tsc msr pae mce cx8 sep mtrr pge mca
cmov mmx
bogomips        : 463.66
```

The listing first shows two Itanium processors that are running at 1 GHz, which is slower than the 1.5 GHz available at the time of this writing. **cpuinfo** contains a lot of useful information, such as the 1 GHz rating of the two processors. This is the system running Red Hat Advanced Server 2.1.

The second listing reveals a lot of information about the dinosaur CPU in my Linux system. (One of the great aspects of Linux is that it's efficient so you don't necessarily need the fastest CPU to get some work done.) This is the system running Red Hat 8.x.

You can also see the maximum number of open files the kernel will handle by viewing **/proc/sys/fs/file-max**. If you don't like the value as it is currently set, you can adjust it by using **echo** to supply a new value, as shown in the following example: first for our Integrity server and then for our IA-32 system:

```
# cat /proc/sys/fs/file-max                    (On Integrity)
207408
# echo "400000" > /proc/sys/fs/file-max
# cat /proc/sys/fs/file-max
400000
#
```

```
# cat /proc/sys/fs/file-max                    (On IA-32)
9830
```

```
# echo "1024" > /proc/sys/fs/file-max
```

There is a huge difference for the default value of these variables on the two systems. It is no surprise that the Advanced Server value is many times higher than the Red Hat 8.x value.

In the Integrity server example, you changed the value from a default of *207408* to *400000.*

On the IA-32 system, you reduced the value. You first saw that *file-max* was set to *9830,* which you changed to *1024.* Always be careful when reducing a setting. Going from *9830* to *1024* maximum open files may not be a good idea.

The **/proc** file system provides an easy way to view and modify kernel parameters. It may be that an application that you're using requires minimum values for some kernel parameters, in which case, you'd use the technique shown to modify them. To see the number of files you currently have open, you can get an idea of how close you are to your limit. You can issue the following command to list the number on either of our two systems.

```
# cat /proc/sys/fs/file-nr                     (On Integrity)
1374      950       40000
```

```
# cat /proc/sys/fs/file-nr                     (On IA-32)
1520              134          1024
```

This output shows the number of allocated, used, and maximum file handles. On the IA-32 system, the *1024* that you earlier set is shown as the maximum but there are *1520* allocated, which is already above our maximum. You can see that we have only *134* open files and that you are no where near the maximum number of open files at this time, but we reduced our maximum to a number below the current number allocated. Again, be careful when reducing the value of settings. The file **/proc/sys/fs/file-nr** is read-only because it shows the number of open files.

You can also get useful information about your swap device(s) in **/proc**. The following output shows the status of swap:

```
# cat /proc/swaps                                    (On Integrity)
Filename      Type        Size      Used     Priority
/dev/sda2     partition   2040208   0        -1
```

```
# cat /proc/swaps                                    (On IA-32)
Filename      Type        Size      Used     Priority
/dev/hda7     partition   192740    656      -1
```

You are using no swap of the two GB allocated on the Integrity server in the first output. On our IA-32 system, in the second output, you use a lot of available swap space. If the system were heavily used and swap was nearly all consumed, this would be an indication that you may need to increase swap space on the system.

The sysctl Command

The **sysctl** command is also used to work with kernel settings. **sysctl** is used to view and set settings in **/proc/sys**. Issuing **sysctl -a** produces an overview of configurable settings in **/proc/sys** as shown in the following abbreviated listings. The first listing shows the output on the Integrity server and the second listing the output on our IA-32 system.

```
# sysctl -a                                          (On Integrity)
abi.fake_utsname = 0
abi.trace = 0
dev.raid.speed_limit_max = 10000
dev.raid.speed_limit_min = 100
dev.cdrom.check_media = 0
dev.cdrom.lock = 1
dev.cdrom.debug = 0
dev.cdrom.autoeject = 0
```

```
dev.cdrom.autoclose = 1
dev.cdrom.info = CD-ROM information, Id: cdrom.c 3.12 2000/10/18
dev.cdrom.info =
dev.cdrom.info = drive name:              hda
dev.cdrom.info = drive speed:             24
dev.cdrom.info = drive # of slots:        1
dev.cdrom.info = Can close tray:                  1
dev.cdrom.info = Can open tray:           1
dev.cdrom.info = Can lock tray:           1
dev.cdrom.info = Can change speed:        1
dev.cdrom.info = Can select disk:         0
dev.cdrom.info = Can read multisession:   1
dev.cdrom.info = Can read MCN:            1
dev.cdrom.info = Reports media changed:   1
dev.cdrom.info = Can play audio:                  1
dev.cdrom.info = Can write CD-R:                  0
dev.cdrom.info = Can write CD-RW:         0
dev.cdrom.info = Can read DVD:            1
dev.cdrom.info = Can write DVD-R:         0
dev.cdrom.info = Can write DVD-RAM:       0
dev.cdrom.info =
dev.cdrom.info =
debug.rpmarch =
debug.kerneltype =
net.unix.max_dgram_qlen = 10
net.ipv4.conf.eth0.arp_filter = 0
net.ipv4.conf.eth0.tag = 0
net.ipv4.conf.eth0.log_martians = 0
net.ipv4.conf.eth0.bootp_relay = 0
                   .
                   .
                   .
net.core.divert_version = 0.46
net.core.hot_list_length = 128
net.core.optmem_max = 20480
net.core.message_burst = 50
net.core.message_cost = 5
net.core.mod_cong = 290
net.core.lo_cong = 100
net.core.no_cong = 20
net.core.no_cong_thresh = 20
net.core.netdev_max_backlog = 300
net.core.dev_weight = 64
net.core.rmem_default = 65535
net.core.wmem_default = 65535
net.core.rmem_max = 65535
net.core.wmem_max = 65535
vm.max-readahead = 127
vm.min-readahead = 3
vm.max_map_count = 65536
vm.page-cluster = 3
vm.pagetable_cache = 25 562
vm.kswapd = 512 32        8
vm.overcommit_memory = 0
vm.bdflush = 30 500        0        0     5120    30720   60      20      0
kernel.perfmon.fastctxsw = 0
kernel.perfmon.debug_ovfl = 0
kernel.perfmon.debug = 0
kernel.overflowgid = 65534
kernel.overflowuid = 65534
kernel.random.uuid = d6b7b7be-0286-4832-958b-945708388754
kernel.random.boot_id = 7d4a2307-b24f-4b35-b833-3dde320bda4c
kernel.random.write_wakeup_threshold = 128
kernel.random.read_wakeup_threshold = 8
kernel.random.entropy_avail = 4096
kernel.random.poolsize = 512
kernel.threads-max = 8101
kernel.cad_pid = 1
kernel.sysrq = 0
kernel.sem = 250        32000    32       128
kernel.msgmnb = 16384
kernel.msgmni = 16
kernel.msgmax = 8192
kernel.shmmni = 4096
kernel.shmall = 524288
```

```
kernel.shmmax = 33554432
kernel.rtsig-max = 1024
kernel.rtsig-nr = 1
kernel.acct = 4 2          30
kernel.hotplug = /sbin/hotplug
kernel.modprobe = /sbin/modprobe
kernel.printk = 3        4        1        7
kernel.ctrl-alt-del = 0
kernel.real-root-dev = 256
kernel.cap-bound = -257
kernel.tainted = 0
kernel.core_uses_pid = 0
kernel.panic = 0
kernel.domainname = (none)
kernel.hostname = m4415mxp
kernel.version = #1 SMP Thu Oct 17 15:13:01 EDT 2002
kernel.osrelease = 2.4.18-e.12smp
kernel.ostype = Linux
fs.lease-break-time = 45
fs.dir-notify-enable = 1
fs.leases-enable = 1
fs.overflowgid = 65534
fs.overflowuid = 65534
fs.dentry-state = 9166   8491    45       0        0        0
fs.dquot-nr = 0 0
fs.file-max = 400000
fs.file-nr = 1374        960     400000
fs.inode-state = 5165    31      0        0        0        0        0
fs.inode-nr = 5165       31
```

```
# sysctl -a                                            (On IA-32)
abi.fake_utsname = 0
abi.trace = 0
abi.defhandler_libcso = 68157441
abi.defhandler_lcall7 = 68157441
abi.defhandler_elf = 0
abi.defhandler_coff = 117440515
dev.cdrom.check_media = 0
dev.cdrom.lock = 1
dev.cdrom.debug = 0
dev.cdrom.autoeject = 0
dev.cdrom.autoclose = 1
dev.cdrom.info = CD-ROM information, Id: cdrom.c 3.12 2000/10/18
dev.cdrom.info =
dev.cdrom.info = drive name:hdc
dev.cdrom.info = drive speed:32
dev.cdrom.info = drive # of slots:1
dev.cdrom.info = Can close tray:1
dev.cdrom.info = Can open tray:1
dev.cdrom.info = Can lock tray:1
dev.cdrom.info = Can change speed:1
dev.cdrom.info = Can select disk:0
dev.cdrom.info = Can read multisession:1
dev.cdrom.info = Can read MCN:1
dev.cdrom.info = Reports media changed:1
dev.cdrom.info = Can play audio:1
dev.cdrom.info = Can write CD-R:0
dev.cdrom.info = Can write CD-RW:0
dev.cdrom.info = Can read DVD:0
dev.cdrom.info = Can write DVD-R:0
dev.cdrom.info = Can write DVD-RAM:0
dev.cdrom.info =
dev.cdrom.info =
dev.raid.speed_limit_max = 100000
dev.raid.speed_limit_min = 100
dev.rtc.max-user-freq = 64
debug.rpmarch =
debug.kerneltype =
net.unix.max_dgram_qlen = 10
net.token-ring.rif_timeout = 60000
net.ipv4.conf.eth0.arp_filter = 0
```

```
net.ipv4.conf.eth0.tag = 0
net.ipv4.conf.eth0.log_martians = 0
net.ipv4.conf.eth0.bootp_relay = 0
net.ipv4.conf.eth0.proxy_arp = 0
net.ipv4.conf.eth0.accept_source_route = 1
net.ipv4.conf.eth0.send_redirects = 1
net.ipv4.conf.eth0.rp_filter = 1


                    .

                    .

                    .


net.core.rmem_max = 65535
net.core.wmem_max = 65535
vm.max-readahead = 127
vm.min-readahead = 3
vm.max_map_count = 65536
vm.page-cluster = 3
vm.pagetable_cache = 2550
vm.kswapd = 512    328
vm.overcommit_memory = 0
vm.bdflush = 40    00050030006000
vm.freepages = 192 384576
kernel.overflowgid = 65534
kernel.overflowuid = 65534
kernel.random.uuid = 807f6e0c-dda4-475c-8130-d7821ba24069
kernel.random.boot_id = 20e67c64-b181-4d3e-af23-bbe84dececdb
kernel.random.write_wakeup_threshold = 128
kernel.random.read_wakeup_threshold = 8
kernel.random.entropy_avail = 4096
kernel.random.poolsize = 512
kernel.threads-max = 1536
kernel.cad_pid = 1
kernel.sysrq = 0
kernel.sem = 250    3200032128
kernel.msgmnb = 16384
kernel.msgmni = 16
kernel.msgmax = 8192
kernel.shmmni = 4096
kernel.shmall = 2097152
kernel.shmmax = 33554432
kernel.rtsig-max = 1024
kernel.rtsig-nr = 2
kernel.acct = 4     230
kernel.hotplug = /sbin/hotplug
kernel.modprobe = /sbin/modprobe
kernel.printk = 6   417
kernel.ctrl-alt-del = 0
kernel.real-root-dev = 256
kernel.cap-bound = -257
kernel.tainted = 0
kernel.core_uses_pid = 1
kernel.panic = 0
kernel.domainname = (none)
kernel.hostname = linuxdev
kernel.version = #1 Thu Apr 18 07:37:53 EDT 2002
kernel.osrelease = 2.4.18-3
kernel.ostype = Linux
fs.lease-break-time = 45
fs.dir-notify-enable = 1
fs.leases-enable = 1
fs.overflowgid = 65534
fs.overflowuid = 65534
fs.dentry-state = 2749197245000
fs.dquot-nr = 0    0
fs.file-max = 1024
fs.file-nr = 1520 1471024
fs.inode-state = 2180693700000
fs.inode-nr = 2180 6937
```

These abbreviated listings have more settings than what are shown. **sysctl** can be used to both view and modify kernel settings. For more information about **sysctl**, see the **sysctl** and **sysctl.conf** man pages.

Changing IP Forwarding

Now that you have two ways to modify settings (using **echo** and **sysctl**), let's modify a parameter using both techniques. If you want to perform IP forwarding, you would set **/proc/sys/net/ipv4/ip_forward** to a *1* and if you don't you would set it to a *0*. The following example uses **cat** to see what *ip_forward* is set to; using **sysctl** to set it to *0*, and then using **echo** to set it back to *1*:

```
# cat /proc/sys/net/ipv4/ip_forward
1

# sysctl -w net.ipv4.ip_forward="0"
net.ipv4.ip_forward = 0

# echo "1" > /proc/sys/net/ipv4/ip_forward

# cat /proc/sys/net/ipv4/ip_forward
1
```

This procedure is identical on both our Integrity and IA-32 systems.

There are far too many **/proc** entries to list in this book; however, Table 5-1 is a list of a few kernel parameters of interest. The table is divided between directories in which categories of configuration options.

Table 5-1   Sample of **/proc** Entries

File	Function
/proc	Process information for the virtual file system.
cpuinfo	Provides information about CPUs in the system.
modules	Provides information about modules in the system (same as **lsmod**).
version	Provides the current version number of the kernel and other detailed information.

File	Function
/proc/sys/fs	Contains file system information.
file-max	Defines the maximum number of open files per process.
inode-max	Present number of inodes.
/proc/sys/kernel	Contains kernel information.
shmmax	Defines the maximum shared memory size.
shmmni	Defines the maximum number of shared memory segments system wide.
hostname	System hostname.
ctrl-alt-del	Specifies whether system will reboot on *ctrl-alt-del* key sequence.
/proc/sys/net/ipv4	Contains network information.
ip_forward	Defines whether or not packets will be forwarded between network interfaces.
icmp_echo_ignore_all	Defines whether or not ICMP pints are ignored.
ip_local_port_range	Defines range of ports used when originating a connection.

Patching the Kernel

Another common kernel-related task is patching the kernel. You may need to patch the kernel for a variety of reasons. With patches, you can load a device driver, install and upgrade the kernel, fix a bug, add new features, improve performance, and so on. You take your existing kernel to the next minor release with patches as well. *www.kernel.org/pub/linux/kernel* has directories under it containing patches for most kernel releases. The *v2.5* directory has patches for version *2.5*.

You normally work in the **/usr/src/linux** directory when performing any kernel work. After moving to this directory, you would apply a patch with the following command:

```
# patch -pnum < patch_file
```

In this example, the *num* has to do with the number of slashes in the path of the name found in the patch file. A *0* will strip away no slashes, a *1* will strip away the first slash, and so on. I normally us a *0* for a patch downloaded from *www.kernel.org*.

After you run **patch**, a large number of messages will stream by. If you have no errors, you can perform your **make dep**; **make clean**; **make bzImage**; **make module** and any other configuration and clean up work. When you're done, your patch is installed.

Chapter 6

System Startup and Shutdown Scripts

Various topics related to startup and shutdown are covered in this chapter, including the following:

- Linux startup and shutdown scripts
- **ksysv** graphical interface for controlling scripts and run levels
- Run levels **/etc/inittab** file
- **service** and **xinetd**
- System shutdown

Linux System Startup and Shutdown Scripts

Startup and shutdown scripts for Linux are organized in three parts: sequencer script; execution scripts; and subdirectories and link files. These scripts work together to facilitate startup execution and are described shortly.

Startup and shutdown are going to become increasingly more important to you as your system administration work to become more sophisticated. As you load and customize more applications, you will need to know more about startup and shutdown. In this section, you get an overview of startup and shutdown and the commands that you can use to control your system.

The following descriptions are for the three components that are in the startup and shutdown model of Linux that is based on the UNIX System V model:

Execution Scripts

> Read variables from configuration variable files and run through the startup or shutdown sequence. These scripts are located in **/etc/rc.d/init.d**, such as **/etc/rc.d/init.d/smb** to start and stop Samba.

Sequencer Script

> Calls all other scripts is **/etc/rc.d/rc**. This script calls all of the other scripts in the correct order for each run level. The scripts it calls are in a run level subdirectory.

Subdirectories and Link Files

> There is subdirectory for each run level in **/etc/rc.d** such as **/etc/rc.d/rc2.d** for run level two, **/etc/rc.d/rc3.d** for run level three, and so on. These subdirectories contain symbolic links to the execution scripts in **/etc/rc.d/init.d**. The links start with either an *S* for start or a *K* for kill. An *S* script would start a service and a *K* script would kill, or stop, a service. Lower number scripts are executed before higher number scripts.

Figure 6-1 shows the directory structure for startup and shutdown scripts.

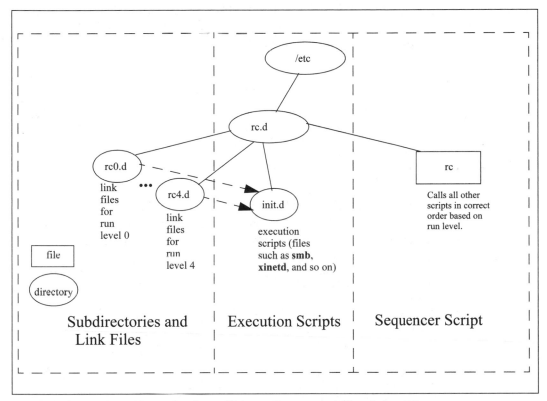

Figure 6-1   Organization of Linux Startup and Shutdown Files

Execution scripts perform startup and shutdown tasks. **/sbin/rc** invokes the execution script with the appropriate start or stop arguments, and you can view the appropriate start or stop messages on the console. You'll see an *[OK]* that indicates that the execution script started successfully.

Let's take a look at an example startup and shutdown file for Samba. This will help us later when we perform extensive Samba-related work in another chapter.

As mentioned earlier, the script used as part of the startup and shutdown process is in **/etc/init.d**. The following example is from the IA-32 system used in the Samba chapter, but is the same for Integrity servers. For the Samba example, the name of the program is **/etc/init.d/smb**. Take a minute and use your favorite editor to open and view the script. If you're logged on as root, remember not to make any changes to the script without backing up the original.

The startup and shutdown scripts in **/etc/init.d** generally perform both startup and shutdown functions. These startup and shutdown scripts recognize many arguments, including the following:

- start
- stop
- restart
- status
- condrestart

See if you can find these in **/etc/init.d/smb**. If you do, see if you can understand what they do. Now, test some of these arguments. We'll *start* smb, obtain its *status*, *stop* smb, and re-obtain its *status*. Remember, to do these things, you must be logged on as *root*:

```
# ./smb start

Starting SMB services: [ OK  ]
Starting NMB services: [ OK  ]

# ./smb status
smbd (pid 11165) is running...
nmbd (pid 11170) is running...

# ./smb stop
Shutting down SMB services: [ OK  ]
Shutting down NMB services: [ OK  ]

# ./smb status
smbd is stopped
nmbd is stopped
#
```

As you can see, the script obviously works great, but does not start automatically at system boot. Make sure that you're in **/etc/rc.d**, then search for all files in **/etc/rc.d** that contain *smb*. If you do, you get the following:

```
# pwd
/etc/rc.d

# find . -name *smb* -print
./init.d/smb
./rc0.d/K35smb
./rc1.d/K35smb
./rc2.d/K35smb
./rc3.d/K35smb
./rc4.d/K35smb
./rc5.d/K35smb
./rc6.d/K35smb
#
```

All the files found begin with *K,* which indicates that these are kill files, and no start files beginning with *S* were found. We can start *smb* a variety of ways, including the following:

- Manually change a *K* file to an *S* file at the appropriate run level so that when we pass through the run level *smb* will start.
- Edit **/etc/rc.d/rc.local** to include the following line:Á **/etc/init.d/smb start**
- Run **ksysv** to display and edit System V startup information although at the time of this writing, it doesn't appear that this will be supported in RHEL 3.

We'll use the third technique because the **ksysv** interface is easy to use and informative. Although this chapter discusses **/etc/inittab** soon, you need to know our default run level. You can obtain the current run level and the default run level because you haven't changed it in this case, by issuing the **runlevel** command:

```
# runlevel
N 5
#
```

You now know that you're at run level *5.* Figure 6-2 shows the top level **ksysv** interface.

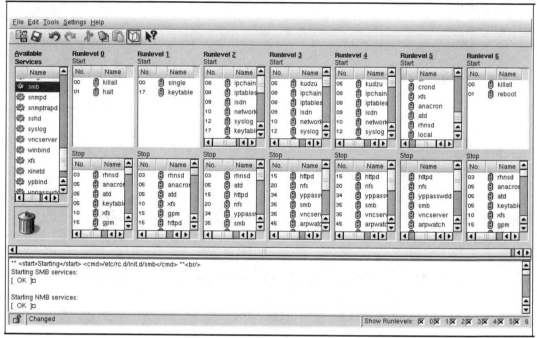

Figure 6-2   **ksysv** Interface

smb appears at run level 5 under *Stop* but not under *Start*. All that we have to do to place it under *Start* is to select it in the *Available Services* window on the left and *Copy* and *Paste* it into *Runlevel 5* to have it start when the system reaches run level 5. Figure 6-3 shows *smb* under *Runlevel 5*.

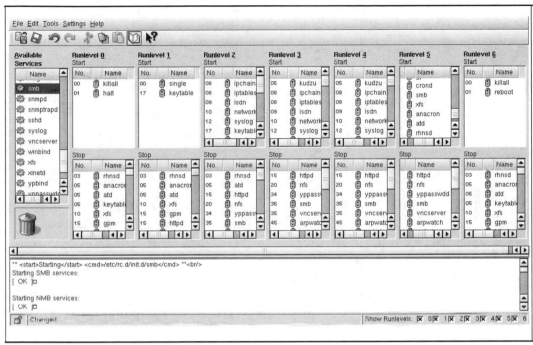

Figure 6-3   **ksysv** with *smb* Under *Runlevel 5*

After the system is rebooted, *smb* did come up as a running service as verified with the command in the following output:

```
# /sbin/service smb status
smbd (pid 933) is running...
nmbd (pid 938) is running...
#
```

The **/sbin/service** command starts services. It calls the startup script, such as **smb** in this case, and performs the desired function, such as producing *status* in this case. There is no manual page for **service**, but you will see it issued in examples often.

Now re-issue the search command and see if there is indeed an *S* file for smb to start it automatically:

```
# pwd
/etc/rc.d

# find . -name *smb* -print
./init.d/smb
./rc0.d/K35smb
./rc1.d/K35smb
./rc2.d/K35smb
./rc3.d/K35smb
./rc4.d/K35smb
./rc5.d/S90smb
./rc5.d/K35smb
./rc6.d/K35smb
#
```

The startup script for out default run level 5 is **/etc/rc.d/rc5.d/S90smb**. This was added for us automatically by **ksysv** with our *copy* and *paste* operation. The following shows the anatomy of the file:

/etc/rc.d/rc5.d/S90smb

```
              |    | | |
              |    | | v
              |    | | script name - smb in example
              |    | v
              |    | sequence number - 90 in example
              |    v
              | "S" for startup, "K" for kill or shutdown
              v
              run level number - 5 in example
```

Now that you know the way in which startup and shutdown scripts work, it's time to investigate **/etc/inittab**.

Run Levels and /etc/inittab

The scripts just covered are run when there is a change in the run level of the system. Different run levels exist because you may want to perform different tasks at different times. You may, for instance, want to repair a disk, which means you'll want to be in a lower run state. In normal operation, you may want to be in a higher run state. **/etc/inittab** defines the default run level of your system. The following listing shows **/etc/inittab**:

```
#
# inittab       This file describes how the INIT process should set up
#               the system in a certain run-level.
#
# Author:       Miquel van Smoorenburg, <miquels@drinkel.nl.mugnet.org>
#               Modified for RHS Linux by Marc Ewing and Donnie Barnes
#

# Default runlevel. The runlevels used by RHS are:
#   0 - halt (Do NOT set initdefault to this)
#   1 - Single user mode
#   2 - Multiuser, without NFS (The same as 3, if you do not have networking)
#   3 - Full multiuser mode
#   4 - unused
#   5 - X11
#   6 - reboot (Do NOT set initdefault to this)
#
id:5:initdefault:

# System initialization.
si::sysinit:/etc/rc.d/rc.sysinit

l0:0:wait:/etc/rc.d/rc 0
l1:1:wait:/etc/rc.d/rc 1
l2:2:wait:/etc/rc.d/rc 2
l3:3:wait:/etc/rc.d/rc 3
l4:4:wait:/etc/rc.d/rc 4
l5:5:wait:/etc/rc.d/rc 5
l6:6:wait:/etc/rc.d/rc 6

# Things to run in every runlevel.
ud::once:/sbin/update

# Trap CTRL-ALT-DELETE
ca::ctrlaltdel:/sbin/shutdown -t3 -r now

# When our UPS tells us power has failed, assume we have a few minutes
# of power left.  Schedule a shutdown for 2 minutes from now.
# This does, of course, assume you have powerd installed and your
# UPS connected and working correctly.
pf::powerfail:/sbin/shutdown -f -h +2 "Power Failure; System Shutting Down"

# If power was restored before the shutdown kicked in, cancel it.
pr:12345:powerokwait:/sbin/shutdown -c "Power Restored; Shutdown Cancelled"


# Run gettys in standard runlevels
1:2345:respawn:/sbin/mingetty tty1
2:2345:respawn:/sbin/mingetty tty2
3:2345:respawn:/sbin/mingetty tty3
4:2345:respawn:/sbin/mingetty tty4
5:2345:respawn:/sbin/mingetty tty5
6:2345:respawn:/sbin/mingetty tty6

#console definition
c0:2345:respawn:/sbin/agetty ttys0 9600 vt100

# Run xdm in runlevel 5
# xdm is now a separate service
x:5:respawn:/etc/X11/prefdm -nodaemon
```

You can see early in this listing, right after the comments, that you are in run level *5* by default.

If you are booting your system to run level 5, **/etc/rc.d/rc** will run the startup scripts present in **/sbin/rc1.d** through **/sbin/rc5.d**.

I have mentioned run levels several times in this discussion. Both the startup and shutdown scripts described here, as well as the **/etc/inittab** file, depend on run levels. The run level descriptions are present in the **/etc/inittab** listing and are summarized here:

0	Halt
1	Single user mode
2	Not used (user defined)
3	Full multi-user mode
4	Not used (user defined)
5	Full multi-user mode with an X-based login screen
6	Reboot

/etc/inittab is also used to define a variety of processes that will be run, and it is used by **/sbin/init**. The **/sbin/init** process ID is 1. It is the first process started on your system and it has no parent. After the kernel has been loaded into memory and initialized device drivers, data structures, and other work, it starts **init**. **init** performs many administrative tasks, such as checking file systems, and then looks at **/etc/inittab** to determine the run level of the system.

Entries in the **/etc/inittab** file have the following format:

id:run states:action:process

id	The name of the entry. The *id* is up to four characters long and must be unique in the file. If the line in **/etc/inittab** is preceded by a "#", the entry is treated as a comment.
run states	Specifies the run level(s) at which the command is executed. More than one run level can be specified. The command is executed for every run level specified.

action	Defines which of 11 actions will be taken with this process. The 11 choices for action are: *init-default, sysinit, boot, bootwait, wait, respawn, once, powerfail, powerwait, ondemand,* and *off.*
process	The shell command to be executed *if* the run level and/or action field so indicates.

To start a **getty**, which is a process run on each terminal so that users can login, at run levels *2-5*, you would include the following line in **/etc/inittab**:

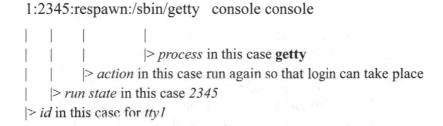

```
1:2345:respawn:/sbin/getty   console console
 |    |    |        |
 |    |    |        |> process in this case getty
 |    |        |> action in this case run again so that login can take place
 |        |> run state in this case 2345
 |> id in this case for tty1
```

This is in the **/etc/inittab** file, as opposed to being defined as a startup script, because the console may be killed and have to be restarted whenever it dies, even if no change has occurred in run level. **respawn** starts a process if it does not exist and restarts the process after it dies. This entry shows several run states, since you want the console to be activated at all times.

Another example is the first line from **/etc/inittab**:

id:5:initdefault:

The default run level of the system is defined as *5*.

The system startup and shutdown basics described here are important. You will be starting up and shutting down your system and possibly modifying some of the files described here. Because of their importance, it is important that you take a close look at the startup and shutdown files before you begin to modify them. If you do need to modify them, I recommend making a backup of any file before you edit it.

Now, look at the commands you can issue to shut down your system.

service, xinetd, and chkconfig

xinetd and **service** are startup-related programs related to enabling and disabling services. **/sbin/service** was mentioned earlier as a command used to start services in general (see the "Networking Background" section for more information about ports and services in general). In the earlier *smb* example, we verified that it was running using the following **service** command:

```
# /sbin/service smb status
smbd (pid 933) is running...
nmbd (pid 938) is running...
#
```

The **/sbin/service** command is used to start services. It calls the startup script, such as **smb** in this case, and performs the desired function, such as producing *status* in this case. There is no man page for **service**, but you will see it issued in examples often.

The **/etc/xinetd.d** directory contains a lot of configuration files that are used by the internet daemon *xinetd*. If, for example, you want to run *ftp*, you may have to change the **/etc/xinetd.d/ftp** file and set *disable = no* to enable *ftp* on your system. You would then issue the following command to restart *xinetd*:

```
# /sbin/service xinetd restart
Stopping xinetd:      [ OK ]
Starting xinetd:      [ OK ]
#
```

Take a look at a long listing of the files in **/etc/xinetd.d** and **cat** the file **ftp** on our IA-32 system. You would edit **wu-ftp** on both our Red Hat Advanced Server Integrity server and on the IA-32 system, but use **ftp** in this example:

```
# cd /etc/xinetd.d

# ll
total 24
-rw-r--r--    1 root     root          297 Apr  4  2002 chargen
-rw-r--r--    1 root     root          317 Apr  4  2002 chargen-udp
-rw-r--r--    1 root     root          297 Apr  4  2002 daytime
-rw-r--r--    1 root     root          317 Apr  4  2002 daytime-udp
-rw-r--r--    1 root     root          289 Apr  4  2002 echo
```

```
-rw-r--r--   1 root     root          308 Apr  4  2002 echo-udp
-rw-r--r--   1 root     root          318 Jun 25  2001 finger
-rw-r--r--   1 root     root          304 Jun 19 05:49 ftp
-rw-r--r--   1 root     root          267 Apr 17 11:04 kotalk
-rw-r--r--   1 root     root          267 Apr 17 11:04 ktalk
-rw-r--r--   1 root     root          259 Jul 24  2001 ntalk
-rw-r--r--   1 root     root          361 Jul 24  2001 rexec
-rw-r--r--   1 root     root          378 Jul 24  2001 rlogin
-rw-r--r--   1 root     root          431 Jul 24  2001 rsh
-rw-r--r--   1 root     root          317 Apr 11 00:04 rsync
-rw-r--r--   1 root     root          314 Apr  4  2002 servers
-rw-r--r--   1 root     root          312 Apr  4  2002 services
-rw-r--r--   1 root     root          392 Apr  7 20:15 sgi_fam
-rw-r--r--   1 root     root          362 Jun 29 04:04 swat
-rw-r--r--   1 root     root          247 Jul 24  2001 talk
-rw-r--r--   1 root     root          304 Jun 19 05:43 telnet
-rw-r--r--   1 root     root          321 Apr  4  2002 time
-rw-r--r--   1 root     root          317 Apr  4  2002 time-udp
-rw-r--r--   1 root     root          329 Jun 19 06:23 wu-ftpd

# cat ftp
# default: on
# description: The telnet server serves telnet sessions; it uses \
#       unencrypted username/password pairs for authentication.
service telnet
{
        flags             = REUSE
        socket_type       = stream
        wait              = no
        user              = root
        server            = /usr/sbin/in.telnetd
        log_on_failure    += USERID
        disable           = no
}

#
```

As you look at the contents of the **/etc/xinetd.d** directory, it's important to note that often, new ftp-related programs are introduced into Linux. I mentioned **wu-ftp** earlier, and we see that here. If this were Red Hat 9, you might see **vsftp** or others as well.

As you can see from the output of the **cat** command, at this time, **ftp** is enabled because *disable = no*. You may consider this to be a potential security problem. If so, we would perform the following steps to turn off *ftp*:

1. Edit **/etc/xinetd.d/ftp** (or **wu-ftp** on Advanced Server) and set *disable = yes*.

2. Run **/sbin/service xinetd restart** to re-read the new value of *disable* for *ftp* on Red Hat or **/etc/init.d/xinetd restart** as a general command.

Alternatively, you could use the **chkconfig** command. **chkconfig** is a powerful command-line utility for updating and querying system service runlevel information. The following example uses **chkconfig** with the *--list* option to see the status of *ftp*, then use the **chkconfig** and specify *ftp off*, and then re-run **chkconfig** to see the new value of *ftp*:

```
# chkconfig --list
keytable        0:off   1:on    2:on    3:on    4:on    5:on    6:off
atd             0:off   1:off   2:off   3:on    4:on    5:on    6:off
syslog          0:off   1:off   2:on    3:on    4:on    5:on    6:off
gpm             0:off   1:off   2:on    3:on    4:on    5:on    6:off
sendmail        0:off   1:off   2:on    3:off   4:off   5:off   6:off
kudzu           0:off   1:off   2:off   3:on    4:on    5:on    6:off
netfs           0:off   1:off   2:off   3:on    4:on    5:on    6:off
network         0:off   1:off   2:on    3:on    4:on    5:on    6:off
random          0:off   1:off   2:on    3:on    4:on    5:on    6:off
rawdevices      0:off   1:off   2:off   3:on    4:on    5:on    6:off
apmd            0:off   1:off   2:on    3:on    4:on    5:on    6:off
ipchains        0:off   1:off   2:on    3:on    4:on    5:on    6:off
iptables        0:off   1:off   2:on    3:on    4:on    5:on    6:off
crond           0:off   1:off   2:on    3:on    4:on    5:on    6:off
anacron         0:off   1:off   2:on    3:on    4:on    5:on    6:off
lpd             0:off   1:off   2:on    3:on    4:on    5:on    6:off
ntpd            0:off   1:off   2:off   3:off   4:off   5:off   6:off
portmap         0:off   1:off   2:off   3:on    4:on    5:on    6:off
xfs             0:off   1:off   2:on    3:on    4:on    5:on    6:off
xinetd          0:off   1:off   2:off   3:on    4:on    5:on    6:off
rhnsd           0:off   1:off   2:off   3:on    4:on    5:on    6:off
autofs          0:off   1:off   2:off   3:on    4:on    5:on    6:off
nfs             0:off   1:off   2:off   3:off   4:off   5:off   6:off
nfslock         0:off   1:off   2:off   3:on    4:on    5:on    6:off
identd          0:off   1:off   2:off   3:off   4:off   5:off   6:off
radvd           0:off   1:off   2:off   3:off   4:off   5:off   6:off
snmpd           0:off   1:off   2:off   3:off   4:off   5:off   6:off
snmptrapd       0:off   1:off   2:off   3:off   4:off   5:off   6:off
isdn            0:off   1:off   2:on    3:on    4:on    5:on    6:off
sshd            0:off   1:off   2:on    3:on    4:on    5:on    6:off
vncserver       0:off   1:off   2:off   3:off   4:off   5:off   6:off
yppasswdd       0:off   1:off   2:off   3:off   4:off   5:off   6:off
ypserv          0:off   1:off   2:off   3:off   4:off   5:off   6:off
ypxfrd          0:off   1:off   2:off   3:off   4:off   5:off   6:off
smb             0:off   1:off   2:off   3:off   4:off   5:off   6:off
arpwatch        0:off   1:off   2:off   3:off   4:off   5:off   6:off
httpd           0:off   1:off   2:off   3:off   4:off   5:off   6:off
webmin          0:off   1:off   2:on    3:on    4:off   5:on    6:off
xinetd based services:
        chargen-udp:    off
        chargen:        off
        daytime-udp:    off
        daytime:        off
        echo-udp:       off
        echo:   off
        services:       off
        servers:        off
        time-udp:       off
        time:   off
        ftp:    on                                      <--- ftp is on
        swat:   on
        sgi_fam:        on
        kotalk: off
        ktalk:  off
        finger: off
        rexec:  off
        rlogin: off
        rsh:    off
        ntalk:  off
        talk:   off
        telnet: on
        rsync:  off
        wu-ftpd:        on

# chkconfig ftp off                                     <--- set ftp off

# chkconfig --list
keytable        0:off   1:on    2:on    3:on    4:on    5:on    6:off
atd             0:off   1:off   2:off   3:on    4:on    5:on    6:off
syslog          0:off   1:off   2:on    3:on    4:on    5:on    6:off
gpm             0:off   1:off   2:on    3:on    4:on    5:on    6:off
sendmail        0:off   1:off   2:on    3:off   4:off   5:off   6:off.
kudzu           0:off   1:off   2:off   3:on    4:on    5:on    6:off
netfs           0:off   1:off   2:off   3:on    4:on    5:on    6:off
```

```
network        0:off   1:off   2:on    3:on    4:on    5:on    6:off
random         0:off   1:off   2:on    3:on    4:on    5:on    6:off
rawdevices     0:off   1:off   2:off   3:on    4:on    5:on    6:off
apmd           0:off   1:off   2:on    3:on    4:on    5:on    6:off
ipchains       0:off   1:off   2:on    3:on    4:on    5:on    6:off
iptables       0:off   1:off   2:on    3:on    4:on    5:on    6:off
crond          0:off   1:off   2:on    3:on    4:on    5:on    6:off
anacron        0:off   1:off   2:on    3:on    4:on    5:on    6:off
lpd            0:off   1:off   2:on    3:on    4:on    5:on    6:off
ntpd           0:off   1:off   2:off   3:off   4:off   5:off   6:off
portmap        0:off   1:off   2:off   3:on    4:on    5:on    6:off
xfs            0:off   1:off   2:on    3:on    4:on    5:on    6:off
xinetd         0:off   1:off   2:off   3:on    4:on    5:on    6:off
rhnsd          0:off   1:off   2:off   3:on    4:on    5:on    6:off
autofs         0:off   1:off   2:off   3:on    4:on    5:on    6:off
nfs            0:off   1:off   2:off   3:off   4:off   5:off   6:off
nfslock        0:off   1:off   2:off   3:on    4:on    5:off   6:off
identd         0:off   1:off   2:off   3:off   4:off   5:off   6:off
radvd          0:off   1:off   2:off   3:off   4:off   5:off   6:off
snmpd          0:off   1:off   2:off   3:off   4:off   5:off   6:off
snmptrapd      0:off   1:off   2:off   3:off   4:off   5:off   6:off
isdn           0:off   1:off   2:on    3:on    4:on    5:on    6:off
sshd           0:off   1:off   2:on    3:on    4:on    5:on    6:off
vncserver      0:off   1:off   2:off   3:off   4:off   5:off   6:off
yppasswdd      0:off   1:off   2:off   3:off   4:off   5:off   6:off
ypserv         0:off   1:off   2:off   3:off   4:off   5:off   6:off
ypxfrd         0:off   1:off   2:off   3:off   4:off   5:off   6:off
smb            0:off   1:off   2:off   3:off   4:off   5:off   6:off
arpwatch       0:off   1:off   2:off   3:off   4:off   5:off   6:off
httpd          0:off   1:off   2:off   3:off   4:off   5:off   6:off
webmin         0:off   1:off   2:on    3:on    4:off   5:on    6:off
xinetd based services:
        chargen-udp:     off
        chargen:         off
        daytime-udp:     off
        daytime:         off
        echo-udp:        off
        echo:     off
        services:        off
        servers:         off
        time-udp:        off
        time:     off
        ftp:      off                                  <--- ftp is now off
        swat:     on
        sgi_fam:         on
        kotalk:   off
        ktalk:    off
        finger:   off
        rexec:    off
        rlogin:   off
        rsh:      off
        ntalk:    off
        talk:     off
        telnet:   on
        rsync:    off
        wu-ftpd:         on
[root@linuxdev xinetd.d]#
```

chkconfig makes this process much easier (on Advanced Server, you would specify *wu-ftpd*). You may want to take a look at the **chkconfig** man page because it lists other functionalities not covered here. This is a great tool for quickly changing whether services are enabled. As a sidenote, you may want to perform the same process for *wu-fptd*.

When determining what services to turn on and off, keep in mind that enabling *ftp, telnet*, and other services can reduce your overall security.

telnet, for example, transmits passwords in clear text that can be read by "sniffing" your network.

Now, take a look at the commands you can issue to shut down your system.

System Shutdown

What does it mean to shut down the system? Well, in its simplest form, a shutdown of the system simply means issuing the **/sbin/shutdown** command. The **shutdown** command terminates all processing. It has many options, including the following:

-a	Use **/etc/shutdown.allow** to determine whether a user is authorized to shut down the system.
-t sec	Wait for *sec* seconds before sending processes the warning and the kill signal and changing run levels.
-r	Automatically reboots the system; that is, brings it down and brings it up.
-h	Halts the system completely.
time	Specifies the time at which to shut down in *hh:mm*, *+m* for the number of minutes to wait, or *now* for immediately.
-F	Force **fsck** on reboot.
-f	Skip **fsck** on reboot.

If you issue a **shutdown -h**, the **halt** command is called by **shutdown**. You can also call **halt** directly if you want. (Note that if halt or reboot is called when the system is not in runlevel 0 or 6 (when its running normally), shutdown will be invoked. For more information, see the shutdown or halt man pages.)

Here are some of the things your system does when you issue the **shutdown -h** or **halt** command:

- Logs the *shutdown* operation (in **/var/log/wtmp**).

- Kills nonessential processes.

- Executes the **sync** system call (**sync** flushes the filesystem buffers, forcing any changed blocks to disk and updating the superblock).

- Waits for filesystem writes to complete.

- Halts the kernel.

- **halt -n** prevents the sync system call from taking place when used by **fsck** after a repair to the root partition.

To shut down and automatically reboot the system, you would type

```
$ shutdown -r now
```

To halt the system, you would type

```
$ shutdown -h now
```

To shut down the system in two minutes, type

```
$ shutdown -h 120
```

You do have ways other than **shutdown** to bring down the system. You can issue **halt**, which was already mentioned, **reboot,** or **poweroff**. If you want to bring down your system, I strongly recommend using **shutdown** because it provides a secure smooth transition to differing run levels, or to power down the system.

Chapter 7

Networking Background

This chapter provides a background for Linux networking. The next chapter covers networking configuration and using networking commands. If you don't have a good background in Linux and TCP/IP networking, you'll want to review this chapter before moving on to the next one. If you have a good networking background and want to know how to set up Linux networking and use networking commands, you can jump directly to the next chapter.

This chapter covers the following:

- TCP/IP and IEEE 802.3 background

- Internet Protocol (IP) addressing (Classes A, B, and C)

- Subnet mask

An Overview of IEEE 802.3, TCP/IP

To understand how the networking on your Linux system works, you first need to understand the components of your network. Linux uses the OSI model, which consists of seven layers of network functionality (see Figure 7-1).

In what follows, I cover the bottom four layers at a cursory level so that you can see how each layer plays a part in the operation of your network. This will help you to understand, configure, and troubleshoot networking on your Linux system.

The top layers are the ones that most Linux system administrators spend time working with because those layers are the ones you work with most often. The bottom layers are, however, also important to understand, so that you can perform any configuration necessary to improve network performance on your system. Improving network performance can have a major impact on the overall performance of your system.

Layer Number	Layer Name	Data Form	Comments
7	Application		User applications here.
6	Presentation		Applications prepared.
5	Session		Applications prepared.
4	Transport	Packet	Port-to-port transportation handled by TCP.
3	Network	Datagram	Internet Protocol (IP) handles routing by going directly to either the destination or default router.
2	Link	Frame	Data encapsulated in Ethernet or IEEE 802.3 with source and destination addresses.
1	Physical		Physical connection between systems. Usually thinnet or twisted pair.

Figure 7-1   ISO/OSI Network Layer Functions

This is the International Standards Organization Open Systems Interconnection (ISO/OSI) model. It is helpful to visualize the way in which networking layers interact. We'll start with the bottom layer (Layer 1– Physical) and work our way up.

Physical Layer (Layer 1)

At the bottom of the model is the physical interconnection between the systems on your network. Without the physical layer, you can't communicate between systems, and all the great functionality you would like to implement is not possible. The physical layer converts the data you would like to transmit to the analog signals that travel along the wire. The information traveling into a network interface is taken off the wire and prepared for use by the next layer. For the purposes of this discussion, I'll assume for now that whatever physical layer you have in place uses wires. If your network is all or partially wireless, the wireless bandwidth is also part of the physical layer.

Link Layer (Layer 2)

To connect to other systems local to your system, you use the link layer. The link layer establishes a connection to all the other systems on your local segment (assuming they all use the same protocol). In this layer, data packets are encoded and decoded into bits. The link layer furnishes transmission protocol knowledge and management and handles errors in the physical layer, flow control, and frame synchronization.

The data link layer is divided into two sublayers: the Media Access Control (MAC) layer and the Logical Link Control (LLC) layer. The MAC sublayer controls how a computer on the network gains access to the data and permission to transmit it. The LLC layer controls frame synchronization, flow control, and error checking.

The link layer supports either IEEE 802.3 or Ethernet frames. Your Linux system may support both of these "encapsulation" methods. This is called encapsulation because your data is put in one of these two forms (either IEEE 802.3 or Ethernet). Data is transferred at the link layer into frames (just another name for data), with the source and destination addresses and some other information attached. You might think that because two different encapsulation methods exist, they must be different. This assumption, however, is not the case. IEEE 802.3 and Ethernet are nearly identical. For this reason, many Linux systems can handle both types of encapsulation.

Figure 7-2 lists the components of an **Ethernet** encapsulation and makes comments about IEEE802.3 encapsulation where appropriate.

Destination address	6 bytes	Address data is sent to.
Source address	6 bytes	Address data is sent from.
Type	2 bytes	This is the "length count" in 802.3.
Data	46-MTU bytes	38-1492 bytes for 802.3; the difference in these two data sizes (MTU) can be seen with the **ifconfig** command.
Crc	4 bytes	Checksum to detect errors called cycle redundancy check.

Figure 7-2   Ethernet Encapsulation

One interesting item to note is the difference in the maximum data size between IEEE 802.3 and Ethernet of 1492 and 1500 bytes, respectively. This is the Maximum Transfer Unit (MTU). The **ifconfig** command (covered in the next chapter) displays the MTU for your network interface. The data in Ethernet is called a *frame* (the re-encapsulation of data at the next layer up is called a *datagram* in IP, and encapsulation at two levels up is called a *packet* for TCP).

Keep in mind that Ethernet and IEEE 802.3 will run on the same physical connection, but there are indeed differences between the two encapsulation methods. With your Linux systems, you don't have to spend much, if any, time setting up your network interface for encapsulation.

Note that MAC address is short for Media Access Control address, a hardware address that uniquely identifies each node of a network. The MAC layer interfaces directly with the network media. Consequently, each different type of network media requires a different MAC layer. On a Local Area Network (LAN) or other network, the MAC address is your computer's unique hardware number. (On an Ethernet LAN, it's the same as your Ethernet address.) When you're connected to the Internet from your computer (or host as the Internet protocol thinks of it), a correspondence table relates your IP address to your computer's physical (MAC) address on the LAN.

Network Layer (Layer 3)

The network layer on Linux systems is synonymous with the Internet Protocol (IP). Data at this layer is transported as *datagrams*. This is the layer that handles the routing of data around the network. Data that gets routed with IP sometimes encounters an error of some type, which is reported back to the source system with an Internet Control Message Protocol (ICMP) message. You will see some ICMP messages in the next chapter. **ifconfig** and **netstat** are two Linux commands that are commonly used to configure this routing.

Unfortunately, the information that IP uses does not conveniently fit inside an Ethernet frame, so you end up with fragmented data. This is really re-encapsulation of the data, so you end up with a lot of inefficiency as you work your way up the layers.

IP handles routing in a simple fashion. If data is sent to a destination connected directly to your system, the data is sent directly to that system. If, on the other hand, the destination is not connected directly to your system, the data is sent to the default router. The default router then has the responsibility of getting the data to its destination. This routing can be a little tricky to understand, so I'll cover it in detail shortly (see the upcoming "Subnet Mask section").

Transport Layer (Layer 4)

The transport layer is the next level up from the network layer. It communicates with *ports*. TCP is the most common protocol found at this level, and it forms packets that are sent from port to port. The port used by a program is usually defined in **/etc/services**, along with the protocol (such as TCP). These ports are used by network programs, such as **telnet**, **rlogin**, **ftp, http**, and so on. You can see that these programs, associated with ports, are the highest level we have covered while analyzing the layer diagram. Ports are covered later in this chapter.

Internet Protocol (IP) Addressing and Subnet Mask

The IP address is either a Class A, B, or C address (There are also Class D and E addresses, but they are not relevant to our discussion.) A Class A network supports many more nodes per network than either a Class B or C network. IP addresses consist of four fields. The purpose of breaking down the IP address into four fields is to define a node (or host) address and a network address. Figure 7-3 summarizes the relationships between the classes and addresses.

Address Class	Networks	Nodes per Network	Bits Defining Network	Bits Defining Nodes per Network
A	Few	Most	8 bits	24 bits
B	Many	Many	16 bits	16 bits
C	Most	Few	24 bits	8 bits
Reserved	-	-	-	-

Figure 7-3   Classes and Addresses

These bit patterns are significant in that the number of bits defines the ranges of networks and nodes in each class. For example, a Class A address uses 8 bits to define networks, and a Class C address uses 24 bits to define networks. A Class A address therefore supports fewer networks than a class C address. A Class A address, however, supports many more nodes per network than a Class C address. Taking these relationships one step further, you can now view the specific parameters associated with these address classes in Figure 7-4.

Figure 7-4   Address Classes

Address Class	Networks Supported	Nodes per Network	Address Range		
A	127	16777215	0.0.0.1	-	127.255.255.254
B	16383	65535	128.0.0.1	-	191.255.255.254
C	2097157	255	192.0.0.1	-	223.255.254.254
Reserved	-	-	224.0.0.0	-	255.255.255.255

Figure 7-4   Address Classes (Continued)

> Looking at the 32-bit address in binary form, you can see how to determine the class of an address:

Class A
0uuuuuuuu..........

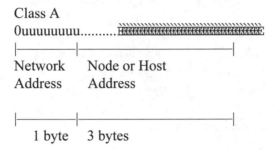

|————|————————————|
Network   Node or Host
Address   Address

|————|————————————|
1 byte   3 bytes

net.host.host.host

A Class A address has the first bit set to 0. You can see how so many nodes per network can be supported with all the bits devoted to the node or host address. The first bit of a Class A address is 0, and the remaining 7 bits of the network portion are used to define the network. Then a total of 3 bytes are devoted to defining the nodes within a network.

Figure 7-4   Address Classes (Continued)

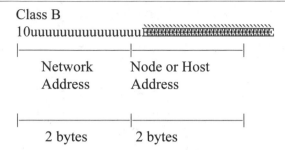

net.net.host.host

A Class B address has the first bit set to a 1 and the second bit to a 0. More networks are supported here than with a Class A address, but fewer nodes per network. With a Class B address, 2 bytes are devoted to the network portion of the address and 2 bytes devoted to the node portion of the address.

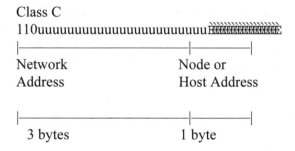

net.net.net.host

A Class C address has the first bit and second bit set to 1, and the third bit is 0. The greatest number of networks and fewest number of nodes per network are associated with a Class C address. With a Class C address, 3 bytes are devoted to the network and 1 byte is devoted to the nodes within a network.

These addresses are used in various setup files that are covered later when the **/etc/hosts** file is described. Every interface on your network must have a unique IP address. Systems that have two network interfaces must have two unique IP addresses.

Subnet Mask

Your Linux system uses the subnet mask to determine whether an IP datagram is for a host on its own subnet, a host on a different subnet but the same network, or a host on a different network. Using subnets, you can have some hosts on one subnet and other hosts on a different subnet. The subnets can be separated by routers or other networking electronics that connect the subnets.

To perform routing, the only aspects of an address that your router uses are the net and subnet. The subnet mask is used to mask the host part of the address. Because you can set up network addresses in such a way that you are the only one who knows which part of the address is the host, subnet, and network, you use the subnet mask to make your system aware of the bits of your IP address that are for the host and which are for the subnet.

In its simplest form, what you are really doing with subnet masking is specifying which portion of your IP address defines the host, and which part defines the network. One of the most confusing aspects of working with subnet masks is that most books show the subnet masks in Figure 7-5 as the most common.

Address Class	Decimal	Hex
A	255.0.0.0	0xff000000
B	255.255.0.0	0xffff0000
C	255.255.255.0	0xffffff00

Figure 7-5   Subnet Masks

This way of thinking, however, assumes that you are devoting as many bits as possible to the network and as many bits as possible to the host, and that no subnets are used. Figure 7-6 shows an example of using subnetting with a Class B address.

Address Class	Class B		
Host IP address	152.128.	12.	1
Breakdown	Network	Subnet	Hostid
Number of bits	16 bits	8 bits	8 bits
Subnet mask in decimal	255.255.	255.	0
Subnet mask in hexadecimal	0xffffff00		
Example of different host on same subnet	152.128.	12.	2
Example of host on different subnet	152.128.	13.	1

Figure 7-6   Class B IP Address and Subnet Mask Example

In Figure 7-6, the first two bytes of the subnet mask (255.255) define the network, the third byte (255) defines the subnet, and the fourth byte (0) is devoted to the host ID. Although this subnet mask for a Class B address did not appear in the earlier default subnet mask example, the subnet mask of 255.255.255.0 is widely used in Class B networks to support subnetting.

How does your Linux system perform the comparison using the subnet mask of 255.255.255.0 to determine that 152.128.12.1 and 152.128.13.1 are on different subnets? Figure 7-7 shows this comparison.

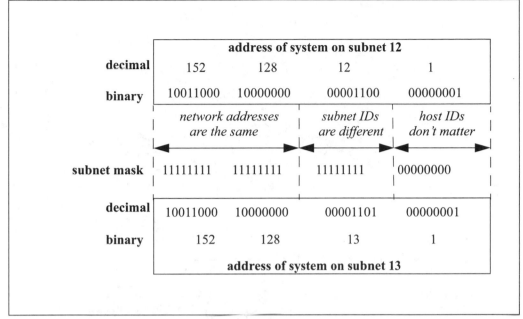

Figure 7-7   Example of Using Subnet Mask to Compare Addresses

Figure 7-8 shows these two systems on the different subnets. You don't have to use the 8-bit boundaries to delineate the network, subnet, and host ID fields. If, for example, you want to use part of the subnet field for the host ID, you can do so. A good reason for this approach would be to accommodate future expandability. You might want subnets 12, 13, 14, and 15 to be part of the same subnet today and make these into separate subnets in the future. Figure 7-9 shows this setup.

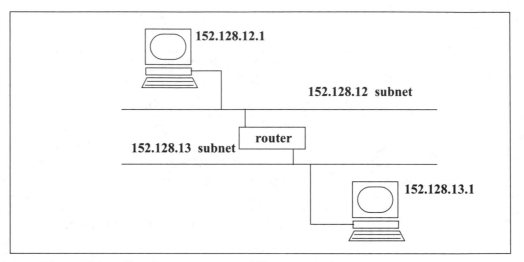

Figure 7-8   Class B Systems on Different Subnets

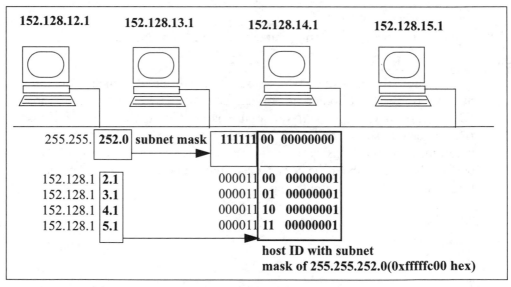

Figure 7-9   Future Expandability Using Subnet Mask

These systems are connected to the same subnet, even though part of the third byte, normally associated with the subnet, is used for the host ID. In the future, the subnet mask could be changed to 255.255.252.0 and have four separate subnets of 12, 13, 14, and 15. This arrangement would require putting routers in place to route to these separate subnets.

Ports and Related Topics

Now that some of the background of networking and TCP/IP has been covered, let's go over ports and some related topics. Ports have an impact on the security of your system, so be sure to see the security chapter for an introduction to some security topics and recommendations.

Every Linux system on an IP network has a minimum of one IP address through which systems and their processes communicate. With many processes running on every system and a lot of data exchanged between systems, there is the potential for much confusion. If a process on one system, for instance, needs to communicate with a process on another system, there needs to be a way for the second system to identify where to deliver the data. This problem is solved by TCP/IP identifying a TCP or UDP port. Ports are a connection that one host has to another host. I use host here because it's easier to understand host-to-host connections, but you should bear in mind that TCP/IP connections can be between processes on the same host (for example, between a Web browser on your desktop and a Web server running on your own machine). In any event, ports are identified by integers on your system and can be controlled. For security purposes, you might want to close some ports that you don't plan on using and restrict others.

The operating system keeps track of many pieces of information for every connection. This information facilitates the communication between the processes. Of this vast amount of information, there are four pieces that make the connection unique. These are the source IP address, the source port number, the destination IP address, and the destination port number.

When a system wants to make a connection to another system, it specifies the destination IP address and port number. Internet services running on systems listen on a particular port. The file **/etc/services** lists all the possible ports and their corresponding numbers. This is a long file, so the following listing shows a small subset of it:

```
ftp-data        20/tcp
ftp-data        20/udp
# 21 is registered to ftp, but also used by fsp
ftp             21/tcp
ftp             21/udp          fsp fspd
ssh             22/tcp                          # SSH Remote Login Protocol
ssh             22/udp                          # SSH Remote Login Protocol
telnet          23/tcp
telnet          23/udp
# 24 - private mail system
smtp            25/tcp          mail
smtp            25/udp          mail
time            37/tcp          timserver
```

```
time             37/udp        timserver
rlp              39/tcp        resource      # resource location
rlp              39/udp        resource      # resource location
```

As you can see in this example, *telnet* runs on port *23*. This is the standard port number for *telnet*. This is a well-known service for which there is a standard port number as is the case for any well-known service.

You have a lot of control over which ports and services you'll enable and disable on your Linux system. To begin with, let's use **netstat** to view all of ports with -*a*, not to resolve hostnames with -*n*, and to show both UDP with -*u* and TCP with -*t,* as shown in the following example:

```
# netstat -antu

Active Internet connections (servers and established)
Proto Recv-Q Send-Q Local Address               Foreign Address         State
tcp        0      0 0.0.0.0:1024                0.0.0.0:*               LISTEN
tcp        0      0 0.0.0.0:901                 0.0.0.0:*               LISTEN
tcp        0      0 127.0.0.1:1448              0.0.0.0:*               LISTEN
tcp        0      0 0.0.0.0:139                 0.0.0.0:*               LISTEN
tcp        0      0 0.0.0.0:111                 0.0.0.0:*               LISTEN
tcp        0      0 0.0.0.0:6000                0.0.0.0:*               LISTEN
tcp        0      0 0.0.0.0:10000               0.0.0.0:*               LISTEN
tcp        0      0 0.0.0.0:21                  0.0.0.0:*               LISTEN
tcp        0      0 0.0.0.0:22                  0.0.0.0:*               LISTEN
tcp        0      0 0.0.0.0:23                  0.0.0.0:*               LISTEN
tcp        0    138 192.168.1.102:23            192.168.1.100:2706      ESTABLISHED
tcp        1      0 192.168.1.102:1406          216.239.51.101:80       CLOSE_WAIT
tcp        0      0 192.168.1.102:1571          64.12.29.103:5190       ESTABLISHED
tcp        1      0 192.168.1.102:1405          66.70.73.150:80         CLOSE_WAIT
tcp        1      0 192.168.1.102:1404          66.70.73.150:80         CLOSE_WAIT
udp        0      0 0.0.0.0:1024                0.0.0.0:*
udp        0      0 192.168.1.102:137           0.0.0.0:*
udp        0      0 0.0.0.0:137                 0.0.0.0:*
udp        0      0 192.168.1.102:138           0.0.0.0:*
udp        0      0 0.0.0.0:138                 0.0.0.0:*
udp        0      0 0.0.0.0:10000               0.0.0.0:*
udp        0      0 0.0.0.0:111                 0.0.0.0:*
#
```

You can see that many ports are *LISTEN*, some are *ESTABLISHED*, and others are *CLOSE_WAIT* at this time. One of the *ESTABLISHED* connections is on port *23,* with IP address *192.168.1.100*, which means that it's a *telnet* session as determined earlier by viewing the **/etc/services** file.

Notice also that *21, 22,* and *23* are all listening. These were in our earlier **/etc/services** listing and are *ftp, ssh*, and *telnet,* respectively. Many other ports are also listening, which provides the potential to access to the system. Turning off these ports would increase the level of security of our system but potentially remove the ability to connect through that port and use a useful service.

You've now seen a lot of useful information by viewing **/etc/services** to see the list of services that we can enable and disable and using

netstat -antu to view the status of the ports. There is an interesting nuance to the port number scheme.

Many services based on Remote Procedure Call do not listen for requests on a well-known port, such as *telnet* on *23*, but rather pick an arbitrary port when initialized. They then register this port with a Portmapper service running on the same machine. Only the *portmapper* needs to run on a well-known port; when clients want access to the service, they first contact the *portmapper*, and it tells them which port they should then contact in order to reach the service. This second port may be for TCP or UDP access. The following two lines are from our **/etc/services** file showing *portmapper*:

```
sunrpc          111/tcp         portmapper      # RPC 4.0 portmapper TCP
sunrpc          111/udp         portmapper      # RPC 4.0 portmapper UDP
```

The earlier **netstat -antu** output did indeed show that port *111* is listening. You have to be careful with this port because, in most cases, you can't disable the port; however, it is a port to which someone could connect and potentially gain access to your system. The **netstat -p** command shows which processes are connected to which ports, as shown in the following example searching for *telnet*:

```
#  netstat -p | grep tel
tcp        0      2 linuxdev:telnet          F4457MXP:2706
                               ESTABLISHED 27269/in.telnetd: F

#
```

I issued the **netstat** command and piped it to **grep** so you could see the *telnet* connection only. Shown in this output are both the destination and source host and the status of *ESTABLISHED*.

The next chapter covers ways of controlling the services. There are a few different ways to enable and disable services and some examples are provided. Before you permanantly enable and disable network services, please be sure to see the security chapter for an introduction to some security topics and recommendations.

Chapter 8

Configuring and Using Networking

In this chapter, you'll configure LAN cards and use a variety of networking commands. If you are not familiar with the background for Linux networking, take a look at Chapter 7, "Networking Background," before you start this chapter. This chapter focuses on what every system administrator should know about identifying and configuring LAN cards and many of the commands associated with network configuration. The examples used in this chapter are from a Red Hat 8.x system and the Integrity server running Advanced Server. As a sidenote, the "retail" versions of Red Hat, such as 8.x used in this section, has been replaced by Fedora. Fedora Project is a Red Hat-sponsored and community-supported open source project. Fedora Core 2 is available at the time of this writing. You also use a few UNIX examples so that you can see the differences in the outputs. In this chapter, you will:

- View some important networking configuration files, such as Á **ifcfg-eth0** and **/etc/hosts** and others to see some of the networking parameters you set.

- Work with commonly used networking commands, such as **ping**, **netstat**, **route**, **ifconfig**, **iptables**, and others.

- Set up NFS networking.

- Work with graphical programs, such as **neat** and **Webmin**.

Commonly Used Networking Files

There isn't really any "procedure" associated with networking. Networking is more of a matter of knowing commands and files associated with networking than it is a step-by-step endeavor, so this section covers most common networking commands and files. First, some commonly used files are covered so you can see the type of networking parameters you define. Then you'll look at graphical tools that you can use to define these parameters. Finally, this section covers commands that you can issue from the command line to view and set networking-related parameters.

ifcfg-eth0

You can define the parameters related to a network interface card easily with the *ifcfg* file for the card. The file **ifcfg-eth0** is usually the first network card on Red Hat systems. This file is in **/etc/sysconfig/network-scripts** along with a lot of other networking files beginning with *if*. The interface device files, such as **ifcfg-eth0** are usually named *ifcfg-device* where *device* is the name of the device for which control will be specified in the configuration file.The contents of this file are shown here for the system used in many of the examples in this chapter:

```
# pwd
/etc/sysconfig/network-scripts
# cat ifcfg-eth0
DEVICE=eth0
BOOTPROTO=static
BROADCAST=192.168.1.255
IPADDR=192.168.1.102
NETMASK=255.255.255.0
NETWORK=192.168.1.0
ONBOOT=yes
#
```

This file has in it all the important information related to the interface, such as *IPADDR, DEVICE, NETMASK*, and so on.

You can edit this file directly, using the command line with **ifconfig** as described shortly, or use **neat**, **webmin**, or **netconf** to define the information for *eth0* or any other interface. (Keep in mind that not all graphical tools are available on Integrity yet.)

If you were to use DHCP, the file might look like the following:

```
DEVICE=eth0
BOOTPROTO=dhcp
ONBOOT=yes
```

The following describes the entries shown in the *ifcfg-device* file:

BOOTPROTO=*protocol, where protocol is one of the following:*
    none — No boot-time protocol should be used.
    bootp — The BOOTP protocol should be used.
    dhcp — The DHCP protocol should be used.

BROADCAST=*address*, where *address* is the broadcast address.

DEVICE=*name*, where *name* is the name of the physical device.

IPADDR=*address*, where *address* is the IP address.

NETMASK=*mask*, where *mask* is the netmask value.

NETWORK=*address*, where *address* is the network address.

ONBOOT=*answer*, where *answer* is one of the following:
    yes — This device should be activated at boot-time.
    no — This device should not be activated at boot-time.

USERCTL=*answer*, where *answer* is one of the following:
    true — Non-root users are allowed to control this device.
    false — Non-root users are not allowed to control this device.

There is also a loopback device in this directory called **ifcfg-lo**, which has the following contents:

```
# more /etc/sysconfig/network-scripts/ifcfg-lo
DEVICE=lo
IPADDR=127.0.0.1
NETMASK=255.0.0.0
NETWORK=127.0.0.0
# If you're having problems with gated making 127.0.0.0/8 a martian,
# you can change this to anything (255.255.255.255, for example)
BROADCAST=127.255.255.255
ONBOOT=yes
NAME=loopback
#
```

The address of *127.0.0.1* is a special address know as the *loopback*. This is for an IP host to refer to itself. A local loopback interface is often used in testing, as well as a variety of applications that require an IP address pointing back to the same system. Any data sent to the loopback device is immediately returned to the host's network layer.

You can find a lot of information about these scripts in **/usr/share/doc/ initscripts** and **ssyconfig.txt**.

/etc/sysconfig/network

The file **/etc/sysconfig/network** has in it information about the network configuration. The file contains information such as the following:

NETWORKING — Set to *yes* or *no* depending on whether you want networking configured.

HOSTNAME — The hostname, such as m4415mxp.

GATEWAY — The address of the gateway.

GATEWAYDEV — The gateway device, such as *eth0*.

NISDOMAIN=*value*, where *value* is the NIS domain name.

The following is an example **network** file:

```
# cat /etc/sysconfig/network
NETWORKING=yes
HOSTNAME=m4415mxp
GATEWAY=15.32.160.1
#
```

/etc/hosts

The **/etc/hosts** file contains the Internet Protocol (IP) hostnames and addresses for the local host and other hosts in the Internet network. This file is used to translate a hostname into its Internet address or what is called *resolve* the hostname. When your system is using a name server, the file is accessed only if the name server cannot resolve the hostname. You may be using the *DOMAIN* protocol on your Linux system in which case the resolver routines query a remote *DOMAIN* name server before searching this file. In a flat network with no name server, the resolver routines search this file for hostname and address data. This file contains information about the other systems to which you are connected. It contains the Internet address of each system, the system name, and any aliases for the system name. The format of the file is simple as shown in the following example:

```
127.0.0.1       localhostloopback
15.32.199.42    a4410827
15.32.199.28    a4410tu8
15.32.199.7     a4410922
15.32.199.21    a4410tu1
15.32.199.22    a4410tu2
15.32.199.62    a4410730
15.32.199.63    hpxterm1
15.32.199.64    a4410rd1
15.32.199.62    a4410750hp1
```

This file is in the following format:

internet_address   official_hostname   aliases

The Internet Protocol address (IP address) is a Class A, B, or C address. A Class A network supports many more nodes per network than either a Class B or C network. The purpose of breaking down the IP address into four fields is to define a node (or host) address and a network address. The previous chapter describes these classes in detail.

Assuming that the above **/etc/hosts** file contains Class C addresses, the rightmost field is the host or node address, and the other three fields comprise the network address.

You could use either the official_hostname or alias from the **/etc/hosts** file when issuing remote connection command, such as **telnet** or **rlogin**, as shown in the following example:

```
$ telnet a4410750
```

   or

```
$ telnet hp1
```

Similarly, either of the following Berkeley commands works:

```
$ rlogin a4410750
```

   or

```
$ rlogin hp1
```

If you're using only the *loopback* device, the only line in the file will be the one that contains *127.0.0.1*.

/etc/networks

This file lists the names of networks including the one on which you are working and other networks. This is an optional file. It is used by the **route** command to identify networks by name rather than IP address. An entry in **/etc/networks** would look like the following:

```
dev-net         15.33.75.0      #development network
```

You can then use the following **route** command:

```
# route add dev-net
```

Without the **/etc/networks** file, you would have to use the IP address rather than the name *dev-net*. If your system doesn't have an **/etc/networks** file, you must create one and add entries like the above for any network you want to **route** by name.

/etc/nsswitch.conf

This file is used by the system to determine where it should look up information and in what order it should reference these entries. To look up *hosts* for instance, you would specify locations such as the **/etc/hosts** file, *dns*, *nisplus*, and so on. The following examples show looking up *hosts* using these locations in the same order just listed:

```
hosts:          files dns nisplus
```

In most cases, the **/etc/hosts** file comes first. This file has many other networking selections in it. The following example shows the full **nsswitch.conf** file from the Integrity Advanced Server system:

```
# cat /etc/nsswitch.conf
#
# /etc/nsswitch.conf
#
# An example Name Service Switch config file. This file should be
# sorted with the most-used services at the beginning.
#
# The entry '[NOTFOUND=return]' means that the search for an
# entry should stop if the search in the previous entry turned
# up nothing. Note that if the search failed due to some other reason
# (like no NIS server responding) then the search continues with the
# next entry.
#
# Legal entries are:
#
#       nisplus or nis+        Use NIS+ (NIS version 3)
#       nis or yp              Use NIS (NIS version 2), also called YP
#       dns                    Use DNS (Domain Name Service)
#       files                  Use the local files
#       db                     Use the local database (.db) files
#       compat                 Use NIS on compat mode
#       hesiod                 Use Hesiod for user lookups
#       [NOTFOUND=return]      Stop searching if not found so far
#

# To use db, put the "db" in front of "files" for entries you want to be
# looked up first in the databases
#
# Example:
#passwd:    db files nisplus nis
#shadow:    db files nisplus nis
#group:     db files nisplus nis

passwd:     files nisplus
shadow:     files nisplus
group:      files nisplus

#hosts:     db files nisplus nis dns
hosts:      files nisplus dns

# Example - obey only what nisplus tells us...
#services:   nisplus [NOTFOUND=return] files
#networks:   nisplus [NOTFOUND=return] files
#protocols:  nisplus [NOTFOUND=return] files
#rpc:        nisplus [NOTFOUND=return] files
#ethers:     nisplus [NOTFOUND=return] files
#netmasks:   nisplus [NOTFOUND=return] files
```

```
bootparams: nisplus [NOTFOUND=return] files

ethers:      files
netmasks:    files
networks:    files
protocols:   files nisplus
rpc:         files
services:    files nisplus

netgroup:    files nisplus

publickey:   nisplus

automount:   files nisplus
aliases:     files nisplus

#
```

You are not limited to *hosts* information in this file. You can specify other services besides *hosts,* such as *passwd, shadow, group,* and others. There are already entries in your default **/etc/nsswitch.conf** file if you want to view them. For more information about **/etc/nsswitch.conf**, see the man page for **nsswitch.conf**.

/etc/resolv.conf

This file contains the name of the domain and any name server(s) that will be used along with their IP addresses. The name servers will resolve a name into an IP address. The following example shows a simple **resolv.conf** file:

```
domain       development.com
nameserver   15.33.75.55
```

This first line contains the default search domain and the second contains the is the IP address of the host's name server.

In the previous example, the domain of *development.com* will be appended to any hostname such the result will be *hostname.development.com*. You can specify multiple domain names in this file by separating them with spaces all on one line.

Commonly Used Commands

This section looks at many commands that you can issue from the command line to view and set networking-related parameters, including **ping**, **netstat**, **route**, **ifconfig**, **rpcinfo**, **arp**, and **iptables**.

ping

ping is one of the most commonly used networking commands. **ping** stands for Packet InterNet Groper. This command determines whether a connection exists between two networking components. **ping** is a simple command that sends an ICMP echo packet to the host you specify once per second. You'll find that the options to **ping** differ on Linux and UNIX.

The following example shows issuing **ping** with a count (*-c*) of *5*, and interval of *5*, and a packet size of *1024*:

```
# ping 192.168.1.1 -c 5 -i 5 -s 1024
PING 192.168.1.1 (192.168.1.1) from 192.168.1.102 : 1024(1052) bytes
of data.
1032 bytes from 192.168.1.1: icmp_seq=1 ttl=150 time=2.79 ms
1032 bytes from 192.168.1.1: icmp_seq=2 ttl=150 time=2.80 ms
1032 bytes from 192.168.1.1: icmp_seq=3 ttl=150 time=2.79 ms
1032 bytes from 192.168.1.1: icmp_seq=4 ttl=150 time=2.79 ms
1032 bytes from 192.168.1.1: icmp_seq=5 ttl=150 time=2.77 ms

--- 192.168.1.1 ping statistics ---
5 packets transmitted, 5 received, 0% loss, time 20036ms
rtt min/avg/max/mdev = 2.775/2.792/2.804/0.048 ms
#
```

Many useful statistics are produced as a result of **ping**. Notice that it took around 2.75 ms for the *1024* packet size. This is substantially less if you use the default *64* bit packet size:

```
# ping 192.168.1.1 -c 5 -i 5
PING 192.168.1.1 (192.168.1.1) from 192.168.1.102 : 56(84) bytes of
data.
64 bytes from 192.168.1.1: icmp_seq=1 ttl=150 time=0.655 ms
64 bytes from 192.168.1.1: icmp_seq=2 ttl=150 time=0.626 ms
64 bytes from 192.168.1.1: icmp_seq=3 ttl=150 time=0.608 ms
64 bytes from 192.168.1.1: icmp_seq=4 ttl=150 time=0.626 ms
64 bytes from 192.168.1.1: icmp_seq=5 ttl=150 time=0.659 ms
```

```
--- 192.168.1.1 ping statistics ---
5 packets transmitted, 5 received, 0% loss, time 20007ms
rtt min/avg/max/mdev = 0.608/0.634/0.659/0.037 ms
[root@linuxdev etc]#
```

The default packet size results in a much shorter transfer time.

In the event that you're an experienced UNIX user, I've included the following examples from some UNIX variants.

You can adjust the packet size and number of iterations on most UNIX variants as in the HP-UX example shown here, which specifies a packet size of *4096* and interval of *5*:

```
# ping 12 4096 5
PING 12: 4096 byte packets
4096 bytes from 10.1.1.12: icmp_seq=0. time=2. ms
4096 bytes from 10.1.1.12: icmp_seq=1. time=2. ms
4096 bytes from 10.1.1.12: icmp_seq=2. time=2. ms
4096 bytes from 10.1.1.12: icmp_seq=3. time=2. ms
4096 bytes from 10.1.1.12: icmp_seq=4. time=2. ms

----12 PING Statistics----
5 packets transmitted, 5 packets received, 0% packet loss
round-trip (ms)  min/avg/max = 2/2/2
#
```

netstat

From the description of the subnet mask in the previous chapter, you can see that routing from one host to another can be configured in a variety of ways. The path that information takes in getting from one host to another depends on routing.

You can obtain information related to routing with the **netstat** command, or the **route** command. The *-r* option to **netstat** shows the routing tables, which you usually want to know, and the *-n* option can be used to print network addresses as numbers rather than as names. In the following examples, **netstat** is issued with the *-r* option (this is used when describing the **netstat** output), and the *-rn* options, and the *-rnv* options, so you can compare the outputs:

```
# netstat -r
Kernel IP routing table
Destination      Gateway          Genmask          Flags  MSS Window  irtt Iface
192.168.1.0      *                255.255.255.0    U       40 0          0 eth0
127.0.0.0        *                255.0.0.0        U       40 0          0 lo
default          192.168.1.1      0.0.0.0          UG      40 0          0 eth0

# netstat -rn
Kernel IP routing table
Destination      Gateway          Genmask          Flags  MSS Window  irtt Iface
192.168.1.0      0.0.0.0          255.255.255.0    U       40 0          0 eth0
127.0.0.0        0.0.0.0          255.0.0.0        U       40 0          0 lo
0.0.0.0          192.168.1.1      0.0.0.0          UG      40 0          0 eth0
#
```

These two outputs are very similar.

The first and second outputs show that our system, *192.168.1.102*, has one network interface card. The first line shows this card as *eth0*. The second is the loopback interface called *lo0*. The last line is for the default route. This entry says to send packets to *192.168.1.1* if you don't know another route.

I also use **netstat** to obtain networking statistics on Linux system interfaces. The following example shows a lot of statistical information for *eth0*:

```
# netstat -i
Kernel Interface table
Iface   MTU Met   RX-OK RX-ERR RX-DRP RX-OVR   TX-OK TX-ERR TX-DRP TX-OVR Flg
eth0   1500   0 7801580      0      0      0 53 5249311      0      0      0 BMRU
lo    16436   0     616      0      0      0     616      0      0      0 LRU
#
```

You can see from this output the receives and transmits that are *OK* are huge numbers (*RX-OK* and *TX-OK* respectively). There are no errors reported in this output.

If you're an experienced UNIX system administrator, you can see that this output is substantially different than what you will see on UNIX systems.

Yet another use of **netstat** is to show the state of network sockets. **netstat -a** produces a list of protocols, queues, local and remote addresses, and protocol states. All this information is useful for showing active communications, as shown in the following Linux example:

```
# netstat -a
Active Internet connections (servers and established)
Proto Recv-Q Send-Q Local Address          Foreign Address        State
tcp        0      0 *:1024                  *:*                    LISTEN
tcp        0      0 localhost.localdom:1025 *:*                    LISTEN
tcp        0      0 *:swat                  *:*                    LISTEN
tcp        0      0 *:netbios-ssn           *:*                    LISTEN
tcp        0      0 *:sunrpc                *:*                    LISTEN
tcp        0      0 *:x11                   *:*                    LISTEN
tcp        0      0 *:10000                 *:*                    LISTEN
tcp        0      0 *:ftp                   *:*                    LISTEN
tcp        0      0 *:ssh                   *:*                    LISTEN
```

```
tcp        0        0 *:telnet                *:*                     LISTEN
tcp        0        0 linuxdev:1180           64.12.29.100:5190       ESTABLISHED
tcp        0      138 linuxdev:telnet         F4457MXP:4846           ESTABLISHED
udp        0        0 *:1024                  *:*
udp        0        0 linuxdev:netbios-ns     *:*
udp        0        0 *:netbios-ns            *:*
udp        0        0 linuxdev:netbios-dgm    *:*
udp        0        0 *:netbios-dgm           *:*
udp        0        0 *:10000                 *:*
udp        0        0 *:sunrpc                *:*
Active UNIX domain sockets (servers and established)
Proto RefCnt Flags       Type       State         I-Node Path
unix  2     [ ACC ]      STREAM     LISTENING     2053   /tmp/orbit-root/orb-1523613880190
4627091
unix  2     [ ACC ]      STREAM     LISTENING     2063   /tmp/orbit-root/orb-7610255132067
156537
unix  2     [ ACC ]      STREAM     LISTENING     2075   /tmp/orbit-root/orb-6806623012888
86487
unix  11    [ ]          DGRAM                    947    /dev/log
unix  2     [ ACC ]      STREAM     LISTENING     2100   /tmp/orbit-root/orb-1053351818121
2229376
unix  2     [ ACC ]      STREAM     LISTENING     2136   /tmp/orbit-root/orb-4011262787838
1447
unix  2     [ ACC ]      STREAM     LISTENING     2166   /tmp/orbit-root/orb-3523674863949
39250
unix  2     [ ACC ]      STREAM     LISTENING     2305   /tmp/orbit-root/orb-1746122099132
2113508
unix  2     [ ACC ]      STREAM     LISTENING     1495   /dev/gpmctl
unix  2     [ ACC ]      STREAM     LISTENING     2320   /tmp/orbit-root/orb-1566553237209
6623112
unix  2     [ ACC ]      STREAM     LISTENING     2351   /tmp/orbit-root/orb-6282964742254
79129
unix  2     [ ACC ]      STREAM     LISTENING     2386   /tmp/.fam_socket
unix  2     [ ACC ]      STREAM     LISTENING     1852   /tmp/.ICE-unix/1037
unix  2     [ ACC ]      STREAM     LISTENING     1607   /tmp/.font-unix/fs7100
unix  2     [ ACC ]      STREAM     LISTENING     1714   /tmp/.X11-unix/X0
unix  2     [ ACC ]      STREAM     LISTENING     1962   /tmp/.sawfish-root/linuxdev:0.0
unix  2     [ ACC ]      STREAM     LISTENING     3276   /tmp/gaim_root.1505
unix  3     [ ]          STREAM     CONNECTED     14884  /tmp/.X11-unix/X0
unix  3     [ ]          STREAM     CONNECTED     14883
unix  3     [ ]          STREAM     CONNECTED     3282   /tmp/gaim_root.1505
unix  3     [ ]          STREAM     CONNECTED     3278
unix  3     [ ]          STREAM     CONNECTED     3274   /tmp/.ICE-unix/1037
unix  3     [ ]          STREAM     CONNECTED     3273
unix  3     [ ]          STREAM     CONNECTED     3270   /tmp/.X11-unix/X0
unix  3     [ ]          STREAM     CONNECTED     3269
unix  3     [ ]          STREAM     CONNECTED     2392   /tmp/.famDZd9xZ
unix  3     [ ]          STREAM     CONNECTED     2391
unix  3     [ ]          STREAM     CONNECTED     2395   /tmp/orbit-root/orb-6282964742254
79129
unix  3     [ ]          STREAM     CONNECTED     2384
unix  3     [ ]          STREAM     CONNECTED     2369   /tmp/orbit-root/orb-7610255132067
156537
unix  3     [ ]          STREAM     CONNECTED     2368
unix  3     [ ]          STREAM     CONNECTED     2364   /tmp/orbit-root/orb-6806623012888
86487
unix  3     [ ]          STREAM     CONNECTED     2363
unix  3     [ ]          STREAM     CONNECTED     2371   /tmp/orbit-root/orb-1566553237209
6623112
unix  3     [ ]          STREAM     CONNECTED     2358
unix  3     [ ]          STREAM     CONNECTED     2357   /tmp/orbit-root/orb-7610255132067
156537
unix  3     [ ]          STREAM     CONNECTED     2356
unix  3     [ ]          STREAM     CONNECTED     2360   /tmp/orbit-root/orb-1746122099132
2113508
unix  3     [ ]          STREAM     CONNECTED     2353
unix  3     [ ]          STREAM     CONNECTED     2349   /tmp/orbit-root/orb-6806623012888
86487
unix  3     [ ]          STREAM     CONNECTED     2348
unix  3     [ ]          STREAM     CONNECTED     2343   /tmp/orbit-root/orb-1053351818121
2229376
unix  3     [ ]          STREAM     CONNECTED     2342
unix  3     [ ]          STREAM     CONNECTED     2339   /tmp/.X11-unix/X0
unix  3     [ ]          STREAM     CONNECTED     2338
unix  3     [ ]          STREAM     CONNECTED     2335   /tmp/orbit-root/orb-1053351818121
```

```
2229376
unix  3      [ ]          STREAM     CONNECTED     2333
unix  3      [ ]          STREAM     CONNECTED     2330     /tmp/orbit-root/orb-7610255132067
156537
unix  3      [ ]          STREAM     CONNECTED     2329
unix  3      [ ]          STREAM     CONNECTED     2325     /tmp/orbit-root/orb-6806623012888
86487
unix  3      [ ]          STREAM     CONNECTED     2324
unix  3      [ ]          STREAM     CONNECTED     2317     /tmp/orbit-root/orb-3523674863949
39250
unix  3      [ ]          STREAM     CONNECTED     2315
unix  3      [ ]          STREAM     CONNECTED     2312     /tmp/.X11-unix/X0
unix  3      [ ]          STREAM     CONNECTED     2311
unix  3      [ ]          STREAM     CONNECTED     2302     /tmp/.X11-unix/X0
unix  3      [ ]          STREAM     CONNECTED     2301
unix  3      [ ]          STREAM     CONNECTED     2219     /tmp/.ICE-unix/1037
unix  3      [ ]          STREAM     CONNECTED     2218
unix  3      [ ]          STREAM     CONNECTED     2216     /tmp/.ICE-unix/1037
unix  3      [ ]          STREAM     CONNECTED     2215
unix  3      [ ]          STREAM     CONNECTED     2205     /tmp/.ICE-unix/1037
unix  3      [ ]          STREAM     CONNECTED     2204
unix  3      [ ]          STREAM     CONNECTED     2158     /tmp/orbit-root/orb-4011262787838
1447
unix  3      [ ]          STREAM     CONNECTED     2153
unix  2      [ ]          DGRAM                    2135
unix  3      [ ]          STREAM     CONNECTED     2130     /tmp/.X11-unix/X0
unix  3      [ ]          STREAM     CONNECTED     2129
unix  3      [ ]          STREAM     CONNECTED     2128     /tmp/.X11-unix/X0
unix  3      [ ]          STREAM     CONNECTED     2126
unix  3      [ ]          STREAM     CONNECTED     2127     /tmp/.X11-unix/X0
unix  3      [ ]          STREAM     CONNECTED     2125
unix  3      [ ]          STREAM     CONNECTED     2097     /tmp/.ICE-unix/1037
unix  3      [ ]          STREAM     CONNECTED     2096
unix  3      [ ]          STREAM     CONNECTED     2092     /tmp/.X11-unix/X0
unix  3      [ ]          STREAM     CONNECTED     2091
unix  3      [ ]          STREAM     CONNECTED     2080     /tmp/orbit-root/orb-6806623012888
86487
unix  3      [ ]          STREAM     CONNECTED     2087
unix  3      [ ]          STREAM     CONNECTED     2079     /tmp/orbit-root/orb-6806623012888
86487
unix  3      [ ]          STREAM     CONNECTED     2077
unix  3      [ ]          STREAM     CONNECTED     2073     /tmp/.X11-unix/X0
unix  3      [ ]          STREAM     CONNECTED     2072
unix  2      [ ]          DGRAM                    2071
unix  3      [ ]          STREAM     CONNECTED     2061     /tmp/.ICE-unix/1037
unix  3      [ ]          STREAM     CONNECTED     2060
unix  3      [ ]          STREAM     CONNECTED     2057     /tmp/.X11-unix/X0
unix  3      [ ]          STREAM     CONNECTED     2056
unix  3      [ ]          STREAM     CONNECTED     2052     /tmp/.ICE-unix/1037
unix  3      [ ]          STREAM     CONNECTED     2051
unix  3      [ ]          STREAM     CONNECTED     2048     /tmp/.X11-unix/X0
unix  3      [ ]          STREAM     CONNECTED     2047
unix  3      [ ]          STREAM     CONNECTED     2039     /tmp/.ICE-unix/1037
unix  3      [ ]          STREAM     CONNECTED     2038
unix  3      [ ]          STREAM     CONNECTED     1957     /tmp/.X11-unix/X0
unix  3      [ ]          STREAM     CONNECTED     1956
unix  3      [ ]          STREAM     CONNECTED     1869     /tmp/.ICE-unix/1037
unix  3      [ ]          STREAM     CONNECTED     1868
unix  3      [ ]          STREAM     CONNECTED     1867     /tmp/.X11-unix/X0
unix  3      [ ]          STREAM     CONNECTED     1866
unix  3      [ ]          STREAM     CONNECTED     1857     /tmp/.X11-unix/X0
unix  3      [ ]          STREAM     CONNECTED     1856
unix  3      [ ]          STREAM     CONNECTED     1724     /tmp/.font-unix/fs7100
unix  3      [ ]          STREAM     CONNECTED     1723
unix  4      [ ]          STREAM     CONNECTED     1726     /tmp/.X11-unix/X0
unix  3      [ ]          STREAM     CONNECTED     1717
unix  2      [ ]          DGRAM                    1689
unix  2      [ ]          DGRAM                    1610
unix  2      [ ]          DGRAM                    1518
unix  2      [ ]          DGRAM                    1451
unix  2      [ ]          DGRAM                    1155
unix  2      [ ]          DGRAM                    1011
unix  2      [ ]          DGRAM                    959
#
```

Some of the connections are *ESTABLISHED* (such as the *linuxdev:telnet* connection early in the listing). This is the connection you have initiated to this system. You are connected from *F4457MXP* with a telnet session open to the system *linuxdev.*

Most of the remaining *tcp* protocol entries are listening, such as *swat*. This means that they are listening for incoming connections, as indicated by the *LISTEN*. They have a wild card in the *Foreign Address* field, which will contain the address when a connection has been established. Your connection is one of the few connections that has been made, as indicated by the *ESTABLISHED*.

All the send and receive queues, shown as *Recv-Q* and *Send-Q*, are empty as indicated by *0*.

The UNIX domain sockets at the end of the output are stream and datagram connections for a variety of services such as *X11*.

This output gives you an appreciation of the immense amount of activity taking place from a networking perspective on your Linux system. Networking and connectivity have been among the most advanced aspects of Linux since its inception.

route

The information displayed with **netstat -a** includes the routing tables for your system. Some are automatically created with the **ifconfig** command when your system is booted or when the network interface is initialized. Routes to networks and hosts that are not directly connected to your system are entered with the **route** command.

Routing is required if your system is connected to a network with multiple subnets. Most of the time, your Linux system is aware of three routes. The first is the *loopback* route, which points to the loopback device which was *lo* in the earlier **netstat -r** example. The next route is to the same LAN to which the system is connected, which means that packets are sent directly to a system. The third is the *default* route, which is the destination for packets not on the same LAN as the system. If you type the **route** command on your Linux system with no options, you'll see an output similar to **netstat -r**, as shown in the following example:

```
# route
Kernel IP routing table
Destination     Gateway        Genmask        Flags Metric Ref    Use Iface
192.168.1.0     *              255.255.255.0  U     0      0        0 eth0
127.0.0.0       *              255.0.0.0      U     0      0        0 lo
default         192.168.1.1    0.0.0.0        UG    0      0        0 eth0
#
```

From this output, you see the *Destination*, which is the network to which you want to route, and the *Gateway* for getting there. These include a route for *192.168.1.0* which is the LAN to which the system is connected, the *loopback*, and then the *default* which is the router that takes care of packets sent to a different LAN. If the default route was not set to the desired address, you could add it with the following command and example:

route add default gw *address*

route add default gw 15.32.160.1

You could also delete an erroneous default gateway using the same command with *delete* in place of *add*.

The *netmask* in this output is shown as the *genmask*. Note also that there are *Flags* in the **route** output that also appeared in some of the **netstat** outputs. The following list summarizes some of the most often seen *Flags* values including the two that appear in our output:

U   The connection is up.

UG   The destination is up and it is a gateway.

UH   The destination is up and it is a host.

A *Metric* that defines the cost of the route in "hops" is not used by the Linux kernel, but is used by advanced routing protocols.

The *Ref* is the number of references to this route also not used by the Linux kernel.

Use is the number of successful route cache lookups that can be seen with the *-F* option.

In addition to viewing information with **route**, you could modify the routing setup with this command. If the default route were not set to the address shown in the previous **route** output, you could issue the following command:

```
# route add -net default gw 192.168.1.1 dev eth0
```

First is the **route** command. Second, specify that you want to *add* a route; the other option is to *del* a route. Third, specify a *-net* for network or *-host* for router. Fourth, specify the destination; in this case, the *default*. Fifth, specify that routes will go through the gateway of *192.168.1.1*. Finally, specify a *dev* of *eth0*.

Before issuing **route** with the **add** option, you can first use the **delete** option to remove the existing default route, which is not working.

ifconfig

On Linux systems, **ifconfig** configures the kernel-resident network interfaces. It is used at boot time to set up interfaces. Other than that, it is usually only needed when debugging or when system tuning is needed. It is used for debugging because it can be very informative. The following is an **ifconfig** output with no options:

```
# ifconfig
eth0      Link encap:Ethernet  HWaddr 00:10:4B:64:D4:3E
          inet addr:192.168.1.102  Bcast:192.168.1.255  Mask:255.255.255.0
          UP BROADCAST RUNNING MULTICAST  MTU:1500  Metric:1
          RX packets:7820857 errors:0 dropped:0 overruns:53 frame:0
          TX packets:5250880 errors:0 dropped:0 overruns:0 carrier:3
          collisions:572 txqueuelen:100
          RX bytes:2097256998 (2000.1 Mb)  TX bytes:490813036 (468.0 Mb)
          Interrupt:9 Base address:0xfc80

lo        Link encap:Local Loopback
          inet addr:127.0.0.1  Mask:255.0.0.0
          UP LOOPBACK RUNNING  MTU:16436  Metric:1
          RX packets:622 errors:0 dropped:0 overruns:0 frame:0
          TX packets:622 errors:0 dropped:0 overruns:0 carrier:0
          collisions:0 txqueuelen:0
          RX bytes:31930 (31.1 Kb)  TX bytes:31930 (31.1 Kb)

#
```

With no options, **ifconfig** produces a detailed output for all active interfaces.

ifconfig can also be used to set up network interfaces. Many excellent tools, such as **neat**, **webmin,** and **netconf**, are used to configure network interfaces as well. You could set the IP address of a network interface with **ifconfig**, as shown in the following example:

```
# /etc/ifconfig eth0 192.168.1.102 netmask 255.255.255.0 broadcast 192.168.1.255
```

In this example, you set the IP address, *netmask*, and *broadcast* address of *eth0*. Because this is a Class C address, you did not have to specify the *netmask* and *broadcast* because the values specified are the calculated values. For other classes, you would have to specify these values.

The network address you have falls into classes such as A, B, or C, as covered in the previous chapter. You want to be sure that you know the class of your network before you start configuring your LAN interface. For a Class B network, the netmask is defined as ffff0000 (typical for a Class B address), as opposed to ffffff00, which is typical for a Class C network. The netmask determines how much of the address to reserve for subdividing the network into smaller networks.

rpcinfo

As a user, you may have a need to NFS mount a directory on another system or perform some other function that you haven't before used on your system. You can determine whether various pieces of functionality have been enabled by evaluating the daemons running on your system. **rpcinfo** allows you to generate a Remote Procedure Call (RPC) on a system, including your local system, by issuing the command **rpc -p** *system_name*.

The following example shows issuing **rpcinfo -p** on the local system:

```
# rpcinfo -p
   program vers proto   port  service
    100000    2   tcp    111  portmapper
    100000    2   udp    111  portmapper
    100024    1   udp    777  status
    100024    1   tcp    779  status
    100021    1   tcp    783  nlockmgr
    100021    1   udp   1035  nlockmgr
    100021    3   tcp    787  nlockmgr
    100021    3   udp   1036  nlockmgr
    100020    1   udp   1037  llockmgr
    100020    1   tcp    792  llockmgr
    100021    2   tcp    795  nlockmgr
    100068    2   udp   1040  cmsd
    100068    3   udp   1040  cmsd
    100068    4   udp   1040  cmsd
    100068    5   udp   1040  cmsd
    100083    1   tcp   1036  ttdbserver
```

```
100005    1    udp     976    mountd
100005    1    tcp     978    mountd
100003    2    udp    2049    nfs
150001    1    udp    1003    pcnfsd
150001    2    udp    1003    pcnfsd
150001    1    tcp    1006    pcnfsd
150001    2    tcp    1006    pcnfsd
#
```

As you can see many daemons are running on the local system. **mountd** is running, which indicates that a server could NFS mount file systems on this computer. There is other setup required for the mount to take place, but at least the daemon is running to support this functionality. In addition, **pcnfsd** is running, which means you have support for Windows-based NFS access.

arp (Address Resolution Protocol)

The mechanism used to maintain a list of IP addresses and their corresponding MAC addresses is the *ARP cache*. The mapped addresses are only held in the cache for minutes, so if you want to see what addresses have been mapped recently, you can use the **arp** command. The following command produces information on **eth0** on the system on which the examples will take place:

```
# ifconfig eth0
eth0      Link encap:Ethernet  HWaddr 00:30:6E:06:79:7C
          inet addr:192.6.175.244  Bcast:192.6.175.255
          Mask:255.255.255.128
          UP BROADCAST RUNNING MULTICAST  MTU:1500  Metric:1
          RX packets:233 errors:0 dropped:0 overruns:0 frame:0
          TX packets:27 errors:0 dropped:0 overruns:0 carrier:0
          collisions:0 txqueuelen:100
          RX bytes:17807 (17.3 Kb)  TX bytes:2268 (2.2 Kb)
          Interrupt:9 Base address:0x8000
```

The address of the networking card is *192.6.175.244*. Now populate the arp cache. **ping** the broadcast address of *192.6.175.255* for this interface, which will make entries in the arp cache. Note that I have shortened **ping** output:

```
# ping -b 192.6.175.255
WARNING: pinging broadcast address
PING 192.6.175.255 (192.6.175.255) from 192.6.175.244 : 56(84) bytes
of data.
64 bytes from 192.6.175.244: icmp_seq=1 ttl=64 time=0.102 ms
64 bytes from 192.6.175.160: icmp_seq=1 ttl=255 time=0.257 ms (DUP!)
64 bytes from 192.6.175.192: icmp_seq=1 ttl=255 time=0.406 ms (DUP!)
64 bytes from 192.6.175.185: icmp_seq=1 ttl=255 time=0.417 ms (DUP!)
64 bytes from 192.6.175.199: icmp_seq=1 ttl=255 time=0.432 ms (DUP!)
64 bytes from 192.6.175.236: icmp_seq=1 ttl=255 time=0.458 ms (DUP!)
64 bytes from 192.6.175.206: icmp_seq=1 ttl=255 time=0.469 ms (DUP!)
64 bytes from 192.6.175.229: icmp_seq=1 ttl=255 time=0.504 ms (DUP!)
64 bytes from 192.6.175.171: icmp_seq=1 ttl=255 time=0.516 ms (DUP!)
64 bytes from 192.6.175.178: icmp_seq=1 ttl=255 time=0.553 ms (DUP!)
64 bytes from 192.6.175.215: icmp_seq=1 ttl=255 time=0.616 ms (DUP!)
64 bytes from 192.6.175.164: icmp_seq=1 ttl=255 time=0.654 ms (DUP!)
64 bytes from 192.6.175.138: icmp_seq=1 ttl=255 time=0.708 ms (DUP!)
64 bytes from 192.6.175.140: icmp_seq=1 ttl=255 time=0.794 ms (DUP!)
64 bytes from 192.6.175.140: icmp_seq=1 ttl=255 time=0.805 ms (DUP!)
64 bytes from 192.6.175.142: icmp_seq=1 ttl=255 time=1.56 ms (DUP!)
64 bytes from 192.6.175.133: icmp_seq=1 ttl=255 time=2.63 ms (DUP!)
64 bytes from 192.6.175.134: icmp_seq=1 ttl=255 time=2.64 ms (DUP!)
64 bytes from 192.6.175.165: icmp_seq=1 ttl=64 time=4.36 ms (DUP!)
64 bytes from 192.6.175.161: icmp_seq=1 ttl=64 time=4.83 ms (DUP!)
64 bytes from 192.6.175.254: icmp_seq=1 ttl=64 time=6.89 ms (DUP!)
64 bytes from 192.6.175.252: icmp_seq=1 ttl=64 time=150 ms (DUP!)
64 bytes from 192.6.175.244: icmp_seq=2 ttl=64 time=0.070 ms
64 bytes from 192.6.175.206: icmp_seq=2 ttl=255 time=0.145 ms (DUP!)
64 bytes from 192.6.175.192: icmp_seq=2 ttl=255 time=0.153 ms (DUP!)
64 bytes from 192.6.175.254: icmp_seq=2 ttl=64 time=1.76 ms (DUP!)
64 bytes from 192.6.175.161: icmp_seq=2 ttl=64 time=1.79 ms (DUP!)
64 bytes from 192.6.175.244: icmp_seq=3 ttl=64 time=0.072 ms
64 bytes from 192.6.175.192: icmp_seq=3 ttl=255 time=0.145 ms (DUP!)
64 bytes from 192.6.175.199: icmp_seq=3 ttl=255 time=0.153 ms (DUP!)
64 bytes from 192.6.175.236: icmp_seq=3 ttl=255 time=0.163 ms (DUP!)
64 bytes from 192.6.175.185: icmp_seq=3 ttl=255 time=0.173 ms (DUP!)
64 bytes from 192.6.175.206: icmp_seq=3 ttl=255 time=0.183 ms (DUP!)
64 bytes from 192.6.175.229: icmp_seq=3 ttl=255 time=0.192 ms (DUP!)
64 bytes from 192.6.175.178: icmp_seq=3 ttl=255 time=0.202 ms (DUP!)
64 bytes from 192.6.175.215: icmp_seq=3 ttl=255 time=0.212 ms (DUP!)
64 bytes from 192.6.175.140: icmp_seq=3 ttl=255 time=0.222 ms (DUP!)
64 bytes from 192.6.175.171: icmp_seq=3 ttl=255 time=0.232 ms (DUP!)
64 bytes from 192.6.175.160: icmp_seq=3 ttl=255 time=0.241 ms (DUP!)
64 bytes from 192.6.175.164: icmp_seq=3 ttl=255 time=0.251 ms (DUP!)
64 bytes from 192.6.175.138: icmp_seq=3 ttl=255 time=0.261 ms (DUP!)
64 bytes from 192.6.175.140: icmp_seq=3 ttl=255 time=0.271 ms (DUP!)
64 bytes from 192.6.175.142: icmp_seq=3 ttl=255 time=0.361 ms (DUP!)
64 bytes from 192.6.175.133: icmp_seq=3 ttl=255 time=0.831 ms (DUP!)
64 bytes from 192.6.175.134: icmp_seq=3 ttl=255 time=0.848 ms (DUP!)
64 bytes from 192.6.175.254: icmp_seq=3 ttl=64 time=1.17 ms (DUP!)
64 bytes from 192.6.175.252: icmp_seq=3 ttl=64 time=1.32 ms (DUP!)
64 bytes from 192.6.175.161: icmp_seq=3 ttl=64 time=1.76 ms (DUP!)

--- 192.6.175.255 ping statistics ---
4 packets transmitted, 4 received, +84 duplicates, 0% loss, time
3005ms
rtt min/avg/max/mdev = 0.070/2.446/150.539/15.913 ms
```

You established a connection to many devices on the *192.6.175* subnet and should have entries for these systems in the arp cache. We'll issue the **arp -a** command in the following example, which shows the systems from the **ping** included in the cache:

```
# arp -a
? (192.6.175.178) at 00:30:6E:1C:22:5E [ether] on eth0
? (192.6.175.252) at 00:30:C1:52:F1:80 [ether] on eth0
? (192.6.175.254) at 00:30:C1:79:4C:8C [ether] on eth0
? (192.6.175.185) at 00:30:6E:2C:15:8F [ether] on eth0
? (192.6.175.215) at 00:30:6E:38:32:B9 [ether] on eth0
? (192.6.175.206) at 00:30:6E:2C:32:98 [ether] on eth0
? (192.6.175.164) at 00:30:6E:0A:30:33 [ether] on eth0
? (192.6.175.236) at 00:30:6E:38:72:2A [ether] on eth0
? (192.6.175.129) at 00:E0:52:92:EC:56 [ether] on eth0
? (192.6.175.171) at 00:30:6E:13:96:FC [ether] on eth0
? (192.6.175.199) at 00:30:6E:2C:12:0C [ether] on eth0
? (192.6.175.140) at 00:01:02:47:EB:4B [ether] on eth0
? (192.6.175.138) at 00:10:83:B9:80:AA [ether] on eth0
? (192.6.175.192) at 00:30:6E:2C:62:AD [ether] on eth0
? (192.6.175.229) at 00:30:6E:38:72:64 [ether] on eth0
```

Current *arp* entries are displayed with the **-a** command. If an entry was missing that you want to have in the cache, you can create it with the **-s** option.

iptables

iptables is used at the command line to implement packet filtering. This is accomplished by inserting and deleting rules from the kernel's packet filtering section. **iptables** is a newer method of packet filtering that is considered superior to the method it replaced, called **ipchains**. **ipchains** was available in kernel release *2.2* and **iptables** became available in *2.4* that was used as the basis for the examples in this book. **ipchains** is still available and, as a side note, the following URL contains an excellent "how to" document for working with **ipchains**:

http://www.tldp.org/HOWTO/IPCHAINS-HOWTO.html

An excellent **potables** "how to" document is:

http://www.linxguruz.org/iptables/howto

Packets are the basis of network traffic on a Linux system. The beginning of a packet is the *header* and the data of the packet is in the *body*. **potables** is a packet filter which means it determines whether your Linux system will *ACCEPT* (let the packet through,) *DROP* (discard the packet,) *RETURN* (stop traversing this chain and resume at the next rule in the calling chain,) or *QUEUE* (pass the packet to user space.)

You may want to control packets coming to and from your Linux system for a variety of reasons, most of which are related to security. For example, you may not want those without accounts on your system to be able to establish a *telnet* connection to your system. It may be that your system may be used for a specific function and you don't want anyone from an outside network to connect to your system. This is not a security section and it only provides an introduction to **iptables.** If you are interested in security, you may want to read a document dedicated to network security. If you believe you are vulnerable to attack, you may want to implement more extensive security measures than what's covered here. This section covers only the basics of **iptables**.

The changes you make using **iptables** are not permanent because they're stored in the currently running kernel. If you want these changes made permanent, the **iptables** commands you issue can be included in a script and run at the time of system boot to be reinitiated. Be sure to make the script executable by root and run it. Two commands help with saving and restoring iptables, called **iptables-save** and **iptables-restore**, that also help with re-running **iptables** commands.

With iptables, you are inserting and deleting rules that govern packet filtering in the kernel's packet filtering section. When a packet is received it is compared to a checklist of rules and appropriate action is taken with the packet. This list of rules, called a *chain*, are compared to the packet header and if there is a match between the rule and the packet, action is taken based on the rule.

There are three core chain types: *INPUT, FORWARD,* and *OUTPUT.* A packet is evaluated based on it's type. The *DROP, ACCEPT, QUEUE,* or *RETURN* action is taken relative to which of the three types of chain is being used. Figure 8-1 shows the relationship between the three types of chains.

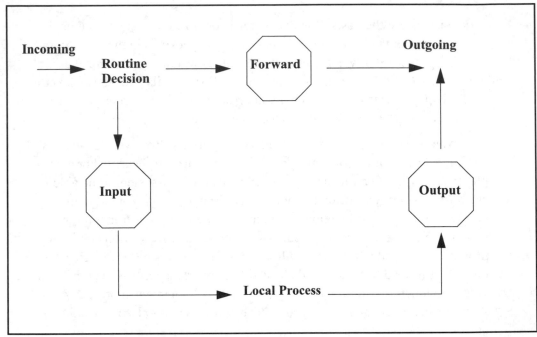

Figure 8-1   **iptables** Processing

This is a widely used diagram that you'll see in almost any document that describes **iptables**.

Look at a couple of simple examples to see how **iptables** is used. To *DROP ftp* for everyone, we would issue the following command:

```
#iptables -A INPUT -p tcp --destination-port 21 -j DROP -i eth0

# iptables --list
Chain INPUT (policy ACCEPT)
target     prot opt source                destination
DROP       tcp  --  anywhere             anywhere            tcp dpt:ftp

Chain FORWARD (policy ACCEPT)
target     prot opt source                destination

Chain OUTPUT (policy ACCEPT)
target     prot opt source                destination
#
```

Any attempts to connect to port *21* will now *DROP* as indicated by the output of the **iptables --list** command. The **iptables** command appends a new rule to the input chain (with *-A)*, specifies a protocol of *tcp(*with *-p)*, specifies a destination port of *21,* which corresponds to *ftp* (with *--destination-port 21)*, specifies a rule of *DROP* (with *-j)*, and specifies an interface of *eth0* (with *-i)*. Attempts to initiate an *ftp* connection to *eth0* will now be dropped. FTP requests coming from another interface such as *eth1* are not dropped.

Remove this rule with the following command:

```
# iptables -D INPUT -p tcp --destination-port 21 -j DROP -i eth0

# iptables --list
Chain INPUT (policy ACCEPT)
target     prot opt source                destination

Chain FORWARD (policy ACCEPT)
target     prot opt source                destination

Chain OUTPUT (policy ACCEPT)
target     prot opt source                destination
```

Again, the *-D* has removed the *ftp* restriction on port *21,* so you could now initiate an *ftp* session with port *21* on *eth0.* Keep in mind that what we have done with the first command was to *DROP* any attempt to use port *21* which corresponds to *ftp.* As you can see in the following output, both *ftp* and *wu-ftp* are configured to run:

```
# chkconfig --list | grep ftp
        ftp:              on
        wu-ftpd:          on
#
```

If you don't know the port numbers for your internet services, you can view the **/etc/services** file. It contains mappings between internet services and their assigned port numbers. The following shows the first 30 or so lines of **/etc/services** on the system used for the **iptables** examples:

```
# /etc/services:
# $Id: services,v 1.31 2002/04/03 16:53:20 notting Exp $
#
# Network services, Internet style
#
# Note that it is presently the policy of IANA to assign a single well-known
# port number for both TCP and UDP; hence, most entries here have two entries
# even if the protocol doesn't support UDP operations.
# Updated from RFC 1700, ``Assigned Numbers'' (October 1994).  Not all ports
# are included, only the more common ones.
#
# The latest IANA port assignments can be gotten from
#       http://www.iana.org/assignments/port-numbers
# The Well Known Ports are those from 0 through 1023.
```

```
# The Registered Ports are those from 1024 through 49151
# The Dynamic and/or Private Ports are those from 49152 through 65535
#
# Each line describes one service, and is of the form:
#
# service-name  port/protocol  [aliases ...]    [# comment]

tcpmux          1/tcp                                 # TCP port service multiplexer
tcpmux          1/udp                                 # TCP port service multiplexer
rje             5/tcp                                 # Remote Job Entry
rje             5/udp                                 # Remote Job Entry
echo            7/tcp
echo            7/udp
discard         9/tcp           sink null
discard         9/udp           sink null
systat          11/tcp          users
systat          11/udp          users
daytime         13/tcp
daytime         13/udp
qotd            17/tcp          quote
qotd            17/udp          quote
msp             18/tcp                                # message send protocol
msp             18/udp                                # message send protocol
chargen         19/tcp          ttytst source
chargen         19/udp          ttytst source
ftp-data        20/tcp
ftp-data        20/udp
# 21 is registered to ftp, but also used by fsp
ftp             21/tcp
ftp             21/udp          fsp fspd
ssh             22/tcp                                # SSH Remote Login Protocol
ssh             22/udp                                # SSH Remote Login Protocol
telnet          23/tcp
telnet          23/udp
```

.
.
.

This is a long file so I included only the beginning of it. You can see port *23* is defined for *telnet*.

You could disable the *ftp* and *wu-ftp* services using one of the procedures in the *service, xinetd, and chkconfig* section of this chapter. What you have done with **iptables** is not allow access to the port, which is different than disabling the service. You could allow access to the port in a less restrictive manner by specifying a group of IP addresses that will be restricted, using the full name of system(s) to be restricted, or specifying a specific IP address to be restricted with *iptables*. There are many options in **iptables** for controlling access to ports.

You could restrict access to many other commonly used ports, such as *finger, telnet, X Windows*, and any others that are not important to the operation of your system.

The more services you enable, the more ports you'll have open. An NFS example in this chapter made you notice that several ports were open. Because it opens ports and shares data with the network, NFS is not without some security risks.

The following example shows a partial output of the **nmap** command:

```
# nmap -sT -O localhost

Starting nmap V. 3.00 ( www.insecure.org/nmap/ )
Insufficient responses for TCP sequencing (0), OS detection may be
less accurate
Insufficient responses for TCP sequencing (3), OS detection may be
less accurate
Interesting ports on localhost.localdomain (127.0.0.1):
(The 1592 ports scanned but not shown below are in state: closed)
Port        State       Service
22/tcp      open        ssh
23/tcp      open        telnet
25/tcp      open        smtp
111/tcp     open        sunrpc
989/tcp     open        ftps-data
1024/tcp    open        kdm
1031/tcp    open        iad2
1032/tcp    open        iad3
6000/tcp    open        X11
               .
               .
               .
```

You can see from this output that several ports are now open, including the *telnet* session used to obtain these examples from the system and several ports related to the NFS work. You used the *-sT* option, which is the most basic form of TCP scanning. You also used *-O*, which guesses the operating system of the machine. The following example is the output of the same command from the NFS client in the example:

```
# nmap -sT -O localhost

Starting nmap V. 3.00 ( www.insecure.org/nmap/ )
Interesting ports on localhost.localdomain (127.0.0.1):
(The 1590 ports scanned but not shown below are in state: closed)
Port        State       Service
21/tcp      open        ftp
22/tcp      open        ssh
23/tcp      open        telnet
25/tcp      open        smtp
111/tcp     open        sunrpc
139/tcp     open        netbios-ssn
901/tcp     open        samba-swat
1024/tcp    open        kdm
1025/tcp    open        NFS-or-IIS
6000/tcp    open        X11
10000/tcp   open        snet-sensor-mgmt
```

```
Remote OS guesses: Linux Kernel 2.4.0 - 2.5.20, Linux 2.5.25 or Gen-
too 1.2 Linux 2.4.19 rc
1-rc7)

Nmap run completed -- 1 IP address (1 host up) scanned in 6 seconds
You have new mail in /var/spool/mail/root
```

This system has additional ports open such as *901,* which is for the *swat* tool used to configure samba. No unknown ports are in these two outputs, so we at least know that the ports are used for known services (which are defined in **/etc/services**.) To find out more about the *sunrpc* service listings, we could use the following two commands:

You could easily include the *iptables* commands in a file and run it as a shell program. The *iptables* commands you issue modify the running kernel and must be re-run after a reboot. The **iptables-save** and **iptables-restore** allow you to save and restore *iptables* information to *STDOUT* and from *STDIN* respectively.

This chapter only scratched the surface of *iptables* of the extensive capability of **iptables** in this section, so I'd recommend the "how to" guides listed earlier to get a detailed understanding of *iptables* and *ipchains*.

service, xinetd, and chkconfig

A couple of miscellaneous startup-related programs and files related to enabling and disabling network services are **xinetd** and **service**. For more information about ports and services in relation to networks, see "Networking Background."

nslookup and dig

nslookup is used to resolve a hostname into an IP address. You issue **nslookup** *hostname* and **nslookup** will access either the **/etc/resolv.conf** file or **/etc/hosts** to resolve the host name. The following example shows a system using **/etc/hosts** to produce the IP address of system *l2*:

```
# nslookup mxf4458nt1

Server:         15.227.128.51
Address:        15.227.128.51#53

Name:   mxf4458nt1.esr.hp.com
Address: 15.32.161.3

#
```

This example shows the server and address used for the **nslookup** command. Then the fully qualified name of your system appears and its IP address.

You may get a message indicating that **nslookup** may be replaced in the future. You can use **dig**, which provides more detailed information on host lookup. **dig** is a newer command than **nslookup** and will be available in future releases.

/etc/hosts

As mentioned earlier, this file contains information about the other systems to which you are connected. It contains the Internet address of each system, the system name, and any aliases for the system name.

/etc/securetty for Equivalent root Access

If you have a highly self-contained environment, you can set up your Linux systems so that root can run remote commands from one system to another, login to a remote system without a password, and perform other such functions by making entries in **/etc/securetty**. **/etc/hosts.equiv** performs nearly the same function for other users. Using **/etc/securetty** is considered a severe security risk, so please use this technique for system-to-system openness only if you have an environment that is not exposed to any users who are potential security threats. The *secure shell* (SSH) and other such tools is highly preferable to this technique because they use encryption.

To have root as an equivalent user on multiple systems, enter the desired services into **/etc/securetty**. The following example shows entries for **rexec, rsh, rlogin**. To allow root to log in using these tools via telnet, make the following entries in **/etc/securetty**:

```
rexec
rsh
rlogin
pts/0
pts/1
```

After making these entries, run the following command:

```
# /sbin/service xinetd restart
```

At this point, you now have this functionality enabled for root. This is not required for other users. Other users require only **/etc/hosts.equiv** to get this functionality, as described in the next section.

/etc/hosts.equiv

Your system may be set up so user's don't have to issue a password when they **rlogin** to a remote system; they can set up equivalent hosts by editing this file. As with **/etc/securetty**, this is technique considered a security risk. The login names must be the same on both the local and remote systems for **/etc/hosts.equiv** to allow the user to bypass entering a password. You can either list all the equivalent hosts in **/etc/hosts.equiv** or list the host and user name you want to be equivalent. Users can now use **rsh** and other such commands because they are equivalent users on these systems. I usually just enter all the hostnames on the network in this format:

```
host_to_trust#1
host_to_trust#2
host_to_trust#3
```

Keep in mind the potential security risks of using **/etc/hosts.equiv**. If a user can log into a remote system without a password, you have reduced the overall level of security on your network. Even though users may find it convenient to not have to enter a password when logging into a remote system, you have given every user in **/etc/hosts.equiv** access to the entire network. If you could ensure that all the permissions on all the files and directories on all systems were properly set up, then you wouldn't care who had access to what system. In the real Linux world, however, permissions are sometimes not what they are supposed to be. Users have a strong tendency to "browse around," invariably stumbling upon a file they want to copy to which they really shouldn't have access.

Secure Shell (SSH)

SSH is a method of establishing a secure session between two systems. The client initiates a session with the server in which all communication is encrypted. Passwords and all data are encrypted so that programs monitoring networking traffic, often called "sniffing," or employing other techniques to breach security, are less of a threat and thereby security is increased.

An SSH client component and an SSH server component are both supplied with most Linux distributions. SSH is available for almost all client and server systems.

The client programs are **ssh**, **scp**, and **sftp** and the server program is **sshd**. Two versions of Secure Shell are available called SSH1 and SSH2. The protocols for these two version are different and incompatible with one another. SSH2 provides **sftp** which is a replacement for **ftp**. You may notice some performance degradation when using **sftp** in place of **ftp** when copying large files. This is because encryption takes place for all packets that are transferred. *OpenSSH* is used on Linux distributions, which has system-wide configuration files in **/etc/ssh**. User-specific files are stored in the **~/.ssh** directory. The *ssh* and *sshd* manual pages contain a lot of information regarding the configuration of SSH.

Many SSH clients are available for many different systems. When establishing a connection through an SSH client, you are asked the hostname or IP address of the system to which you want to connect, the protocol such as *telnet*, *rlogin*, or others, and then you connect to the server.

Operation of *telnet* through SSH is similar to non-secure *telnet* operation from a user standpoint, even though encryption takes place at the transport layer.

SSH is strongly recommended to increase network security. It is easy to implement and provides a much higher level of security over non-SSH communications.

Network File System (NFS)

NFS allows you to mount disks on remote systems so that they appear as though they are local to your system. Similarly, NFS allows remote systems to mount your local disk so that it looks as though it is local to the remote system. This section goes through a simple NFS server and client setup after NFS background is supplied. You can use standard-mounted directories or automounted directories with NFS. The upcoming example uses standard-mount directories, but you can use automounted directories, which mount remote directories as they are needed. Configuring NFS to achieve this functionality is simple. Here are the steps to go through in order to configure NFS:

1. Start NFS on the server.

2. Setup **/etc/exports** on the server.

3. Run **exportfs** on the server.

4. Create a directory on the client under which the remote directory will be mounted.

5. Mount the remote disks on the client.

Because NFS may be set up on your system to meet the needs of many users, you may want to understand the terminology associated with NFS. The following are commonly used NFS terms:

Node   A computer system that is attached to or is part of a computer network.

Client   A node that requests data or services from other nodes (servers).

Server   A node that provides data or services to other nodes (clients) on the network.

File system	A disk partition or logical volume.
Export	Makes a file system available for mounting on remote nodes using NFS.
Mount	Accesses a remote file system using NFS.
Mount point	The name of a directory on which the NFS file system is mounted.
Import	Mounts a remote file system.

Example NFS Configuration

Let's take a look at the steps to set up an NFS server and client. This example is performed on an IA-32 set of systems, but is great for learning the basics of NFS setup in general. Perform the following steps on your NFS server, with hostname *asodev*, to export the directory **/home**:

1. Start NFS:

```
# rpcinfo -p
   program vers proto    port
    100000   2    tcp     111   portmapper
    100000   2    udp     111   portmapper
    100024   1    udp    1024   status
    100024   1    tcp    1024   status
    391002   2    tcp    1031   sgi_fam

# /etc/rc.d/init.d/nfs start
Starting NFS services:  60G[  0;32mOK0;39m  ]
Starting NFS quotas: 60G[  0;32mOK0;39m  ]
Starting NFS daemon: 60G[  0;32mOK0;39m  ]
Starting NFS mountd: 60G[  0;32mOK0;39m  ]

# rpcinfo -p
   program vers proto    port
    100000   2    tcp     111   portmapper
```

```
100000    2    udp     111    portmapper
100024    1    udp    1024    status
100024    1    tcp    1024    status
391002    2    tcp    1031    sgi_fam
100011    1    udp     986    rquotad
100011    2    udp     986    rquotad
100011    1    tcp     989    rquotad
100011    2    tcp     989    rquotad
100003    2    udp    2049    nfs
100003    3    udp    2049    nfs
100021    1    udp    1026    nlockmgr
100021    3    udp    1026    nlockmgr
100021    4    udp    1026    nlockmgr
100005    1    udp    1027    mountd
100005    1    tcp    1032    mountd
100005    2    udp    1027    mountd
100005    2    tcp    1032    mountd
100005    3    udp    1027    mountd
100005    3    tcp    1032    mountd
```

You have enabled NFS for this session, but NFS needs to be permanently enabled if you want to run it after a reboot. This can be done from **ksysv**.

2. Update the **/etc/exports** file to include a directory, which we want to be available to all systems as shown below:

```
# cat /etc/exports

# /etc/exports for linux development

/home    linuxdev(rw,no_root_squash)
```

When **exportfs** runs, you will have exported **/home** to *linuxdev* with read/write access as indicated by the *rw*. Note that you're allowing the root user on the client to access this directory with *no_root_squash*. This last option is important because only non-root users will be able to access the directory if it is not specified.

3. The last step to perform on the server is to run the **exportfs** command to make **/home** available to other systems:

```
# exportfs -a
exportfs: No 'sync' or 'async' option specified for export
"linuxdev:/home".
  Assuming default behaviour ('sync').
  NOTE: this default has changed from previous versions
```

You want to make sure you have NFS running on the server and the **/etc/exports** file set up on your server so that on reboots of the server, NFS starts automatically and file systems are exported automatically.

You have performed all the set up required on the server to export this file system. Next, proceed to the client part of the setup.

1. Next, update the **/etc/fstab** file to include the mount.Á

You need to complete a couple of steps to mount the remote directory on the client. First, you have to create a mount directory on the client. Next we need to run the **mount** command to mount the NFS server's directory on our client. Finally, you'll run **df** to see that it is indeed mounted. These steps are shown here:

```
# mkdir /asodev_home

# mount asodev:/home /asodev_home

# df
Filesystem              1K-blocks      Used Available Use% Mounted on
/dev/hda5                  381139    174830    186631  49% /
/dev/hda1                   46636     14547     29681  33% /boot
/dev/hda3                 1423096    241416   1109388  18% /home
none                        46928         0     46928   0% /dev/shm
/dev/hda2                 3889924   2513180   1179148  69% /usr
/dev/hda6                  256667     70400    173015  29% /var
/dev/hdb1                38464340  23579884  12930552  65% /home/
linuxconnect/backup
asodev:/home               102456      4132     93032   5% /asodev_home

#
```

As you can see from the last entry, under **df**, you have the server directory of *asodev:/home* mounted in the local directory of */asodev_home* on the client. You can now freely share files between these two systems.

2. To make this mount persist across reboots, you need to update the **/etc/fstab** file to include the entry for **/asodev_home**, as shown in the following example:

```
# cat /etc/fstab
LABEL=/                    /                          ext3     defaults          1 1
LABEL=/boot                /boot                      ext3     defaults          1 2
none                       /dev/pts                   devpts   gid=5,mode=620    0 0
LABEL=/home                /home                      ext3     defaults          1 2
none                       /proc                      proc     defaults          0 0
none                       /dev/shm                   tmpfs    defaults          0 0
LABEL=/usr                 /usr                       ext3     defaults          1 2
LABEL=/var                 /var                       ext3     defaults          1 2
LABEL=/backup              /home/linuxconnect/backup  ext3     defaults          1 2
/dev/hda7                  swap                       swap     defaults          0 0
/dev/fd0                   /mnt/floppy                auto     noauto,owner,kudzu 0 0
/dev/cdrom                 /mnt/cdrom          iso9660 noauto,owner,kudzu,ro      0 0
asodev:/home               /asodev_home               nfs      rw,bg,soft        0 0
```

The last entry is the NFS mount. This entry is going to mount the remote NFS file system *asodev:/home* when the client is rebooted. You specified that **asodev:/home** would be an *nfs* mount, that the file system is *rw* so it can be read and written, *bg* means that this is a background mount so a failed mount will continue trying to execute, and finally, the mount is *soft* allowing the client to time out after a number of retries.

If you go back to the server, you can run **showmount** to see the remote hosts that have mounted file systems on the server, as shown in the following example:

```
# showmount
linuxdev:/home
[root@localhost nfs]#
```

This shows that *linuxdev* is a remote host that has mounted a file system exported by the server *asodev*.

You did not have to run the **nfs start** command on the client because there were sufficient services running to support an NFS client.

Using NFS is not without some security risks because you now have data that is shared on your network and many ports are now open. The following example shows a partial output of the **nmap** command:

```
# nmap -sT -O localhost

Starting nmap V. 3.00 ( www.insecure.org/nmap/ )
Insufficient responses for TCP sequencing (0), OS detection may be
less accurate
Insufficient responses for TCP sequencing (3), OS detection may be
less accurate
Interesting ports on localhost.localdomain (127.0.0.1):
(The 1592 ports scanned but not shown below are in state: closed)
Port       State      Service
22/tcp     open       ssh
23/tcp     open       telnet
```

```
25/tcp       open        smtp
111/tcp      open        sunrpc
989/tcp      open        ftps-data
1024/tcp     open        kdm
1031/tcp     open        iad2
1032/tcp     open        iad3
6000/tcp     open        X11
                 .
                 .
                 .
```

This output shows that several ports are now open, including the *telnet* session used to obtain these examples from the system and several ports related to our NFS work. You used the *-sT* option, which is the most basic form of TCP scanning. You also used *-O,* which guesses the operating system of the machine. The following example is the output of the same command from the NFS client in the example:

```
# nmap -sT -O localhost

Starting nmap V. 3.00 ( www.insecure.org/nmap/ )
Interesting ports on localhost.localdomain (127.0.0.1):
(The 1590 ports scanned but not shown below are in state: closed)
Port         State       Service
21/tcp       open        ftp
22/tcp       open        ssh
23/tcp       open        telnet
25/tcp       open        smtp
111/tcp      open        sunrpc
139/tcp      open        netbios-ssn
901/tcp      open        samba-swat
1024/tcp     open        kdm
1025/tcp     open        NFS-or-IIS
6000/tcp     open        X11
10000/tcp    open        snet-sensor-mgmt
Remote OS guesses: Linux Kernel 2.4.0 - 2.5.20, Linux 2.5.25 or Gen-
too 1.2 Linux 2.4.19 rc
1-rc7)

Nmap run completed -- 1 IP address (1 host up) scanned in 6 seconds
```

This system has additional ports open, such as *901,* which is for the *swat* tool used to configure samba. There are no unknown ports in these two outputs, so we at least know that the ports are used for known services (which are defined in **/etc/services**).

NFS is a commonly used technique for data sharing across the network on Linux and UNIX systems. This is easy to set up and use and it is provided as a standard component in operating systems.

Graphical Tools - /usr/sbin/neat and Webmin

neat is a graphical network configuration tool that you can issue from the command line with **/usr/sbin/neat**. This tool modifies many files when you enter configuration through it. You may choose to use the commands in the upcoming section or edit network configuration files directly, such as those covered in the previous section. If you like graphical tools; however, this is an easy interface to work with and it helps with a lot of basic networking configuration.

After invoking **neat** if you are running our Integrity Red Hat Advanced Server system, you see the main window shown in Figure 8-2.

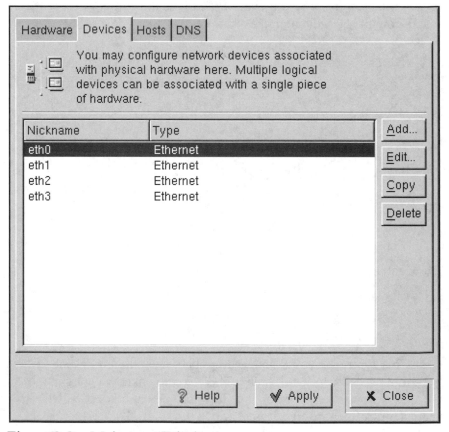

Figure 8-2   Main **neat** Window

At this point, you can either select any of the buttons in the window or double-click one of the four devices, which opens another window. When you double-click one of the cards, the window that opens on Advanced Server is called *Ethernet Device* and has tabs for *General, Protocols,* and *Routing* as shown in Figure 8-3. (As a sidenote, you get different windows that open on Red Hat 8.x, but mostly the same information is viewed and edited: it just takes place in different windows.)

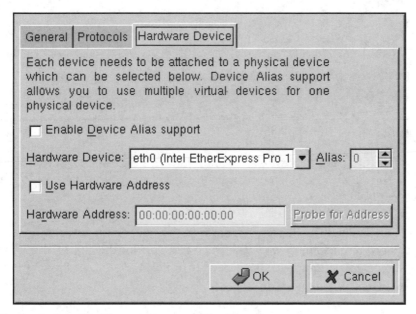

Figure 8-3   *Hardware Device* Window

Selecting *Protocols* and *TCP/IP* opens the window shown in Figure 8-4.

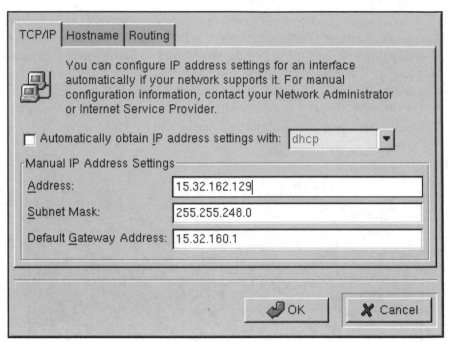

Figure 8-4   *TCP/IP* Window

In this window, you can update the *Address, Subnet Mask, Default Gateway Address,* and other parameters associated with the network card. You can select *Hostname* or *Routing* from the tabs on the top of the window as well.

There are different network cards in the slots on the Integrity system. If you were to click the *Hardware Device* button on the top of the window, we'd receive a summary of the hardware of the card *eth3,* as shown in Figure 8-5.

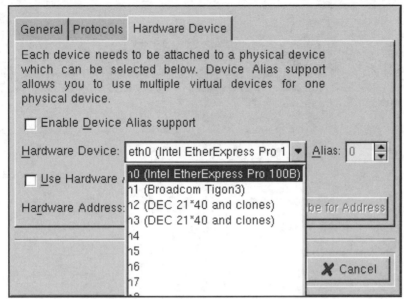

Figure 8-5   *Hardware* Window Showing *eth0:3*

The corresponding hardware devices of all four networking cards in the Integrity server are shown.

This is a great graphical tool for managing networking basics. Please keep in mind that the **neat** windows are slightly different on the Integrity Advanced Server than they are on Red Hat 8.x. The tool's functionality, however, is the same on both operating systems.

The *Webmin* tool covered next also has a *Network Configuration* area under *Hardware*. At the time of this writing, I have used *Webmin* on only IA-32 systems and not on Integrity servers. Figure 8-6 shows the *Network Configuration* area in which you can make one of four selections using *Webmin*.

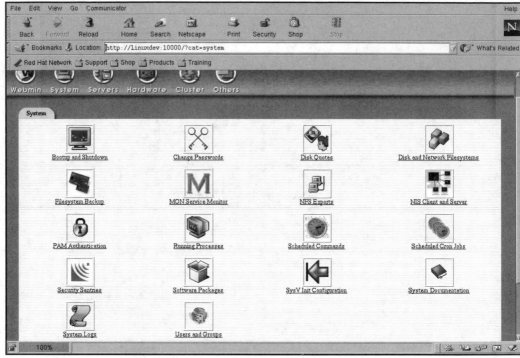

Figure 8-6   Webmin Network Configuration

You can select from the areas shown in the figure to modify the desired functionality of your system.

The graphical tools covered in this section are by no means exhaustive. Countless Linux tools are available for working with networking. I like these tools and use them, but you may find others that suit your needs.

Chapter 9

Backup

Performing backups on your Linux system is important for various reasons. As with any system, you could experience a hardware problem. Similarly, the software on your system could become corrupted or someone could accidently delete it. Similarly, over time, you'll probably customize your system. If you have to reinstall it, you will loose all your customizations. Backups can save you lots of time in all these situations.

Many issues are related to backup. First, you must consider the frequency of system backups. You may decide to protect your data with some kind of storage technology (such as mirrored disks), but even that is not without risk. With mirrored disks, even if your system disk becomes corrupted, your data remains intact. Still, even mirroring doesn't help with deleted or corrupted files. Further, if you have to use your mirrored disk to restore your files, you will be unable to use your system while you restore it (unless you employ some high-availability program, such as ServiceGuard).

Similarly, if your system backup takes place to a tape device on a remote system, you'll have to consider the additional latency introduced by the network overhead.

For all these reasons, it is important to test your recovery plan after you have designed your backup technique. Testing your plan ensures that you can recover your systems and data within the window required by your operation.

Built-In Backup Programs

This section gives an overview of several backup commands. All the examples are run on an Integrity server, but the commands work identically on IA-32 systems. If you're interested in how tape drives are used for system backup, the examples in the device files section of this chapter pay special attention to the device file for tape drives. The following is a brief overview of backup programs covered in this chapter:

tar   **tar** is widely considered the most *portable* of the backup and restore programs. **tar** is the most popular generic backup utility. You will find that many applications are shipped on **tar** tapes. This is the most widely used format for exchanging data with other Linux systems. **tar** is an old backup method and therefore runs on all Linux and UNIX systems. **tar** is one of the slower backup programs so you'll need to consider this if you decide to use if for your full or incremental backups. One highly desirable aspect of **tar** is that when you load files onto a tape with **tar** and then restore them onto another system, the original users and groups are retained.

dump   **dump** provides many levels of backup and creates **/etc/dumpdates,** which lists the last time a file system was backed up. **restore** is used to read information backed up with **dump**.

cpio   **cpio** is portable and easy to use, like **tar**. In addition, **cpio** is faster than **tar**. **cpio** is good for replicating directory trees.

dd   This is a bit-for-bit copy. It is not smart in the sense that it does not copy files and ownerships; it just copies bits. You could not, therefore, select an individual file from a **dd** tape as you could with **tar**, **restore** or **cpio**. **dd** is mainly used for converting data, such as EBCDIC to ASCII.

tar

tar (originally short for tape archive) is widely considered the most *portable* of the backup and restore programs. You will find that many applications are shipped on **tar** tapes and many Linux files downloaded from the Internet are in **tar** format or compressed **tar** format such as *archivename.tgz*. This is the most widely used format for exchanging data with other Linux and UNIX systems. You can append files to the end of a **tar** file or tape, which you can't do with many other programs. When sending files to another Linux user, I would recommend **tar**. **tar** is a slow backup program, so keep this in mind if you use it for your full or incremental backups if you have a lot of data to back up. One highly desirable aspect of **tar** is that when you load files onto a tape with **tar** and then restore them onto another system, the original users and groups are retained.

We'll use several **tar** commands in the upcoming examples, including the following:

```
# tar cf /dev/st0 /var         ;use tar to create (c) an archive of
                                    the directory /var and put it on
                                    tape /dev/st0.


# tar tvf /dev/st0             ;obtain table of contents (t) from
                                    tape /dev/st0 and produce
                                    produce verbose (v) output.


# tar xvf /dev/st0             ;extract (x) the entire contents
                                    of the archive on tape /dev/st0
                                    to default destination.


# tar xvf /dev/st0 file1       ;extract (x) only file1
                                    from the archive on tape /dev/st0
                                    to default destination

# cd /var/log; tar cf - .| (cd /tmp/log; tar xfBp -)

                               ;send data to standard output with cf -,
                                    then use standard input with xfBp -
                                    to copy the contents of /var/log to
                                    /tmp/log.
```

You'll notice when you view the man pages for **tar** that options are preceded by a hyphen. The command works without the hyphen so most **tar** examples omit the hyphen.

Take a look at some examples using **tar**. Begin by performing a **tar** backup (usually called creating an archive) of the directory **/var** to tape device **/dev/st0**. We use the *c* option to create a backup, the *v* option for verbose output, and the *f* option to specify the file of the tape drive **/dev/st0** because the default I/O is to *stdin/stdout*:

```
[root@demtstd1 root]# tar cvf /dev/st0 /var
tar: Removing leading `/' from member names
var/
var/lib/
var/lib/rpm/
var/lib/rpm/Packages
var/lib/rpm/Basenames
var/lib/rpm/Name
var/lib/rpm/Group
var/lib/rpm/Requirename
var/lib/rpm/Providename
var/lib/rpm/Conflictname
var/lib/rpm/Dirnames
var/lib/rpm/Requireversion
var/lib/rpm/Provideversion
var/lib/rpm/Installtid
var/lib/rpm/Sigmd5
var/lib/rpm/Sha1header
var/lib/rpm/Filemd5s
var/lib/rpm/Triggername
var/lib/games/
var/lib/misc/
                    .
                    .
                    .
var/www/icons/up.png
var/www/icons/uu.gif
var/www/icons/uu.png
var/www/icons/uuencoded.gif
var/www/icons/uuencoded.png
var/www/icons/world1.gif
var/www/icons/world1.png
var/www/icons/world2.gif
var/www/icons/world2.png
var/crash/
var/crash/.ssh/
var/crash/.ssh/authorized_keys2
var/crash/magic/
var/crash/scripts/
[root@demtstd1 root]# more /var/log/sa/sa05
var/crash/magic/
var/crash/scripts/
[root@demtstd1 root]#
```

The abbreviated output shows a list of all files that were included in the archive. If you wanted to see only messages related to problems with creating the archive, you would leave off the *v* option and you'd receive only problem-related messages.

Next, take a look at only the file named **sa05** on the tape. To produce a table of contents, we will use the *t* option. The following example also uses *v* for verbose output:

```
[root@demtstd1 root]# tar tvf /dev/st0 | grep sa05
-rw-r--r-- root/root    146661 2003-03-05 10:30:00 var/log/sa/sa05
```

Note that this is a relative backup; that is, there is no / preceding the file name. You need to be aware of the relative path names used with **tar** and your present working directory when using **tar**. We'll delete **sa05** from the computer and restore it from tape using the *x* option to extract the file from the **tar** archive. We'll then list the directory (using **ll**, which is an alias for **ls -l** that we've setup) on the system to confirm that the file we deleted has been restored to the directory from tape:

```
[root@demtstd1 root]# rm /var/log/sa/sa05
rm: remove `/var/log/sa/sa05'? y

[root@demtstd1 root]# tar xvf /dev/st0 /var/log/sa/sa05
var/log/sa/sa05

[root@demtstd1 root]# ll /var/log/sa
total 5432
-rw-r--r--    1 root     root       329701 Mar  1 23:50 _[00msa01_[00m
-rw-r--r--    1 root     root       329701 Mar  2 23:50 _[00msa02_[00m
-rw-r--r--    1 root     root       329701 Mar  3 23:50 _[00msa03_[00m
-rw-r--r--    1 root     root       329701 Mar  4 23:50 _[00msa04_[00m
-rw-r--r--    1 root     root       329701 Feb 25 23:50 _[00msa25_[00m
-rw-r--r--    1 root     root       329701 Feb 26 23:50 _[00msa26_[00m
-rw-r--r--    1 root     root       329701 Feb 27 23:50 _[00msa27_[00m
-rw-r--r--    1 root     root       329701 Feb 28 23:50 _[00msa28_[00m
-rw-r--r--    1 root     root       311429 Mar  2 04:02 _[00msar01_[00m
-rw-r--r--    1 root     root       311428 Mar  3 04:02 _[00msar02_[00m
-rw-r--r--    1 root     root       311430 Mar  4 04:02 _[00msar03_[00m
-rw-r--r--    1 root     root       311430 Mar  5 04:02 _[00msar04_[00m
-rw-r--r--    1 root     root       311429 Feb 25 04:02 _[00msar24_[00m
-rw-r--r--    1 root     root       311430 Feb 26 04:02 _[00msar25_[00m
-rw-r--r--    1 root     root       311429 Feb 27 04:02 _[00msar26_[00m
-rw-r--r--    1 root     root       311430 Feb 28 04:02 _[00msar27_[00m
-rw-r--r--    1 root     root       311430 Mar  1 04:02 _[00msar28_[00m_
[root@demtstd1 root]#
```

This backup and restore using **tar** is simple and gets the job done. The file **sa05** has indeed been restored.

A common use for **tar** is to back up files from one directory and restore them to another directory. We'll backup the contents of **/var/log** and restore them to the directory **/tmp/log**. In the following example, we create a **tar** backup archive to a file rather than to tape. The file is called **tartest**. We will then move this file to the destination directory and extract it there. We don't use a tape at all in this example:

```
[root@demtstd1 root]# cd /var/log
[root@demtstd1 log]# ll
total 100124
-rw-------    1 root      root              0 Mar  2 04:02 boot.log
-rw-------    1 root      root              0 Feb 23 04:02 boot.log.1
-rw-------    1 root      root              0 Feb 16 04:02 boot.log.2
-rw-------    1 root      root           3938 Feb 11 14:48 boot.log.3
-rw-------    1 root      root          18637 Feb 11 14:32 boot.log.4
-rw-------    1 root      root         122071 Mar  5 10:40 cron
-rw-------    1 root      root         260944 Mar  2 04:02 cron.1
-rw-------    1 root      root         260768 Feb 23 04:02 cron.2
-rw-------    1 root      root         170460 Feb 16 04:02 cron.3
-rw-------    1 root      root         167831 Feb 11 14:37 cron.4
                  .
                  .
                  .

drwxr-xr-x    2 root      root           4096 May 21  2002 vbox
-rw-rw-r--    1 root      utmp       19666000 Mar  5 10:40 wtmp
-rw-rw-r--    1 root      utmp       80738000 Mar  1 04:01 wtmp.1
-rw-r--r--    1 root      root             86 Mar  5 10:40 xdm-errors
[root@demtstd1 log]# tar cvf /tmp/tartest `ls -a`
boot.log
boot.log.1
boot.log.2
boot.log.3
boot.log.4
cron
cron.1
cron.2
cron.3
cron.4
samba/
            .
            .
            .

vbox/
wtmp
wtmp.1
xdm-errors
[root@demtstd1 log]#

[root@demtstd1 log]# cd /tmp
[root@demtstd1 tmp]# mkdir log
[root@demtstd1 tmp]# cp tartest log
```

```
[root@demtstd1 tmp]# cd log
[root@demtstd1 log]# ls -l
total 124260
-rw-r--r--    1 root     root      127109120 Mar  5 10:44 tartest
[m[root@demtstd1 log]# tar xvf tartest
boot.log
boot.log.1
boot.log.2
boot.log.3
boot.log.4
cron
cron.1
cron.2
cron.3
cron.4
               .
               .
               .
vbox/
wtmp
wtmp.1
xdm-errors
[root@demtstd1 log]#
```

When creating the **tar** backup, I first changed to the **/var/log** directory and then used the **ls** command (a *grav* or *accent*, which is near the upper left of most keyboards on the same key as a *tilde*, appears before and after the **ls**). This produced relative path names that I could easily restore to the **/tmp/ log** directory. Alternatively, I could also have just changed directory to **/var** and issued the command **tar cf /dev/st0 log** to back up the entire contents of the **/var/log** directory.

This entire process could have been done on a single command line. The following line shows the commonly used procedure for producing an archive in the *fromdir* and restoring it to the *todir*:

cd *fromdir* ; **tar cf - .** | (**cd** *todir* ; **tar xf -i**)

For our example, we would perform the following:

```
# mkdir /tmp/log
# cd /var/log; tar cf - .| (cd /tmp/log; tar xfBp -)
```

The "-" in the **tar cf** command tells **tar** to send its data to *standard output*. The "-" in the **tar xfBp** command tells **tar** to look to *standard input* for data, which is the data produced by **tar cf -** issued earlier on the command line.

This does indeed result in all the files of **/var/log** being copied to the directory **/tmp/log**.

You can also use **tar** combined with **find** to produce an incremental backup of your system. An incremental backup is one which includes only files that have changed over a specified time period.

Running the following **find** command produces a file that contains only the names of files that have changed in the last 24 hours:

```
# find / -mtime -1 -print > /tmp/daily.backup.list
```

We could then take the list of files in **/tmp/daily.backup.list** and use this file as input to **tar** with the following command:

```
# tar -cv -T /tmp/daily.backup.list -f /dev/st0
```

Note that in this example (unlike some of the earlier ones), we do need to include dashes for the options to be read. The *-cv* creates and archives with verbose output and the option *-T* indicates that the following file contains a list of files to be included in the archive. The *-f* indicates the file to which the archive will be written which, in this case, is our tape drive.

You often download files that have been compressed with **gzip** from the Internet. Such files have an extension of *.gz*. You would first unzip such files with **gunzip** and then use **tar -xf** to extract the archive as shown here:

```
# ls
files.tar.gz
# gunzip files.tar.gz
# ls
files.tar
# tar -xf examples.tar
# ls
files.tar   file1   file2   file3
#
```

This is a commonly performed procedure after downloading files.

cpio

cpio is a powerful utility that is used in conjunction with **find** to perform full
and incremental backups. **cpio** is an established Linux and UNIX utility that
works similarly on most Linux and UNIX variants.

You'll use several commands in the upcoming examples, including the
following:

```
# find . -print | cpio -ov > /dev/st0   ;find the contents of
                                          the current dir and
                                          write them to tape.

# cpio -it < /dev/st0          ;read table of contents (t) of tape.

# cpio -iv < /dev/st0          ;restore (i) the contents of tape.
```

The first command you'll issue is to **find** the contents in **/var/log/sa**
and write them to your tape device **/dev/st0**. The options to **cpio** used in the
following example are *o* for output mode and *v* for verbose reporting:

```
[root@demtstd1 log]# cd /var/log/sa
[root@demtstd1 log]# find . -print | cpio -ov > /dev/st0

.
./sa05
./sa03
./sa04
./sar03
./sar04
./sa25
./sa26
./sar24
./sa27
./sar26
./sa28
./sar27
./sa01
./sar28
./sa02
./sar01
./sar02
./sar25
10637 blocks
[root@demtstd1 sa]#
```

In the example, you first changed directory to **/var/log/sa**, then issued
the **find** command and pipe its output to **cpio**. **cpio** is almost always used in
conjunction with **find** in the manner shown in the example. This produced a

backup with relative path names because we changed to the directory **/var/log/sa** before issuing the backup commands.

Next, view the contents of the tape to see the files you wrote to it with **cpio**. The *i* option is used for input, and the *t* option is used to get a table of contents in the following listing:

```
[root@demtstd1 sa]# cpio -it < /dev/st0
.
sa05
sa03
sa04
sar03
sar04
sa25
sa26
sar24
sa27
sar26
sa28
sar27
sa01
sar28
sa02
sar01
sar02
sar25
10637 blocks
[root@demtstd1 sa]#
```

Now that you have written to the tape and viewed its table of contents, you'll restore the contents of **/var/log/sa** to the directory **/root/test.cpio**. In the following example, you use only the *-i* option to extract the files from tape to the present directory.

```
[root@demtstd1 sa]# cd /root
[root@demtstd1 root]# mkdir test.cpio
[root@demtstd1 root]# cd test.cpio
[root@demtstd1 test.cpio]# cpio -iv < /dev/st0
.
sa05
sa03
sa04
sar03
sar04
sa25
sa26
sar24
sa27
sar26
sa28
sar27
sa01
sar28
sa02
sar01
sar02
```

```
sar25
10637 blocks
[root@demtstd1 test.cpio]# pwd
/root/test.cpio
[root@demtstd1 test.cpio]# ll
total 5440
-rw-r--r--    1 root       root         329701 Mar   5 10:54 sa01
-rw-r--r--    1 root       root         329701 Mar   5 10:54 sa02
-rw-r--r--    1 root       root         329701 Mar   5 10:54 sa03
-rw-r--r--    1 root       root         329701 Mar   5 10:54 sa04
-rw-r--r--    1 root       root           4805 Mar   5 10:54 sa05
-rw-r--r--    1 root       root         329701 Mar   5 10:54 sa25
-rw-r--r--    1 root       root         329701 Mar   5 10:54 sa26
-rw-r--r--    1 root       root         329701 Mar   5 10:54 sa27
-rw-r--r--    1 root       root         329701 Mar   5 10:54 sa28
-rw-r--r--    1 root       root         311429 Mar   5 10:54 sar01
-rw-r--r--    1 root       root         311428 Mar   5 10:54 sar02
-rw-r--r--    1 root       root         311430 Mar   5 10:54 sar03
-rw-r--r--    1 root       root         311430 Mar   5 10:54 sar04
-rw-r--r--    1 root       root         311429 Mar   5 10:54 sar24
-rw-r--r--    1 root       root         311430 Mar   5 10:54 sar25
-rw-r--r--    1 root       root         311429 Mar   5 10:54 sar26
-rw-r--r--    1 root       root         311430 Mar   5 10:54 sar27
-rw-r--r--    1 root       root         311430 Mar   5 10:54 sar28
[m[root@demtstd1 test.cpio]#
```

The **cpio** command produces a list of files that will be read from the tape and restored to the system. Often, I use several other options when restoring such as *c* for ASCII header format, *v* for verbose, *B* for block output, *d* for creating directories, *u* for unconditional write over existing files, and *m* to restore the original modification times.

This was a very quick overview of **cpio**. Often, I use it to perform backups of remote systems as well using the following format:

```
# find . -print | cpio -o | (rsh remote_sys dd of=/dev/rmt/0m)
        ;find the contents of the current dir and
         write (o) them to tape on remote_sys.
```

```
# rsh remote_sys "dd if=/dev/rmt/0m bs=8k" | cpio -iv
                ;restore the contents (i) of a tape on remote_sys
                 to the local system.
```

For **rsh** to work, you have to enable this command as shown in Chapter 8. In addition, you have to set up the **.rhosts** file with the name of the system to trust and the user name.

You can build from the simple examples in this **cpio** section to develop backup and restore commands to meet your needs in any environment.

dump and restore

dump and **restore** are highly functional programs that are used to back up a complete file system and then restore any or all of the file system at a later date. There are some advanced characteristics of these commands that are covered, including the following:

- **dump** *levels* are employed that allow you to perform a full backup at level *0* and then incremental backups at lower levels. After a full backup has been performed at level *0,* then all changes since that full backup will be saved if you specify dump level *1*. Level *2* will cover all changes since the last level *1* dump, and so on.

- The file **/etc/dumpdates** contains information about dumps including the file system that was part of the dump, when the dump took place, and the dump level of the backup.

- You can combine **dump** with commands such as **gzip** to fit more information on the tape.

- Multi-volume backups are supported by **dump** provided that you specify information about the media such as bits per inch and feet per tape. You can bypass this information and write directly from tape as covered in the example.

- You can get a table of contents of file on the tape using **restore**, restore files interactively, restore select files, or restore an entire file system.

Look at some examples using **dump** and **restore**. We'll use several commands in the upcoming examples, including the following:

```
# dump -0u -f /dev/st0 /dev/sda4   ;dump sda4 file system to tape
                                    /dev/st0 using level 0 and update
                                    /etc/dumpdates.

# dump -0uf - /dev/sda4 | gzip --fast -c >> /dev/nst0
                                   ;dump sda4 file system to tape
                                    /dev/st0 using level 0 and
                                    update /etc/dumpdates. Tape info
                                    such as length and density aren't
                                    known so send output to std out and
                                    gzip before going to tape.
```

```
# restore -tvf /dev/st0 | grep install.log  ;obtain table of contents from
                                              tape /dev/st0 and look for
                                              file name dump.file


# restore -xvf /dev/st0 ./root/install.log  ;restore file dump.file
                                              current directory
```

Let's take a look at some of these commands in more detail. The first example runs **dump** to back up **/dev/sda4.** You set the backup level to *0* for a full backup, the *f* option to specify the output file **/dev/st0**, and *u* for a write to **/etc/dumpdates**. In the following example, you first issue the **df** command to view **/dev/sda4** (which is roughly 4.8 GB), and then run the **dump** command:

```
[root@demtstd1 test.cpio]# df
Filesystem            1k-blocks      Used Available Use% Mounted on
/dev/sda4             32253856    4788992  25826464  16% /
/dev/sda3               102182       6138     96044   7% /boot/efi
none                   4158608          0   4158608   0% /dev/shm
[root@demtstd1 test.cpio]# dump -0u -f /dev/st0 /dev/sda4
  DUMP: Date of this level 0 dump: Wed Mar  5 10:56:17 2003
  DUMP: Dumping /dev/sda4 (/) to /dev/st0
  DUMP: Added inode 8 to exclude list (journal inode)
  DUMP: Added inode 7 to exclude list (resize inode)
  DUMP: Label: /
  DUMP: mapping (Pass I) [regular files]
  DUMP: mapping (Pass II) [directories]
  DUMP: estimated 4721383 tape blocks.
  DUMP: Volume 1 started with block 1 at: Wed Mar  5 10:56:56 2003
  DUMP: dumping (Pass III) [directories]
  DUMP: dumping (Pass IV) [regular files]
  DUMP: 14.01% done at 2205 kB/s, finished in 0:30
  DUMP: 22.38% done at 1761 kB/s, finished in 0:34
  DUMP: 27.69% done at 1452 kB/s, finished in 0:39
  DUMP: 33.09% done at 1301 kB/s, finished in 0:40
  DUMP: 38.91% done at 1224 kB/s, finished in 0:39
  DUMP: 44.23% done at 1160 kB/s, finished in 0:37
  DUMP: 49.69% done at 1117 kB/s, finished in 0:35
  DUMP: 59.78% done at 1175 kB/s, finished in 0:26
  DUMP: 65.21% done at 1140 kB/s, finished in 0:24
  DUMP: 70.54% done at 1110 kB/s, finished in 0:20
  DUMP: 77.40% done at 1107 kB/s, finished in 0:16
  DUMP: 82.73% done at 1084 kB/s, finished in 0:12
  DUMP: 90.04% done at 1090 kB/s, finished in 0:07
  DUMP: Closing /dev/st0
  DUMP: Volume 1 completed at: Wed Mar  5 12:07:15 2003
  DUMP: Volume 1 4804230 tape blocks (4691.63MB)
  DUMP: Volume 1 took 1:10:19
  DUMP: Volume 1 transfer rate: 1138 kB/s
  DUMP: 4804230 tape blocks (4691.63MB) on 1 volume(s)
  DUMP: finished in 4175 seconds, throughput 1150 kBytes/sec
  DUMP: Date of this level 0 dump: Wed Mar  5 10:56:17 2003
  DUMP: Date this dump completed:  Wed Mar  5 12:07:15 2003
  DUMP: Average transfer rate: 1138 kB/s
  DUMP: DUMP IS DONE
```

dump provides information related to the backup to *standard output*. There are regular status outputs reported. We used the *-u* option, which updates the **/etc/dumpdates** file:

```
[root@demtstd1 test.cpio]# cat /etc/dumpdates
/dev/sda4 0 Wed Mar  5 10:56:17 2003
[root@demtstd1 test.cpio]#
```

Because we used the **u** option, we will get an entry in **/etc/dumpdates** for every file system that was dumped. In this case, we dumped only **/dev/sda4**.

Next, extract the file **install.log** from the **dump** and view its contents. To extract the file from tape, use the *x* option to **restore**, as shown in the following listing:

```
# restore -xvf /dev/st0 ./root/install.log
Verify tape and initialize maps
Input is from tape
Tape block size is 10
Dump    date: Wed Mar  5 10:56:17 2003
Dumped from: the epoch
Level 0 dump of / on demtstd1.ct.pb.com:/dev/sda4
Label: /
Extract directories from tape
Initialize symbol table.
restore: ./root: File exists
Extract requested files
You have not read any tapes yet.
Unless you know which volume your file(s) are on you should start
with the last volume and work towards the first.
Specify next volume #: 1
extract file ./root/install.log
Add links
Set directory mode, owner, and times.
set owner/mode for '.'? [yn] n

[root@demtstd1 root]# more install.log
Installing 509 packages
Installing glibc-common-2.2.4-27.2.
Installing indexhtml-7.2-1.
Installing mailcap-2.1.6-1.
Installing redhat-logos-1.1.3-1.
Installing sash-3.4-11.
Installing setup-2.5.7-1.
Installing filesystem-2.1.6-2.
Installing basesystem-7.0-2.
Installing glibc-2.2.4-27.2.
Installing bdflush-1.5-17.
Installing bzip2-libs-1.0.1-4.
Installing chkconfig-1.2.24-1.
Installing cracklib-2.7-12.
Installing db1-1.85-7.
Installing db2-2.4.14-9.
Installing db3-3.3.11-5.
```

```
Installing dosfstools-2.7-1.
Installing e2fsprogs-1.26-1.72.
Installing eject-2.0.9-2.
Installing elilo-3.2-4
[root@demtstd1 root]#
```

Notice that as part of restoring the file, we had to specify a volume number of *1* and decide whether we wanted to set the mode for the file. Also note that the restore took place with a relative path name.

To get a table of contents from the tape, you would have used *-t*. Another commonly used option with **restore** is *-i,* which performs an interactive restore that was not part of the example.

You could also create a file that automatically performs several file system backups for you. **dump** creates a large file for file system that is part of the backup. That means that you can put multiple file systems on a backup tape. You have been using a tape device file of **/dev/st0**, which is a rewind tape device. Because you want to put multiple tapes on the file, use a no rewind device of **/dev/nst0**. When you use the **mount** command, **mt**, you can control this tape drive using options such as *rewind* and *eject*.

Since the length of the tape and density aren't known, run **dump** commands and pipe the output to **gzip**, which gives you some compression. The following file that we'll **cat** called **dump.file** contains these commands:

```
# cat dump.file
mt -f /dev/nst0 rewind

dump -0uf - /dev/sda | gzip --fast -c > /dev/nst0
#fill in other file systems /dev/sdx

mt -f /dev/nst0 rewind
mt -f /dev/nst0 eject
```

You have only one file system to backup on your system, but you could add **dump** lines for all of your file systems. First, mount the tape with **mt**. Next, run the **dump** commands and pipe them to **gzip** with the *--fast* option to make the backup go much faster; however, the compression is not as dense as without this option. You also get **gzip** output to *standard output* with *-c*. You're going to dump only **/dev/sda** in the example but you could add additional lines. When you run the file, it will perform the dumps. The following example shows multiple lines on an IA-32 system with IDE drives:

```
# cat dump.file

mt -f /dev/nst0 rewind
```

```
dump -0uf - /dev/hda1 | gzip --fast -c > /dev/nst0
#dump -0uf - /dev/hda2 | gzip --fast -c > /dev/nst0
#dump -0uf - /dev/hda3 | gzip --fast -c > /dev/nst0
#dump -0uf - /dev/hda5 | gzip --fast -c > /dev/nst0
dump -0uf - /dev/hda6 | gzip --fast -c > /dev/nst0
#dump -0uf - /dev/hdb1 | gzip --fast -c > /dev/nst0

mt -f /dev/nst0 rewind
mt -f /dev/nst0 eject
```

Keep in mind that you can only use such a procedure if you're sure the files you *dump* will fit on a single tape because without specifying tape density and length, you won't get a multi-tape backup.

To see all the options for the commands used in this section, look at the man pages for **mt**, **dump**, **gzip**, and **restore**.

Procedure to Create a Boot Disk if You Can't Boot Off CD-ROM

The procedure in this section has nothing to do with the Integrity server or even new IA-32 systems. This is a procedure to create a boot floppy if you have an old system that won't boot off of a CD-ROM. I included this to demonstrate how to use a couple of commands to create a boot floppy. This can be important because many people get started with Linux on old systems. This is one of the strengths of Linux: It runs on most hardware, including old systems.

If you can't boot from your CD-ROM, you can create the boot floppy using MS-DOS and the **rawrite** utility included on the Red Hat CD-ROM in the *dosutils* directory using the following procedure. Note that this procedures assumes that your CD-ROM is **D:** and that you can boot to a DOS prompt that can read the Linux CD-ROM:

```
C:\> d:
D:\> cd \dosutils
D:\dosutils> rawrite
Enter disk image source file name: ..\images\boot.img
Enter target diskette drive: a:
Please insert a formatted diskette into drive A: andpress --ENTER-- : [Enter]
D:\dosutils>
```

rawrite asks you for the file name of a diskette image. In this case, the images is located at **..\images\boot.img**. **rawrite** produces a Linux bootable floppy off of which you could boot to load Linux.

You can also make a diskette under Linux using the **dd** command. To do so, you must have permission to write to the device representing a 3.5-inch diskette drive **/dev/fd0**. If you have that permission, insert a floppy into the diskette drive but don't mount it. After mounting the Red Hat Linux CD-ROM, change to the directory containing the desired image file, and use the following command:

```
# dd if=boot.img of=/dev/fd0 bs=1440k
```

This copies whatever is in **boot.img** to your floppy disk (/dev/fd0).

Chapter 10

Additional System Administration Topics

Many of the topics covered up to this point, such as installing Linux, networking, startup, kernel configuration, and many others, warrant their own individual chapters. This chapter discusses many of the remaining system administration-related topics, such as the following:

- Managing processes using **ps, kill**, and signals
- Users and groups
- Disk usage
- Scheduling jobs with **cron**

In some cases, there are differences between IA-32 and Integrity server. Generally, I give examples on IA-32 systems. However, I will give examples on Integrity servers where appropriate in order to point out the nuances when working with Integrity servers.

Check Processes with ps

To find the answer to "What is my system doing?," use **ps -ef**. This command provides information about every running process on your system. If, for instance, you want to know about telnet connections, simply type **ps -ef** and look for telnet. Although **ps** tells you every process that is running on your system, it doesn't provide a good summary of the level of system resources being consumed. I would guess that **ps** is the most often issued system administration command. You can use a number of options with **ps**. I normally use **e** and **f**, which provide information about every (**e**) running process and lists this information in full (**f**). **ps** outputs are almost identical going from system to system. The following shows the output of a **ps** command:

```
# ps -ef
UID        PID  PPID  C  STIME TTY        TIME CMD
root         1     0  0  2002 ?       00:00:05 init [5]
root         2     1  0  2002 ?       00:00:00 [keventd]
root         3     1  0  2002 ?       00:00:00 [kapmd]
root         4     1  0  2002 ?       00:00:00 [ksoftirqd_CPU0]
root         5     1  0  2002 ?       00:01:03 [kswapd]
root         6     1  0  2002 ?       00:00:00 [bdflush]
root         7     1  0  2002 ?       00:00:00 [kupdated]
root         8     1  0  2002 ?       00:00:00 [mdrecoveryd]
root        12     1  0  2002 ?       00:00:08 [kjournald]
root        64     1  0  2002 ?       00:00:00 [khubd]
root       158     1  0  2002 ?       00:00:00 [kjournald]
root       159     1  0  2002 ?       00:00:00 [kjournald]
root       160     1  0  2002 ?       00:00:01 [kjournald]
root       161     1  0  2002 ?       00:00:05 [kjournald]
root       162     1  0  2002 ?       00:00:10 [kjournald]
root       459     1  0  2002 ?       00:00:04 syslogd -m 0
root       463     1  0  2002 ?       00:00:00 klogd -x
rpc        474     1  0  2002 ?       00:00:00 portmap
rpcuser    493     1  0  2002 ?       00:00:00 rpc.statd
root       556     1  0  2002 ?       00:00:00 /usr/sbin/apmd -p 10 -w 5 -W -P /etc/sysco

root       594     1  0  2002 ?       00:00:00 /usr/sbin/sshd
root       608     1  0  2002 ?       00:00:00 xinetd -stayalive -reuse -pidfile /var/run

root       631     1  0  2002 ?       00:00:03 sendmail: accepting connections
smmsp      641     1  0  2002 ?       00:00:00 sendmail: Queue runner@01:00:00 for /var/s

root       651     1  0  2002 ?       00:00:01 gpm -t ps/2 -m /dev/mouse
bin        661     1  0  2002 ?       00:00:00 cannaserver -syslog -u bin
root       670     1  0  2002 ?       00:00:00 crond
root       679     1  0  2002 ?       00:00:00 smbd -D
root       683     1  0  2002 ?       00:00:08 nmbd -D
xfs        730     1  0  2002 ?       00:00:34 xfs -droppriv -daemon
daemon     748     1  0  2002 ?       00:00:00 /usr/sbin/atd
root       770     1  0  2002 ?       00:00:09 /usr/bin/perl /usr/libexec/webmin/miniserv

root       774     1  0  2002 tty1    00:00:00 /sbin/mingetty tty1
root       775     1  0  2002 tty2    00:00:00 /sbin/mingetty tty2
root       776     1  0  2002 tty3    00:00:00 /sbin/mingetty tty3
root       777     1  0  2002 tty4    00:00:00 /sbin/mingetty tty4
root       778     1  0  2002 tty5    00:00:00 /sbin/mingetty tty5
root       779     1  0  2002 tty6    00:00:00 /sbin/mingetty tty6
```

```
root        780       1  0  2002 ?         00:00:00 /usr/bin/gdm-binary -nodaemon
root        813     780  0  2002 ?         00:00:00 /usr/bin/gdm-binary -nodaemon
root        814     813  3  2002 ?         07:40:10 /usr/X11R6/bin/X :0 -auth /var/gdm/:0.Xaut

root        823     813  0  2002 ?         00:00:02 /usr/bin/gnome-session
root        882     823  0  2002 ?         00:00:00 /usr/bin/ssh-agent /etc/X11/xinit/Xclients

root        893       1  0  2002 ?         00:00:02 /usr/libexec/gconfd-2 9
root        895       1  0  2002 ?         00:00:00 /usr/libexec/bonobo-activation-server --ac

root        897       1  0  2002 ?         00:00:39 metacity --sm-save-file 1034946228-887-262

root        899       1  0  2002 ?         00:00:03 gnome-settings-daemon --oaf-activate-iid=O

root        901     608  0  2002 ?         00:00:01 fam
root        917       1  0  2002 ?         00:17:06 magicdev --sm-config-prefix /magicdev-Nu4T

root        919       1  0  2002 ?         00:00:14 nautilus --sm-config-prefix /nautilus-vsLM

root        921       1  0  2002 ?         00:01:41 gnome-panel --sm-config-prefix /gnome-pane

root        924       1  0  2002 ?         00:45:40 gnome-terminal --sm-config-prefix /gnome-t

root        926       1  0  2002 ?         00:00:11 /usr/bin/pam-panel-icon --sm-client-id 11c

root        928       1  1  2002 ?         02:09:49 /usr/bin/python /usr/bin/rhn-applet-gui --

root        929     926  0  2002 ?         00:00:02 /sbin/pam_timestamp_check -d root
root        930     924  0  2002 pts/0     00:00:01 bash
root       1112     924  0  2002 pts/2     00:00:00 bash
root       1977       1  0  2002 ?         00:08:52 gaim
root       2279       1  0  2002 ?         00:00:01 /usr/libexec/nautilus-throbber --oaf-activ

root       3555     924  0  2002 pts/1     00:00:01 bash
root      28895     608  0 18:37 ?         00:00:00 in.telnetd: F4457MXP

root      28896   28895  0 18:37 ?         00:00:00 login -- linuxconnect
501       28897   28896  0 18:37 pts/3     00:00:00 -bash
root      28927   28897  0 18:37 pts/3     00:00:00 su -
root      28928   28927  1 18:37 pts/3     00:00:00 -bash
root      28964   28928  0 18:37 pts/3     00:00:00 ps -ef
#
```

Here is a brief description of the headings:

UID	The user ID of the process owner
PID	The process ID (use this number to kill the process)
PPID	The process ID of the parent process
C	Process utilization for scheduling
STIME	Start time of the process
TTY	The controlling terminal for the process, if any
TIME	The cumulative execution time for the process
COMMAND	The command name and arguments

ps quickly profiles the processes running on your system. To get more detailed information, you can use the **l** option, which includes a lot of useful

additional information, as shown in the following example showing only
Bash processes:

```
# ps -efl
  F S UID         PID  PPID  C PRI  NI ADDR    SZ WCHAN  STIME TTY          TIME CMD
000 S root        930   924  0  75   0   -   1056 schedu  2002 pts/0    00:00:01 bash
000 S root       1112   924  0  75   0   -   1066 schedu  2002 pts/2    00:00:00 bash
100 S root       3555   924  0  75   0   -   1081 schedu  2002 pts/1    00:00:01 bash
100 S 501       28897 28896  0  75   0   -   1033 wait4  18:37 pts/3    00:00:00 -bash
100 S root      28928 28927  0  75   0   -   1047 wait4  18:37 pts/3    00:00:00 -bash
000 S root      28977 28928  0  76   0   -    813 pipe_w 18:49 pts/3    00:00:00 grep bash
                  .
                  .
                  .
```

In this example, the first column is *F* for flags. *F* provides octal information about whether the process is swapped, in core, a system process, and
so on. The octal value sometimes varies from system to system, so check the
manual pages for your system to see the octal value of the flags.

S is for state. The state can be sleeping, as indicated by *S* for the processes shown in the example, waiting, running, intermediate, terminated,
and so on. Again, some of these values can vary from system to system, so
check your manual pages.

Some additional useful information in this output is: *NI* for the nice
value; *ADDR* for the memory address of the process; *SZ* for the size in physical pages of the process; and *WCHAN*, which is the event for which the process is waiting.

Killing a Process

If you issue the **ps** command and find that one of your processes is hung or if
you start a large job that you want to stop, you can do so with the **kill** command. **kill** is a utility that sends a signal to the process you identify. You can
kill any process that you own. In addition, superuser can kill almost any process on the system.

To kill a process that you own, simply issue the **kill** command and the
Process ID (PID). The following example shows issuing the **ps** command to
search for **find** processes, killing a process, and checking to see that it has
disappeared:

```
# ps -ef | grep find
root      29012  3555  4 19:05 pts/1    00:00:00 find / -name *.sh -print
root      29021 28928  0 19:06 pts/3    00:00:00 grep find
# kill 29012
# ps -ef | grep find
root      29025 28928  0 19:06 pts/3    00:00:00 grep find
#
```

The example shows killing process *29012,* which is a **find** command. We confirm that the process has indeed been killed by reissuing the **ps** command.

You can kill several processes on the command line by issuing **kill** followed by a space-separated list of all of the process numbers you want to kill.

Take special care when killing processes if you are logged in as superuser. You may adversely affect the way the system runs and have to manually restart processes or reboot the system.

In the shell programming chapter, there are two shell programs to help you search for and then kill processes.

Signals

When you issue the **kill** command and process number, you are also sending a default *signal* associated with the **kill**. You did not specify a *signal* in the **kill** example. That means that the default *signal* of 15, or *SIGTERM*, was used. These *signals* are used by the system to communicate with processes. The *signal* of 15 you used to terminate the process is a software termination *signal* that is usually enough to terminate a user process such as the **find** you started. A process that is difficult to kill may require the *SIGKILL*, or 9 *signal*. This *signal* causes an immediate termination of the process. I use this only as a last resort because processes killed with *SIGKILL* do not always terminate smoothly. To kill such processes as the shell, you sometimes have to use *SIGKILL*.

You can use either the *signal* name or number. These signal numbers sometimes vary from system to system, so view the manual page for *signal* in manual page section 7 to see the list of *signals* on your system. A list of some of the most frequently used *signal* numbers and corresponding *signals* follows:

```
       Signal     Value    Action   Comment
------------------------------------------------------------------------
       SIGHUP        1      Term     Hangup detected on controlling terminal
                                     or death of controlling process
       SIGINT        2      Term     Interrupt from keyboard
       SIGQUIT       3      Core     Quit from keyboard
       SIGILL        4      Core     Illegal Instruction
       SIGABRT       6      Core     Abort signal from abort(3)
       SIGFPE        8      Core     Floating point exception
       SIGKILL       9      Term     Kill signal
       SIGSEGV      11      Core     Invalid memory reference
       SIGPIPE      13      Term   Broken pipe: write to pipe with no readers
       SIGALRM      14      Term     Timer signal from alarm(2)
       SIGTERM      15      Term     Termination signal
       SIGUSR1   30,10,16   Term     User-defined signal 1
       SIGUSR2   31,12,17   Term     User-defined signal 2
       SIGCHLD   20,17,18   Ign      Child stopped or terminated
       SIGCONT   19,18,25            Continue if stopped
       SIGSTOP   17,19,23   Stop     Stop process
       SIGTSTP   18,20,24   Stop     Stop typed at tty
       SIGTTIN   21,21,26   Stop     tty input for background process
       SIGTTOU   22,22,27   Stop     tty output for background process
```

Note that you can get the online manual page for a command by issuing **man** *command_name.* You can view an online manual page from a specific section by specifying the *section* number. To view the **signal** man page in section 7, issue the following command:

 # man 7 signal

This produces the signal(7) man page. If you were to type just man signal the signal(2) man page would be produced; that is, the man page for signal in section *2* would be shown.

To kill a process with id *234* with *SIGKILL,* issue the following command:

```
# kill -9 234
    |    |   |
    |    |   |> process id (PID)
    |    |> signal number
    |> kill command to terminate the process
```

Keep in mind that the signal definitions may differ among Linux variants.

Users and Groups

There are many options to choose from when you're setting up a user. Once set up, however, user administration is not typically a function that you'll spend a lot of time managing.

You have to make some basic decisions about every user they set up. Where should users' data be located? Who needs to access data from whom, thereby defining "groups" of users? What kind of particular startup is required by users and applications? Is there a shell that your users will prefer? Then the customization of the graphical user interface used on your system is another consideration.

Among the most important considerations you have is related to user data. A big system administration headache is rearranging user data, for several reasons. It doesn't fit on a whole disk (in which, case you need a volume manager in order for directories to span multiple disks), users can't freely access one another's data, or even worse, users *can* access one another's data too freely.

This section considers these questions, but first, look at the basic steps to add a user. Here is a list of activities:

- Select a user name to add.
- Select a user ID number.
- Select a group for the user.
- Create an **/etc/passwd** entry.
- Assign a user password (including expiration options).
- Select and create a home directory for user.
- Select the shell the user will run (this will be Bash by default).
- Place startup files in the user's home directory.
- Test the user account.

The **adduser** script allows you to enter the information in the bullet list as well as other information. The following output shows the *usage* of the **adduser** command:

```
# adduser
usage: adduser  [-u uid [-o]] [-g group] [-G group,...]
                [-d home] [-s shell] [-c comment] [-m [-k template]]
                [-f inactive] [-e expire ] [-p passwd] [-M] [-n] [-r] name
        adduser  -D [-g group] [-b base] [-s shell]
                [-f inactive] [-e expire ]
```

You can see from this list that you can specify all user-related information at the command line with **adduser**.

Most of what you do is entered in the **/etc/passwd** file, where information about all users is stored. When you create a user with **adduser**, you'll see the entry in **/etc/passwd** for the user you create. An entry for the user is also made in **/etc/shadow**, which is used for shadow passwords. There will be two exclamaton marks (!!) in **/etc/shadow** for the user, indicating that it is locked. An entry is made in **/etc/group** for the user with an *x* in the password field indicating that a shadow password exists for the user. There is also an entry in **/etc/gshadow** that also has the two exclamation marks, indicating that it is locked. The system administrator can then use the **passwd** command to unlock the account using the command **passwd** *username*.

Note that by default, the Red Hat version of **adduser** creates user account using the values specified on the command line and system defaults. The new user account will be entered into the system files as needed, the home directory will be created, and initial files copied, depending on the command line options. If you do not specify a group or use the **-n** option, **adduser** will create a group for each user added to the system.

You can also make these entries to the **/etc/passwd** file with the **vipw** command. Figure 10-1 is a sample **/etc/passwd** entry.

oracle:xxx:200:201:Oracle User:/home/oracle:/bin/ksh

root:x:0:0:root:/root:/bin/bash
```
|   | | | |     |     |
|   | | | |     |     |> shell
|   | | | |     |
|   | | | |     |> home directory
|   | | | |
|   | | | |> optional user info
|   | | |> group ID (GID)
|   | |> user ID (UID)
|   |> password
|> name
```

Figure 10-1   Sample **/etc/passwd** Entry

Here is a description of each of these fields:

name.   The user name you assign. This name should be easy for the user and other users on the system to remember. When sending electronic mail or copying files from one user to another, the more easily you can remember the user name, the better. If a user has a user name on another system, you may want to assign the same user name on your Linux system. Some systems don't permit nice, easy user names, so you may want to break the tie with the old system and start using sensible, easy-to-remember user names on your Linux system. Remember, no security is tied to the user name; security is handled through the user's password and the file permissions.

password.   This is the user's password in encrypted form. If an asterisk appears in this field, the account can't be used. If it is empty, the user has no password assigned and can log in by typing only his or her user name. I strongly recommend that each user have a password that he or she changes periodically. Every system has different security needs, but at a minimum, every user on every system should have a password. When setting up a new user, you can force the user to create a password at first login by putting a ,.. in the password field.

Some features of a good password are:

- A minimum of six characters that should include special characters such as a slash (/), a dot (.), or an asterisk (*).

- No dictionary words should be used for a password.

- Don't make the password personal such as name, address, favorite sports team, etc.

- Don't use something easy to type such as *123456* or *qwerty*.

- Some people say that misspelled words are acceptable, but I don't recommend using them. Spell check programs that match misspelled words to correctly spelled words can be used to guess at words that might be misspelled for a password.

- A password generator that produces unintelligible passwords works the best, but that they are often hard to remember causing users to write them down, thus loosing some of the advantage associated with there unintelligibility.

user ID (UID).   The identification number of the user. Every user on your system should have a unique UID. Most system users are automatically assigned UIDs of less than 100. These are normally automatically assigned by Linux. The system normally assigns standard users starting at UID 500.

group ID (GID).   The identification number of the group. The members of the group and their GID are in the **/etc/group** file. The system administrator can change the GID assigned if they don't like it, but they may also have to change the GID of many files. As a user creates a file, his or her UID is assigned to the file as well as the GID. This means that if the system administrator changes the GID well after users of the same group have created many files and directories, they may have to change the GID of all these.

optional user info.   In this space, you can make entries, such as the user's phone number or full name. You can leave this blank, but if you manage a system or network with many users, you may want to add the user's full name and extension so that if you need to get in touch with him or her, you'll have the information at your fingertips.

home directory.   The home directory defines the default location for all the users' files and directories. This is the present working directory at the time of login.

shell.   This is the startup program that the user will run at the time of login. The shell is really a command interpreter for the commands the user issues from the command line. The system administrator usually decides what shells are supported based on the setup files they have developed. On Linux systems, the default shell is normally Bash.

The location of the user's home directory is another important entry in the **/etc/passwd** file. You have to select a location for the user's "home" directory in the file system where the user's files will be stored. With some of the advanced networking technology that exists, such as NFS, the user's home directory does not even have to be on a disk that is physically connected to the computer he or she is using! The traditional place to locate a user's home directory on a Linux system is the **/home** directory.

The **/home** directory is typically the most dynamic in terms of growth. Users create and delete files in their home directory on a regular basis. So, you have to do more planning related to your user area than in more static areas, such as the root file system and application areas.

The **passwd** file has a way of getting out-of-date on a regular basis. Users come and go, and in general, there are continuous changes made to this file. There is a program on most Linux variants called **pwck** that checks the integrity of the **passwd** file. Interestingly, this program is often accessible to users as well as the system administrator. The following example shows running **pwck** on the default file used for passwords:

```
# pwck
user adm: directory /var/adm does not exist
user news: directory /var/spool/news does not exist
user uucp: directory /var/spool/uucp does not exist
user gopher: directory /var/gopher does not exist
user ftp: directory /var/ftp does not exist
pwck: no changes
#
```

This example shows that the login directory for several users does not exist. This absence may not be a problem, because some applications require a login name, but no home directory is required such as those shown. On the other hand, there are usually users on the system for which there is no login directory because the directory was removed when the user left the company but their entry in **passwd** was not removed. **pwck** validates the following information in the password file you specify (this is **passwd** by default):

- Correct number of fields
- Login name
- User ID
- Group ID
- Login directory exists
- Valid primary group
- User's default shell exists

pwck is a useful program that is underused. I often run audits for system administrators to check the health of their systems and include this program under the many security checks. There is no response if **pwck** finds no errors or warnings to report.

Assigning Users to Groups

After defining all user-related information, the system administrator needs to consider groups. Groups are often overlooked in the Linux environment until the system administrator finds that all his or her users are in the same group, even though from an organizational standpoint they are in different groups. Before I cover the groups in general, let's look at a file belonging to a user and the way access is defined for a file:

```
# ls -l backup.sh
-rwxr-xr--    1 linuconnect      users        1977 Jan  1 23:11 backup.sh
#
```

For every file on the system, Linux supports three classes of access:

- User access (u). Access granted to the owner of the file
- Group access (g). Access granted to members of the same group as the owner of the file
- Other access (o). Access granted to everyone else

These access rights are defined by the settings on the permissions of r (read), write (w), and execute (x) when the long listing command is issued. For the long listing (**ls -l**) above, you see the permissions in Table 10-1.

Table 10-1   Long Listing Permissions

Access	User Access	Group Access	Other
Read	r	r	-
Write	w	-	-
Execute	x	x	x

You can see that access rights are arranged in groups of three. Three groups of permissions exist with three access levels each. The owner, in this case, *linuconnect*, is allowed read, write, and execute permissions on the file. Anyone in the group *users* is permitted read and execute access to the file. Others are permitted only execute access of the file.

These permissions are important to consider as you arrange your users into groups. If several users require access to the same files, the system administrator will want to put those users in the same group. The trade-off here is that you can give all users within a group *rwx* access to files, but then you run the risk of several users editing a file without other users knowing it, thereby causing confusion. On the other hand, you can make several copies of a file so that each user has his or her personal copy, but then you have multiple versions of a file. If possible, assign users to groups based on their work.

The **/etc/group** file contains the group name, an encrypted password (which is rarely used), a group ID, and a list of users in the group. Here is an example of an **/etc/group** file:

```
# more /etc/group
root:x:0:root
bin:x:1:root,bin,daemon
daemon:x:2:root,bin,daemon
sys:x:3:root,bin,adm
adm:x:4:root,adm,daemon
tty:x:5:
disk:x:6:root
lp:x:7:daemon,lp
mem:x:8:
kmem:x:9:
wheel:x:10:root
mail:x:12:mail
news:x:13:news
uucp:x:14:uucp
man:x:15:
games:x:20:
gopher:x:30:
dip:x:40:
ftp:x:50:
lock:x:54:
nobody:x:99:
users:x:100:billg
slocate:x:21:
floppy:x:19:
vcsa:x:69:
utmp:x:22:
mailnull:x:47:
rpm:x:37:
ntp:x:38:
rpc:x:32:
xfs:x:43:
gdm:x:42:
rpcuser:x:29:
nfsnobody:x:65534:
nscd:x:28:
ident:x:98:
radvd:x:75:
pcap:x:77:
mfpo:x:500:
linuxconnect:x:501
apache:x:48:
```

```
sshd:x:74:
smmsp:x:51:
canna:x:39:
desktop:x:80:
#
```

The **group** file also has a way of getting out-of-date on a regular basis. As users come and go there are both changes to the **passwd** and **group** files required. There is a program on most Linux variants, called **grpck**, that checks the integrity of the **group** file. **grpck** validates the following information in the group file you specify (this is **group** by default):

- Correct number of fields

- Group name

- Group ID

- Login name exceeds maximum number of groups

- Login names appear in password file

grpck is a useful program that is underused. I often run audits for system administrators to check the health of their systems and include this program under the many security checks.

Also note that Linux provides are serveral other user and group management commands. If you're interested, take a look at the manual pages for **groupadd**, **groupdel**, **groupmod**, **useradd**, **userdel**, and **usermod**

Disk-Related Concepts

System administrators typically spend a great deal of time setting up, managing, and monitoring disks and file systems (see, for example "Disk and File System Topics," in Chapter 4). The basics are covered here but I don't want to cover any setup procedures. Users typically aren't permitted access to the commands used to set up disks, file systems, and so on. It is still useful, however, to be able to view the way your system and environment have been set up.

This secion covers a variety of topics including viewing file systems, viewing swap space, viewing some setup files, and a review of Network File System (NFS).

Viewing Mounted File Systems and Swap

One of the first activities you would perform when interested in file systems is to see what file systems are currently mounted on your system and their characteristics. The **df** command produces a listing of mounted file systems and some space-related information on each. The following is an example shows issuing the **df** command with the *--help* option, then just **df**, and finally **df -h**:

```
# df --help
Usage: df [OPTION]... [FILE]...
Show information about the filesystem on which each FILE resides,
or all filesystems by default.

Mandatory arguments to long options are mandatory for short options too.
  -a, --all              include filesystems having 0 blocks
  -B, --block-size=SIZE  use SIZE-byte blocks
  -h, --human-readable   print sizes in human readable format (e.g., 1K 234M 2G)
  -H, --si               likewise, but use powers of 1000 not 1024
  -i, --inodes           list inode information instead of block usage
  -k                     like --block-size=1K
  -l, --local            limit listing to local filesystems
      --no-sync          do not invoke sync before getting usage info (default)
  -P, --portability      use the POSIX output format
      --sync             invoke sync before getting usage info
  -t, --type=TYPE        limit listing to filesystems of type TYPE
  -T, --print-type       print filesystem type
  -x, --exclude-type=TYPE limit listing to filesystems not of type TYPE
  -v                     (ignored)
      --help     display this help and exit
      --version  output version information and exit

SIZE may be (or may be an integer optionally followed by) one of following:
kB 1000, K 1024, MB 1,000,000, M 1,048,576, and so on for G, T, P, E, Z, Y.

Report bugs to <bug-fileutils@gnu.org>.

[root@linuxdev root]# df
Filesystem           1K-blocks      Used Available Use% Mounted on
/dev/hda5             381139       179034    182427  50% /
/dev/hda1             46636        14547     29681   33% /boot
/dev/hda3             1423096      265596    1085208 20% /home
none                 46928        0         46928    0% /dev/shm
/dev/hda2             3889924      2800228   892100  76% /usr
/dev/hda6             256667       70926     172489  30% /var
/dev/hdb1             38464340     29211248  7299188 81% /home/linuxconnect/backup

# df -h
Filesystem           Size  Used Avail Use% Mounted on
/dev/hda5            372M  175M  178M  50% /
```

```
/dev/hda1          45M    15M    28M   33%  /boot
/dev/hda3          1.4G   260M   1.0G  20%  /home
none               46M     0     45M    0%  /dev/shm
/dev/hda2          3.7G   2.7G   871M  76%  /usr
/dev/hda6          251M   70M    168M  30%  /var
/dev/hdb1          37G    28G    6.9G  81%  /home/linuxconnect/backup
```

The first option produces a listing of all options to the **df** command. The second time you issued the **df** command with no options. Finally, you produced an output with the *-h* option that shows the output in an easy-to-read format.

Another important topic related to file systems is swap space.

You can view swap information on most Linux variants using the **parted** command, as shown in the following example:

```
# parted
GNU Parted 1.4.24
Copyright (C) 1998, 1999, 2000, 2001, 2002 Free Software Foundation, Inc.
This program is free software, covered by the GNU General Public License.

This program is distributed in the hope that it will be useful, but WITHOUT ANY WARRANTY;
without even the implied warranty of MERCHANTABILITY or FITNESS FOR A PARTICULAR PUR-
POSE.
See the GNU General Public License for more details.

Using /dev/hda
Information: The operating system thinks the geometry on /dev/hda is 784/255/63.
(parted) help
  check MINOR                       do a simple check on the filesystem
  cp [FROM-DEVICE] FROM-MINOR TO-MINOR      copy filesystem to another partition
  help [COMMAND]                    prints general help, or help on COMMAND
  mklabel LABEL-TYPE                create a new disklabel (partition table)
  mkfs MINOR FS-TYPE                make a filesystem FS-TYPE on partititon MINOR
  mkpart PART-TYPE [FS-TYPE] START END      make a partition
  mkpartfs PART-TYPE FS-TYPE START END      make a partition with a filesystem
  move MINOR START [END]            move partition MINOR
  name MINOR NAME                   name partition MINOR NAME
  print                             display the partition table
  quit                              exit program
  resize MINOR START END            resize filesystem on partition MINOR
  rm MINOR                          delete partition MINOR
  select DEVICE                     choose the device to edit
  set MINOR FLAG STATE              change a flag on partition MINOR
(parted) print
Disk geometry for /dev/hda: 0.000-6149.882 megabytes
Disk label type: msdos
Minor    Start        End      Type        Filesystem  Flags
1          0.031     47.065    primary     ext3        boot
2         47.065   3906.430    primary     ext3
3       3906.431   5318.393    primary     ext3
4       5318.394   6149.882    extended
5       5318.424   5702.761    logical     ext3
6       5702.792   5961.621    logical     ext3
7       5961.652   6149.882    logical     linux-swap
(parted) quit
[root@linuxdev root]#
```

In this example, you issued **parted**, then the *help* option, then the *print* option, and finally the *quit* option.

As you can see, the output from **parted** has to be interpreted. The *boot* partition, for instance, has a *Start* and *End* in MB. This partition is shown in the **df -h** output as being *45M*. The next partition, which is *2*, corresponds to / on the **df -h** output that shows a size of *372M*. Because the **parted** output has a *Start* and *End* entry you have to perform a little arithmetic in order to determine the size of the partition. When you get to *linux-swap,* you have to subtract the *Start* from *End* to see the size of this partition. The partitions are not listed in the same order in the two outputs. You can also use **fdisk** to view all the partitions including swap space, as shown in the following listing:

```
# fdisk /dev/hda -l

Disk /dev/hda: 255 heads, 63 sectors, 784 cylinders
Units = cylinders of 16065 * 512 bytes

    Device Boot    Start      End     Blocks   Id  System
/dev/hda1    *         1        6      481631  83  Linux
/dev/hda2              7      498     3951990  83  Linux
/dev/hda3            499      678     1445850  83  Linux
/dev/hda4            679      784      851445   5  Extended
/dev/hda5            679      727      393561  83  Linux
/dev/hda6            728      760      265041  83  Linux
/dev/hda7            761      784     192748+  82  Linux swap
#
```

This output is different than **parted** and has the added column of *Blocks*, which makes it easier to determine the size of swap on this disk.

You can also use **parted** and **fdisk** to manipulate the partitions.

Determining Disk Usage

System administrators like to know the amount of disk space consumed on their system by users, applications, groups, and so on. It's a good idea to know the disk hogs on a system. The **du** command helps with this determination. With **du**, you specify a file for which you want to view disk usage. You can also use the *-s* option to produce a summary as shown in the following example for the entries in the **/usr** directory:

```
# du -s *
200680   OpenOffice.org1.0
125948   X11R6
160680   bin
4        dict
4        etc
24       games
61700    include
3556     kerberos
950512   lib
49412    libexec
92       local
16       lost+found
15956    sbin
766292   share
432524   src
0        tmp
# Á
```

To see the entire disk usage of this directory in summary form, issue the following command:

```
# du -s
2767404  .
#
```

This output shows the total disk usage in this directory as roughly 2.74 GB. This can be confirmed by running the **df** command also. Running **du** on a regular basis shows the amount of space various directories are consuming and can be used to identify areas of your system in which disk space has increased dramatically over a short period of time.

Scheduling Cron Jobs

You can schedule tasks for periodic execution using the **cron** daemon. The **cron** daemon starts specified tasks at specified times as defined in the **crontab** files. The **cron** daemon starts when the system boots and remains running as long as the system is up.

cron works by reading configuration files and acting on their contents. A typical configuration file would include the command to be run, the day and time to run the command, and the user name under which the command should be run. You can look at this scheduling of jobs as a way of issuing commands at a specific time. The configuration files are called **crontab** files.

crontab files are usually in the **/var/spool/cron/crontabs** directory. The Red Hat Linux system **crontab** files used in some of the upcoming examples were run are in **/var/spool/cron**.

The format of entries in the **crontab** file are as follows:

minute   hour   monthday   month   weekday   user name   command

where:

minute — the minute of the hour, from 0-59.
hour — the hour of the day, from 0-23.
monthday — the day of the month, from 1-31.
month — the month of the year, from 1-12.
weekday — the day of the week, from 0 (Sunday) - 6 (Saturday).
user name — the user who will run the command if necessary
              (not used in the example).
command — specifies the command line or script file to run.

Be sure to check your Linux variant to ensure that **crontab** entries are in the same format and that the entries are in the same order.

You have many options in the **crontab** file for specifying the *minute, hour, monthday, month,* and *weekday* to perform a task. You could list one entry in a field and then a space, several entries in any field separated by a comma, two entries separated by a dash indicating a range, or an asterisk, which corresponds to all possible entries for the field.

Now, create the simplest imaginable example to see how **cron** works. Create a file called **listing** with the following contents in your home directory (*/root* on a Linux system):

```
* * * * * ls -l / > /root/listing.out
```

This file produces a long listing of the root directory every minute and send the output to **listing.out** in our home directory.

To "activate" or "install" the **crontab**, simply issue the **crontab** command and the name of the file. You could also specify a user name if you wanted to associate the file with a specific user. After installing the **crontab** file, issue **crontab -l** to view the installed **crontab** files. The following example shows the process of working with our **crontab** file called **listing**:

```
# cat listing
* * * * * ls -l / > /root/listing.out

# crontab listing

# crontab -l
# DO NOT EDIT THIS FILE - edit the master and reinstall.
# (listing installed on Thu Jan  2 11:34:25 2003)
# (Cron version -- $Id: crontab.c,v 2.13 1994/01/17 03:20:37 vixie Exp $)
* * * * * ls -l / > /root/listing.out

# ls -l | grep list
-rw-r--r--    1 root         root                38 Jan  2 11:33 listing
-rw-r--r--    1 root         root              1315 Jan  2 11:35 listing.out

# cat listing.out
total 164
drwxr-xr-x    2 root         root              1024 Oct 26 20:53 asodev_home
drwxr-xr-x    2 root         root              1024 Jun 30  2002 backup
drwxr-xr-x    2 root         root              1024 Jul  3  2002 bill
drwxr-xr-x    2 root         root              2048 Oct 17 15:27 bin
drwxr-xr-x    4 root         root              1024 Dec 24 00:05 boot
drwxr-xr-x   20 root         root            116736 Dec 24 00:09 dev
drwxr-xr-x   60 root         root              4096 Jan  1 23:30 etc
drwxr-xr-x    7 root         root              4096 Nov 16 14:06 home
drwxr-xr-x    2 root         root              1024 Jun 21  2001 initrd
drwxr-xr-x    7 root         root              4096 Oct 17 15:28 lib
drwxrwxrwx    2 linuxconnect linuxconnect      1024 Nov  9 11:15 linuxconnect
drwx------    2 root         root             12288 Jun 11  2002 lost+found
drwxr-xr-x    2 root         root              1024 Aug 27 00:49 misc
drwxr-xr-x    4 root         root              1024 Dec 24 00:06 mnt
drwxr-xr-x    2 root         root              1024 Aug 23  1999 opt
dr-xr-xr-x   86 root         root                 0 Dec 23 19:05 proc
drwxr-x---   30 root         root              2048 Jan  2 11:35 root
drwxr-xr-x    2 root         root              5120 Oct 17 18:24 sbin
drwxrwxrwt   15 root         root              2048 Jan  2 11:02 tmp
drwxr-xr-x   17 root         root              4096 Oct 17 13:05 usr
drwxr-xr-x   22 root         root              1024 Nov  8 09:55 var

# crontab -r

# crontab -l
no crontab for root
#
```

The first command shows the contents of the file **listing** that you created. Next, issue the **crontab** command to install **listing**. Next, issue **crontab -l** to see the file we have installed. Next is a long listing of our home directory, which shows that the file **listing.out** has indeed been produced. Then, **cat** the file to see its contents. Then, remove the installed file with **crontab -r**. Issuing **crontab -l** as the last command shows that no **crontab** files are installed for the user root.

System administrators get a lot of use out of **cron** by scheduling many time- and resource-consuming jobs during off hours. A typical task that is scheduled at night are backups.

The following hybrid example shows how a system administrator would schedule the full backup on day 6 and the incremental backup on other days. This is a hybrid example whereby you would substitute actual commands for the "full backup command" and "incremental backup commands":

```
$ crontab -l

00 2 * * 6 full backup command
15 12 * * 1-5 incremental backup command
```

The first entry is the full backup, and the second entry is the incremental backup. In the first entry, the *minute* is 00; in the second entry, the *minute* is 15. In the first entry, the *hour* is 2; in the second entry, the *hour* is 12. In both entries, the *monthday* and *month* are all legal values (*), meaning every *monthday* and *month*. In the first entry, the *weekday* is 6 for Saturday (0 is Sunday); in the second entry, the *weekdays* are 1-5, or Monday through Friday. The optional *user name* is not specified in either example. Finally, the backup command is provided:

minute	hour	monthday	month	weekday	user name	command
00	2	all	all	6	n/a	full backup
15	12	all	all	1-5	n/a	incremental

Another common use of **cron** for system administrators is to find *core* files on a daily or weekly basis. *Core* files are images of memory written to disk when a problem of some kind is encountered on the system. They can be written in a variety of places on the system depending on the problem. These files can sometimes be used to identify the source of the problem, so system administrators like to keep track of them. The following **find** command will be run once a week to find *core* files that have not been accessed in a week and writes the *core* file names to a file in the home directory of root:

```
00 2 * * 6 find / -name core -atime 7 > /root/core.files
```

The system administrator checks this file on Monday to see what core files have been produced over the last week. Similar to the backup example, this check is run every Saturday at 2:00 AM.

Users sometimes set up **cron** entries to invoke large compilations or large batch jobs during the night when the system is not heavily used. As long as your system administrator has not denied you access to running **cron** jobs, you are free to set up your own jobs. Your system administrator can list users who are permitted to use **cron** in the **cron.allow** file. If you are not listed in this file, the format of which is one user per line, you cannot run the **crontab** program. If **cron.allow** does not exist, **cron.deny** is checked to see whether any users have been explicitly denied access to **crontab**.

cron is very easy to use. Simply create your file, such I as had done with **listing** in the earlier example, and run **crontab** against the file. If you have jobs you would like to see run on a regular basis, such as running your **make** at night, **cron** is a useful tool.

at

If you have a command you want to schedule to run only one time, you can use the **at** command. You can specify the **at** command, the *time* at which you want a command executed, and then at the *at>* prompt, the *command* to execute. The following shows an example to find all core files at 11:57 A.M.:

```
# at 11:57AM
warning: commands will be executed using (in order) a) $SHELL b) login shell c) /bin/sh
at> find / -name core > /tmp/core.files
at> <EOT>
job 5 at 2003-01-02 11:57
You have new mail in /var/spool/mail/root

# date
Thu Jan  2 11:57:25 EST 2003

# ps -ef | grep find
root     31015 31014  1 11:57 ?        00:00:00 find / -name core
root     31018 30456  0 11:57 pts/3    00:00:00 grep find
#
```

After issuing **at** and the time, the *at>* prompt appears for you to issue the *command*. You then press **^d** (control d) at the next prompt to return to your usual shell prompt.

The output of the **ps** command shows that this find command is indeed running.

Device Files

Device files are a way to access system devices. An application that uses a device doesn't need to know about the underlying device and how it works. When you access a device file the kernel manages the I/O request and passes it to the device driver. The device driver then performs an operation such as sending data to a tape drive. The device driver is built into the kernel which allows the kernel to manage access to the device.

This section covers some important aspects of device files, including the following:

- Some commonly used device files.

- The structure of device files.

- An example of creating a device file.

Generally speaking, device files on Linux systems are character or block devices. Character devices expect the driver and other aspects of the Linux system to manage input and output buffering of data. Block devices expect the file system and kernel to perform buffering for them. Most hard disk drives have both a block and character device file. This provides flexibility in the way in which the hardware is used.

A device file provides the Linux kernel with important information about a specific device. The Linux kernel needs to know a lot about a device before input/output operations can be performed.

Device files are located in **/dev** on Linux systems. You've already seen many device files loading the operating system and performing other tasks. For instance, the SCSI disk on which you loaded Linux on an Integrity server is **/dev/sda**; the IDE drive on which you loaded Linux is **/dev/hda**. There are many other device files of which you should be aware. There may also be a subdirectory under **/dev** used to further categorize the device files such as **/dev/inet**. Table 10-2 lists some of the more commonly used device files along with a comment for each.

Table 10-2   Examples of Linux Device Files

Device	Comments
/dev/hda	First IDE hard drive
/dev/hda1	Primary partition 1 of first IDE hard drive (next is 2 and so on)
/dev/hdb	Second IDE hard drive (next is c and so on)
/dev/hdb1	Primary partition 1 of second IDE hard drive (next is 2 and so on)
/dev/sda	First SCSI hard drive
/dev/sda1	Primary partition 1 of first IDE hard drive (next is 2 and so on)
/dev/sdb	Second SCSI hard drive (next is c and so on)
/dev/sdb1	Primary partition 1 of second SCSI hard drive (next is 2 and so on)
/dev/fd0	First floppy drive (A:)
/dev/st0	SCSI tape drive.
/dev/ttyS0	Serial port on COM1

Although many other device files exist on your system, these are some of the more commonly used ones.

As described earlier, a device file provides the Linux kernel with important information about a specific device. The Linux kernel needs to know a lot about a device before Input/Output operations can be performed.

There is some embedded information that is part of the device file that you need to know should you decide to create your own device file. You need to know some of this information if you were to create your own device file using the **mknod** command. Before you create a device file, list the installed hardware on an IA-32 system with the **lsdev** command:

```
# lsdev
Device            DMA    IRQ   I/O Ports
-------------------------------------------------
00:11.0                        fc80-fcff
3Com                           fc80-fcff
cascade            4      2
dma                            0080-008f
dma1                           0000-001f
dma2                           00c0-00df
eth0                      9
fpu                            00f0-00ff
ide0                     14    01f0-01f7 03f6-03f6 ffa0-ffa7
ide1                     15    0170-0177 0376-0376 ffa8-ffaf
Intel                          ff80-ff9f ffa0-ffaf
isapnp                         0213-0213 0a79-0a79
keyboard                  1    0060-006f
```

```
Mouse                   12
PCI                          0cf8-0cff
pic1                         0020-003f
pic2                         00a0-00bf
rtc                      8   0070-007f
serial                       03f8-03ff
timer                    0   0040-005f
usb-uhci                10   ff80-ff9f
vga+                         03c0-03df
#
```

This **lsdev** listing shows installed hardware and some relevant information for each. Notice though, that devices such as **hda** are not shown. A lot
of information about device files is not shown in **lsdev**.

Looking at the device files in **/dev** can reveal a lot of information about
any given device. The following is the format of the **mknod** (short for make
node) command that is used to manually create device files if they are not
already on your system:

```
mknod    name    type    [major]    [minor]
```

Now dissect a device file in **/dev**. The following is a long listing for a
SCSI tape drive device file:

```
# ls -al /dev/st0
crw-rw----    1 root      disk        9,    0 Aug 30 19:31 /dev/st0
```

This device has a name of **/dev/st0**. It is a *character* device as indicated
by the *c* (as opposed to a block device *b* or a named pipe *p*,) has a major
number of *9* which corresponds to a SCSI tape drive, a minor number of *0*
which corresponds to the drive number. If this device did not exist, the
mknod command to create it would look like the following:

```
# mknod /dev/st0 c 9 0
```

After executing this command, you have the SCSI tape device file we
need. Figure 10-2 shows the components in our **mknod** command.

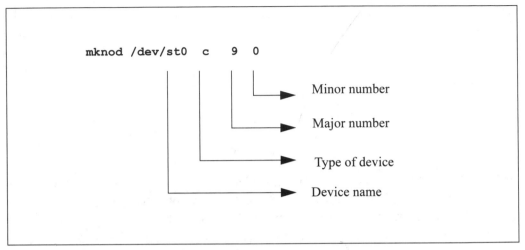

Figure 10-2   **mknod** Command

You'll see the device name, type of device, major and minor numbers when you view a device in **/dev**.

You may never have to create a device file on your system; however, it is good to have some background on device files. You will certainly have to use many device files, such as your hard disks, floppy disks, tape drives, and so on. Therefore, at a minimum you need to know the name you'll use to access these devices.

Printing

UNIX and UNIX-like systems run a variety of programs related to printing called *lp* (for line printing). These programs work together to support printing of text files, formatted documents, graphics files, and so on. This section covers the basics of printing, including some of the basics of printer administration.

To simply print a file called **mbox**, you would use the **lp** (short for line printer) command, as shown in the following example:

```
martyp $ lp mbox
Job number is: 1
martyp $
```

In this example, you requested that the file **mbox** be printed. You receive a return message from **lp**, indicating the request identification number. You can print multiple files with one **lp** request, as shown in the following example:

```
martyp $ ls -l
total 80
-rw-------  1 martyp   usr    350 Sep 27 07:22 dead.letter
-rw-rw-r--  1 martyp   usr  24576 Sep  6 07:07 inst.out
-rw-rw-r--  1 martyp   usr      0 Aug 21 06:45 lanadmin.list
-rw-------  1 martyp   usr   1485 Sep 27 08:20 mbox
-rw-rw-r--  1 martyp   usr    353 Sep 29 04:57 trip
-rw-rw-r--  1 martyp   perf   635 Mar 21 1999  typescript
martyp $ lp t*
Job number is: 2
martyp $
```

In this example, both files beginning with "t" were printed, and one job number is associated with the printing of both files.

Many UNIX systems have multiple printers connected. You can specify the printer you want to send the file(s) to with the **-d** option followed by the printer name. In the previous examples, the default system printer was used. You can specify the printer device to which our earlier print of **mbox** will go with the **-d** option, as shown in the following example:

```
martyp $ lp -d ros2228 mbox
Job number is: 3
martyp $
```

This output sends the file *mbox* to the printer we have specified, and again the job number is specified.

You can specify a default printer by setting the **LPDEST** environment variable. If set, this variable will be used when you do not specify a printer name, as shown in the following example:

```
martyp $ LPDEST=ros2228
martyp $ export LPDEST
martyp $ lp mbox
Job number is: 4
martyp $
```

The **LPDEST** environment variable is normally associated with a user's default printer. You can also specify the default printer in your startup file.

Print jobs are spooled to a printer so that you can proceed with other work. You don't have to wait until a print job completes without a problem before you move on. You can receive an electronic mail message if there was any problem with your print job using the **-m** option, as shown in the following example:

```
martyp $ lp -m t*
Job number is: 5
martyp $
```

In this case, we have again sent the two files beginning with "t" to the default printer we earlier set up. You can assume this print job will complete without any problem unless you receive an electronic mail message informing you otherwise.

Sometimes, you may want to see the status of printers on or attached to your system or network. The spooling functionality means that several files can be spooled to the printer, which means that you may have to wait for your file to print. There may only be one file ahead of yours in the print queue; however, it may be a very large file, such as a report from an ERP system. To obtain the status of printers, use the **lpstat** command. I normally issue this with the **-t** option to obtain a long status listing, as shown in the following example:

```
martyp $ lpstat -t
 Queue    Dev   Status       Job     Name       From       To
                             Submitted          Rnk Pri    Blks  Cp        PP %
 ------- ----- ---------   ---------          --- ---    ----- ---       ---- --
 a464     a464d READY
 a464:
          no entries
 a438     a438d READY
```

```
a438:
        no entries
a570    a570d READY
a570:
        no entries
a654    a654d READY
a654:
        no entries
a662    a662d READY
a662:

a662:

a662:

a662:

a946    a946d READY
a946:
        no entries
a956    a956d READY
a956:
        no entries
a732    a732d READY
a732: ros-ps4: Warning: a732 is down

a732: ros-ps4: Warning: a732 is down

a732: ros-ps4: Warning: a732 is down

a732: ros-ps4: Warning: a732 is down

a732: ros-ps4: Warning: a732 is down

a732: ros-ps4: Warning: a732 is down

a732: ros-ps4: Warning: a732 is down

a732: ros-ps4: Warning: a732 is down

a732: ros-ps4: Warning: a732 is down

a732: ros-ps4: Warning: a732 is down

a732: ros-ps4: Warning: a732 is down

ros2227 ros22 READY
ros2227:
        no entries
ros2228 ros22 READY
ros2228:

ros2228:

ros2228:

ros2228:

ros2228:

ros2228:

ros2228:

ros2228:

ros2228:

ros2228:

ros2228:
```

```
    ros2228:

    ros2228:

    ros2228:

martyp $
```

The output shows the status of all printers available to your system. You can see in this example that there are many printers connected to this system. I removed several printers from this output, because it was too long to include in this book. Several of the printers report warning messages indicating that they are "down," which of course, means that they are unable to print. We won't get into the troubleshooting of such problems here, because this is almost exclusively a problem that would be handled by the system administrator. If you want to obtain the status of the default printer, which was just set up, you can do so with the **-d** option, as shown in the following example:

```
martyp $ lpstat -d
Queue   Dev   Status    Job Files              User        PP %  Blks  Cp Rnk
------- ----- --------- --- ------------------ ----------  ---- -- ----- --- ---
ros2228 ros22 READY
ros2228:
ros2228:
ros2228:
ros2228:
ros2228:
ros2228:
martyp $
```

I often pull the trigger too quickly on a print job and need to cancel it. After a job is submitted, you can remove it with the **cancel** command, along with the job *id*. You can use the *job number* shown in earlier examples, along with the cancel command or use the printer name along with **cancel**. Small print jobs will normally be processed and printed too quickly to **cancel**. Large print jobs, however, may be canceled before they are complete.

You can use the **lpstat** command to obtain the job number, in the event that you did not write it down when you submitted the job.

Table 10-3 lists some of the most commonly used **lp**-related commands. Keep in mind that some of these are associated with system administration work, such as configuring printers and are not normally used by users.

Table 10-3 lp Commands

Command	Description
/usr/sbin/accept	Start accepting jobs to be queued
/usr/bin/cancel	Cancel a print job that is queued
/usr/bin/disable	Disable a device for printing
/usr/bin/enable	Enable a device for printing
/usr/sbin/lpfence	Set minimum priority for spooled file to be printed (not available on all UNIX variants)
/usr/bin/lp	Queue a job or jobs for printing
/usr/sbin/lpadmin	Configure the printing system with the options provided
/usr/sbin/lpmove	Move printing jobs from one device to another
/usr/sbin/lpsched	Start the lp scheduling daemon
/usr/sbin/lpshut	Stop the lp scheduling daemon
/usr/bin/lpstat	Show the status of printing based on the options provided
/usr/sbin/reject	Stop accepting jobs to be queued

Webmin

Let's take a look at a GUI management tool that you can download to a Linux system or one of several UNIX variants. The tool is *Webmin* and is available at *www.webmin.com*. I'm not advocating the use of this particular tool, although I think it is great, rather, I'm using it as an example of a tool that you can download and configure on a variety of operating systems thereby having a similar tool on many platforms. All the upcoming steps are on the Web site, but I'll cover some of the more salient aspects of installing *webmin*. Although I have not used this tool on Integrity servers yet I know that many of you are experimenting with Linux on IA-32 and may find this tool useful.

We start the process of loading *Webmin* by downloading the Linux version we want—in this case, for Red Hat. The software downloaded for Linux is in RPM format and we run the following command:

 # rpm -U webmin-0.990-1.norarch.rpm

This automatically installs *Webmin* in the **/usr/libexec/webmin**. There are a lot of files created in this directory. Of particular interest are the files beginning with **config-** that show the many distributions of operating systems for which *Webmin* is available. There are also directories such as **usermin** that contain files and scripts related user administration through *Webmin*. To run *Webmin,* open a browser window and connect to:

http://linuxdev:10000/

The name of the system used in the example is *linuxdev,* so you would substitute the name of your system. This opens up *Webmin* in your browser window, as shown in Figure 10-3.

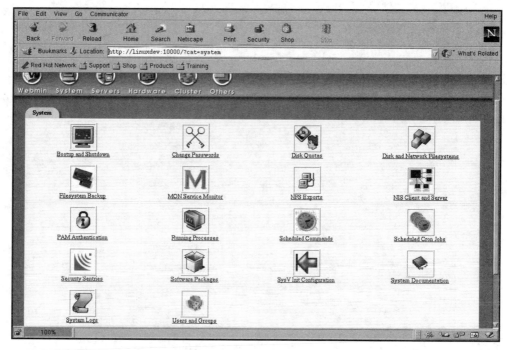

Figure 10-3   *Webmin* with System Selected

You can see that you can perform a variety of system-related tasks. We'll come back to the *Users and Groups* selection shortly. The main *Servers* selection also has many commonly performed selections beneath it, as shown in Figure 10-4.

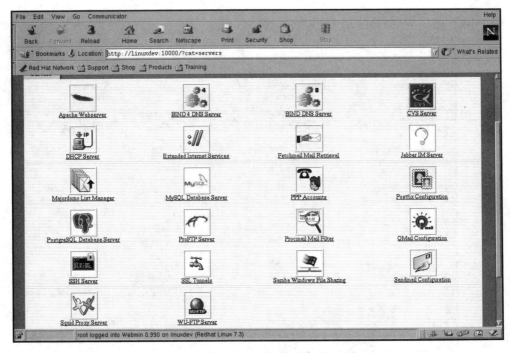

Figure 10-4   *Webmin* with *Servers* Selected

The *Servers* area has such commonly configured programs as *Apache, FTP,* and others. Going back to the *System* area and *Users and Groups,* you get a list of all users on the system, as shown in Figure 10-5.

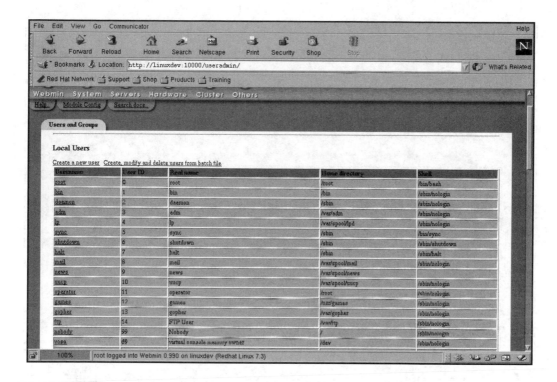

Figure 10-5　*Webmin* with *Users and Groups* Selected Under *System*

This window shows information related to your users that you could modify. If you select *Create a new user* from this area, you get the screen shown in Figure 10-6 in which we can enter all relevant user information.

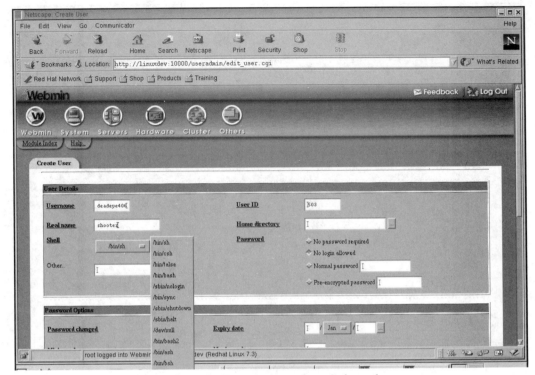

Figure 10-6   *Webmin* with *Create a new user* Selected

Viewing and creating users are just a few of the many commonly performed system administration tasks. Under *Hardware* and *Partitions on Local Disks,* you get the view shown in Figure 10-7.

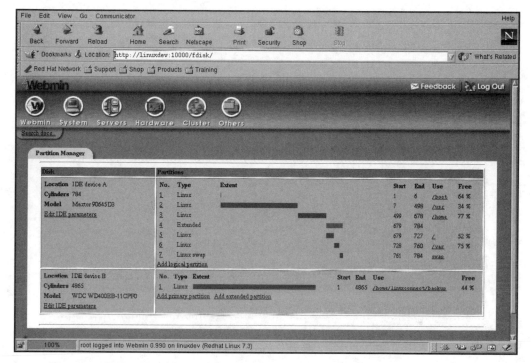

Figure 10-7 *Webmin* with *Hardware and Partitions on Local Disks*
Selected

In Figure 10-7, there are two IDE disks with partitions shown. The first
disk has several partitions and the second disk is just one big partition. We
can add partitions by selecting the *Add* buttons for the respective disks.

Webmin can perform many other functions that were not shown in this
section. This, like many tools, can be downloaded, used, and modified by
you to suit your system administration needs.

Chapter 11

Samba

Samba is an application that allows a Linux or UNIX host to act as a file server for Windows systems and Windows systems can access UNIX file systems and printers using their native Windows networking. This chapter demonstrates a Linux system mounting a Windows drive and a Windows system mapping a Linux drive.

This section gives an overview of the setup of Samba and demonstrates a subset of its functionality. This procedure works the same for the IA-32 and Integrity servers used throughout this book; that is, the Samba setup and concepts are the same. I performed the same Samba setup procedure on both the Integrity Advanced Server system and the Red Hat 8.x IA-32 system. The procedure is identical on both platforms. As a sidenote, the "retail" versions of Red Hat, such as 8.x used in this section, has been replaced by Fedora. Fedora Project is a Red Hat-sponsored and community-supported open source project. Fedora Core 2 is available at the time of this writing.

Samba provides its file-sharing functionality using Server Message Block (SMB) protocol. SMB runs on top of TCP/IP. In this section's example, both the Windows system and UNIX system are running TCP/IP and SMB. These provide all the technology that is required to establish file sharing between the two systems.

At the time of this writing, Samba contains the functionalities just mentioned: file-sharing, printer sharing, and advanced user access control of files. There are many advancements taking place with Samba and other software provided under GNU Public License (GPL) as free software. Because the software is free, many individuals have access to it and spend time enhancing the software. For this reason, you may find that additional functionality is included in Samba and other such software.

smb.conf Setup

Because Samba is supplied on the Red Hat Linux CD-ROM, we'll walk through a simple Samba setup using Red Hat Linux. When installing Red Hat Linux, you can select the software packages you want to load, as you can on most all UNIX variants. If you did not load Samba at the time you originally loaded the operating system, you can use a graphical *RPM* tool or **rpm** from the command line to load Samba or any other software. These tools were briefly discussed in the Chapter 10 covering System Administration.

The configuration file for Samba is **/etc/samba/smb.conf**. The **smb.conf** file has all Samba-related setup information in it. For our simple Samba setup in this chapter we need to have only a few lines in the file setup. You need to have a few *Global Settings* and *Share Definitions* in order to achieve file system sharing between Windows and Linux systems. The following are three select sections from **smb.conf** that were modified for the example in this section:

```
# workgroup = NT-Domain-Name or Workgroup-Name
  workgroup = DEVENV


  encrypt passwords = yes
  smb passwd file = /etc/samba/smbpasswd

[homes]
  comment = Home Directories
  browseable = yes
  writable = yes
  valid users = %S
  create mode = 0664
  directory mode = 0775
```

1. You have a *workgroup* of *DEVENV* specified.

2. You want your passwords to be *encrypted*; you want to use the file **/etc/samba/smbpasswd** for these encrypted passwords. You'll have a user on both the Windows and Linux systems with the same name.

3. You have some information related to our *Share Definitions*, such as making the *Home Directories browseable*.

You made only these three modifications to the **smb.conf** file; however, next you'll run a Samba utility called **testparm**. This utility checks your **/etc/smb.conf** file for errors. This utility produces a long output that I won't include here, but you'll want to run this and check for any warnings or errors it produces:

```
# testparm smb.conf

Load smb config files from smb.conf
Processing section "[homes]"
Processing section "[printers]"
Loaded services file OK.
Press enter to see a dump of your service definitions
# Global parameters
[global]
            coding system =
            client code page = 850
            code page directory = /usr/share/samba/codepages
            workgroup = DEVENV
            netbios name =
            netbios aliases =
            netbios scope =
            server string = Samba Server
            interfaces =
            bind interfaces only = No
            security = USER
            encrypt passwords = Yes
            update encrypted = No
            allow trusted domains = Yes
            hosts equiv =
            min passwd length = 5
            map to guest = Never
            null passwords = No
            obey pam restrictions = Yes
            password server =
            smb passwd file = /etc/samba/smbpasswd
```

- •
- •
- •

There were no warnings or errors produced from having run **testparm**, so proceed to the next step.

User Setup

You now need to create a user on both the Linux and Windows systems that can be used for our Samba-related work. It may already be that you have suitable users on your system. For the purposes of this demonstration, you'll create a user on both systems.

On the Linux system, you can use the **useradd** program from the command line or *User Manager* graphical program (*Programs-System-User Manager*) to add the user. The user appears in the **/etc/passwd** file after he or she has been added. Then, issue the following command to add the encrypted user passwd to the **/etc/samba/smbpasswd** file:

```
# smbpasswd -a linuxconnect
```

linuxconnect is the name of the user you created for this example. You can view the **smbpasswd** file to see the entry for your user.

This same user was created on the Windows system. The menu pick *Start-Programs-Administrative Tools-Computer Management (Local Users and Groups-Users)* was used to create *linuxconnect*.

Samba Startup

You can start Samba daemons every time the system boots or start them at the command line. The following commands show starting the daemons at the command line and then viewing them:

```
# /sbin/service smb start

Starting SMB services:          [  OK  ]
Starting NMB services:          [  OK  ]


# ps -ef | grep mbd
root      10828     1  0 16:59 ?       00:00:00 smbd -D
root      10833     1  0 16:59 ?       00:00:00 nmbd -D
#
```

You started the daemons with **/sbin/service smb start** and check to see the two daemons running with **ps**. Should you make a change to your Samba setup and want to restart the daemons, you could use **/sbin/service smb restart**.

The *smbd* server daemon provides the file and print services to SMB clients, such as Windows systems. SMB stands for "Server Message Block" and is defined as a network protocol for sharing files, printers, serial ports, and communications abstractions such as named pipes and mail slots between computers.

The *nmbd* server daemon allows for NetBIOS over IP name service requests over a network, like those produced by SMB/CIFS clients such as Windows systems. We have now performed all of the basic setup required to proceed with mounting disks.

Mapping a Windows Drive to a Linux Directory

Now we can both browse the Linux system from Windows as well as mount a specific drive directory of the Linux system on our Windows system. Figure 11-1 shows the window in which we specify the Linux system and directory we will mount as *F:* on the Windows system.

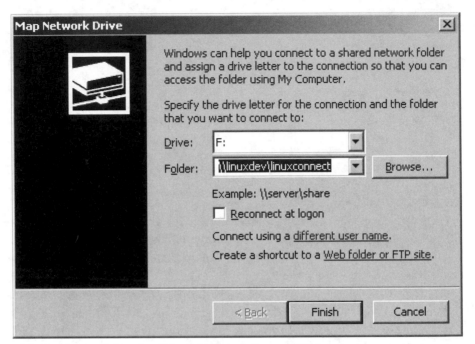

Figure 11-1   Mapping Linux Drive to **F:** on Windows

We specified the path of *\\linuxdev\linuxconnect* to mount on the Windows system drive **F:**. This is the hostname (*linuxdev*) and the user name (*linux-connect*). The system knows automatically to go to the home directory for *linuxconnect* and mounts that directory as **F:** for us on the Windows system as shown in the Figure 11-2.

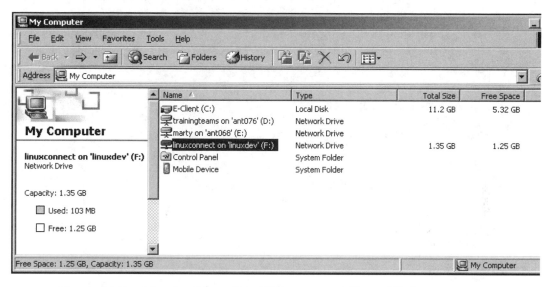

Figure 11-2   Viewing Linux Root Filesystem as F: on Windows

The **/home/linuxconnect** directory on our Linux system is now fully accessible on the Windows system. You can browse, edit, copy, and perform other tasks on these shared files.

You can use **net view** on your Windows system to see the shared resource of the Linux directory, as shown in the following listing:

```
c: net view \\linuxdev

Shared resources at \\linuxdev

Samba Server

Share name    Type          Used as   Comment

-------------------------------------------------------
homes         Disk          Home      Directories
linuxconnect  Disk          F:        Home Directories
The command completed successfully.
```

This listing shows that **F:** has your Linux directory mapped to it.

You may have mapped the drive using an IP address in which case you would specify the path using the IP address. The following example shows viewing the Integrity Advanced Server system with **net view** and the IP address:

```
c: net view \\15.32.162.129

Shared resources at \\15.32.162.129

Samba Server

Share name    Type           Used as   Comment

-----------------------------------------------------------------
homes         Disk                     Home Directories
linuxconnect  Disk           F:        Home Directories
The command completed successfull
```

This example shows the mapping of **F:** to **/home/linuxconnect** on the Integrity server.

Now, get the overall status of the Samba setup with the **smbclient** utility on our Linux system, as shown in the following listing:

```
# su - linuxconnect
$ smbclient -L linuxdev

added interface ip=192.168.1.102 bcast=192.168.1.255 nmask=255.255.255.0

Domain=[DEVENV] OS=[Unix] Server=[Samba 2.2.3a]

                Sharename     Type     Comment
                ---------     ----     -------
                homes         Disk     Home Directories
                IPC$          IPC      IPC Service (Samba Server)
                ADMIN$        Disk     IPC Service (Samba Server)
                linuxconnect  Disk     Home Directories

                Server                 Comment
                ---------              -------
                LINUXDEV               Samba Server

                Workgroup              Master
                ---------              -------
                ATLANTA2               F4457MXP
                DEVENV                 LINUXDEV
```

Before issuing the **smbclient** command, you changed user to *linuxconnect* and then issued the command.

This utility produces a useful summary of the Samba setup, including the share *linuxconnect* you set up, the Samba server for our example, and other useful information.

Keep in mind that Linux, including the Red Hat 8.x distribution used in this example, has a high level of security by default upon installation. The firewall setting on the system in the example was set too high for this drive to be mounted in the example. You first had to lower the security level of the firewall setting. Using the **/usr/sbin/setup** program and selecting *Firewall Configuration*, you lowered the *Security Level* to *No Firewall,* as shown in Figure 11-3.

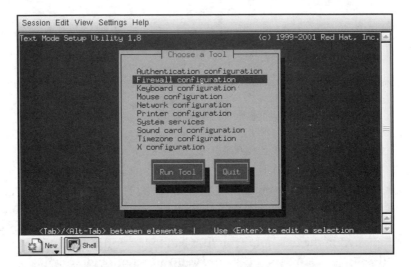

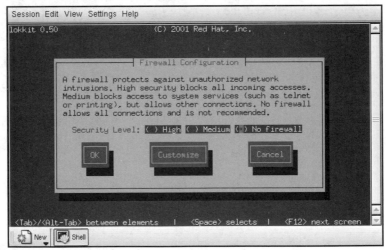

Figure 11-3 *setup* Program Used to Eliminate Firewall

You used *setup* to eliminate the firewall in this example. This greatly
reduces the overall security of the Linux system, so you have to consider this
before making the change. As a result of this selection, files on the system
were updated to permit more open access to the system, which gave you the

ability to map a network drive to your Linux system, but it also reduced the overall level of security on the system.

This did not have to be done on the Integrity server because at the time you installed Advanced Server in Chapter 2, you specified this low level of security.

Mounting a Windows Drive on a Linux System

The previous example demonstrated mapping a Linux file system to a Windows drive. This is commonly done because Linux file systems often act as file servers in a Windows environment. You can also get access to a Windows drive on the Linux system for file sharing purposes or to back up a Windows drive to a Linux system. The following commands show mounting the **C:** drive on the Windows system as the directory **/home/linuxconnect/ pcdev** on your Linux system:

```
# smbmount //F4457MXP/c /home/linuxconnect/pcdev -o username=linuxconnect
Password:
#
#
# cd /home/linuxconnect/pcdev
# ls
6.1_for_2002_Setup.exe   HP                     phone
~adpttmp                 I386                   PMig01.Log
aim95.exe                INFONET                PMig02.Log
AUTOEXEC.BAT             IO.SYS                 PMig03.Log
BDE                      kmd.exe                PMig0.Log
BOOT.BAK                 lj527en.exe            PMig.Log
boot.ini                 Morpheus-b3d-v2.exe    Program Files
BOOTLOG.TXT              MSDOS.SYS              Recycled
cmdcons                  My Music               RECYCLER
cmldr                    My Photos              RunDelay
COMMAND.COM              NETPRINTER             sdc_install.log
comreads.dbg             netzero.exe            sdc.ok
comused.dbg              NI                     setupmpe.exe
CONFIG.SYS               notworm                Support
data                     NTDETECT.COM           System Volume Information
DMI                      ntldr                  temp
Documents and Settings   OMNIBOOK               temp.ps
drivers                  OMNILIB                TOUR
ENV                      openmail.log           unzipped
FDWINW                   pagefile.sys           VERSION.INF
hiberfil.sys             Perl                   WINNT
#
```

In the **smbmount** command, you specified the name of the Windows system and the path (**/F4457MXP/c**) we wanted to mount on the Linux system. You could have specified any drive or a directory of any drive but you specified the full **C:** directory. You then specified the mount point on the Linux system of **/home/linuxconnect/pcdev** and the username of *linuxconnect*. You were then prompted for the password for this user and given access to the drive. The listing shows the entire **C:** drive has been mounted.

You could also have substituted an IP address for the PC hostname of *F4457MXP*. The following example shows having issued **df** and then **ls** to see the **C:** mounted on the Integrity server:

```
# df
Filesystem             1k-blocks        Used Available Use% Mounted on
/dev/sda3               68450624     3572680  61400812   6% /
/dev/sda1                 104184        6118     98066   6% /boot/efi
none                     1024576           0   1024576   0% /dev/shm
//15.244.168.25/c       11770880     8733440   3037440  75% /home/linuxconnect/pcdev
# ls /home/linuxconnect/pcdev/
6.1_for_2002_Setup.exe  DMI                    _NavCClt.Log    sdc_install.log
~adpttmp                Documents and Settings NETPRINTER      sdc.ok
aim95.exe               drivers                netzero.exe     setupmpe.exe
AUTOEXEC.BAT            ENV                    NI              Support
BDE                     FDWINW                 notworm         System Volume Information
BOOT.BAK                hiberfil.sys           NTDETECT.COM    temp
boot.ini                HP                     ntldr           temp.ps
BOOTLOG.TXT             I386                   OMNIBOOK        TOUR
ciretool                INFONET                OMNILIB         UNWISE.EXE
cmdcons                 INSTALL.LOG            openmail.log    UNWISE.INI
cmldr                   IO.SYS                 pagefile.sys    unzipped
COMMAND.COM             kmd.exe                Perl            VERSION.INF
comreads.dbg            1j527en.exe            phone           WINNT
comused.dbg             Morpheus-b3d-v2.exe    Program Files   WINS_updater
CONFIG.SYS              MSDOS.SYS              Recycled
cygwin                  My Music               RECYCLER
data                    My Photos              RunDelay
#
```

Now that the entire **C:** drive is accessible on the Linux system, you can perform any tasks on these files, such as perform a backup of the entire drive or selected files to the Linux system.

Figure 11-4 shows a Linux file manager window (*Konqueror*) open showing **C:** from the Windows system.

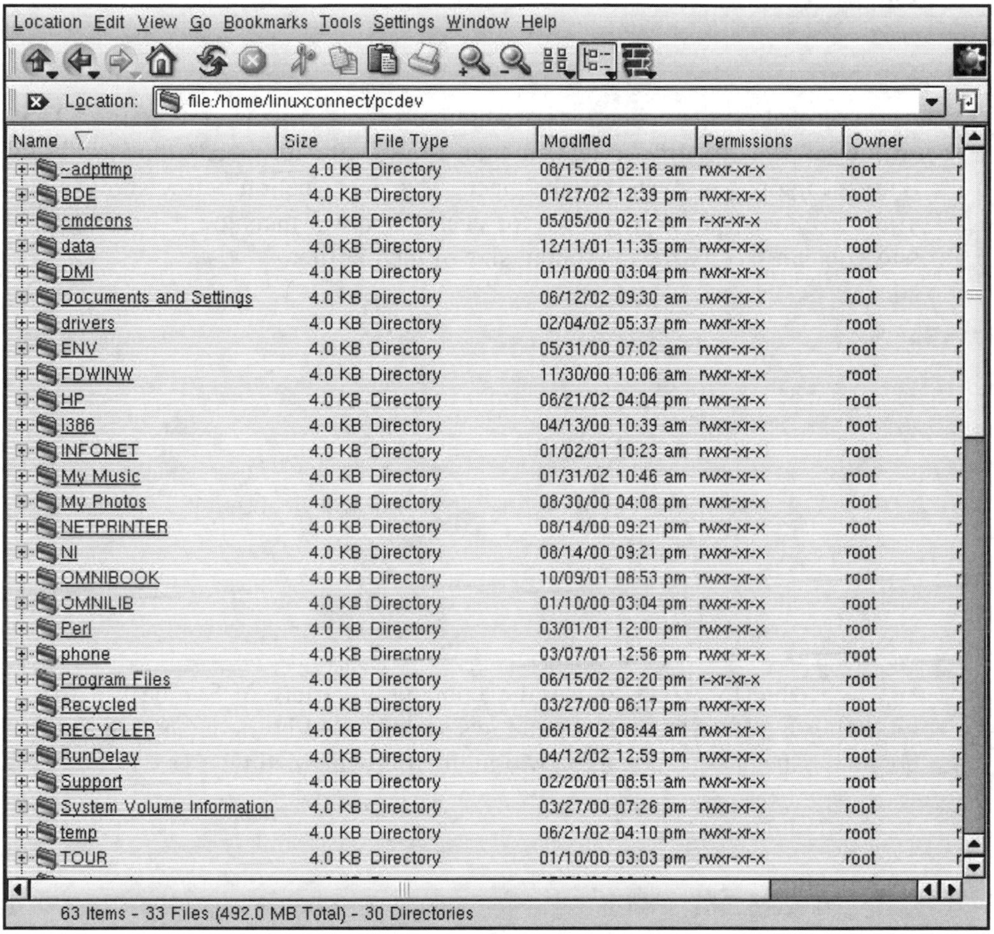

Figure 11-4   *Konqueror* Viewing **C:** on Linux System

Figure 11-4 shows folders on the **C:** drive of our Windows system displayed in one of the file manager windows on our Linux system. You can traverse this hierarchy freely to view, copy, and work with these files in other ways.

You have demonstrated mounts working in both directions. **C:** on the Windows system was mounted as **/home/linuxconnect/pcdev** on the Linux system. **/home/linuxconnect** was mapped to **F:** on the Windows system. Additional Samba functionality exists, such as print serving, that were not shown in this example.

Log Files

Like most UNIX applications, Samba provides extensive logging. The **smb.conf** file contains a section that allows you to specify the level of Samba logging you want to take place. The short section below shows that you can have separate log files for each Windows machine that connects, and you can specify the maximum size of the log file:

```
# this tells Samba to use a separate log file for each machine
# that connects
    log file = /var/log/samba/log.%m

# Put a capping on the size of the log files (in Kb).
    max log size = 50
```

The directory **/var/log/samba** contains a variety of Samba log files, including the log file for the Windows system used in the examples in this chapter, called *f4457mxp,* as shown in the following listing:

```
# ls -l /var/log/samba
```

```
total 27
-rw-r--r--    1 root      root         0 Jun 15 11:15 f4412bfg.log
-rw-r--r--    1 root      root         0 Jun 23 04:03 f4457mxp.log
-rw-r--r--    1 root      root       664 Jun 23 04:03 f4457mxp.log.1
-rw-r--r--    1 root      root         0 Jun 21 12:22 linuxdev.log
-rw-r--r--    1 root      root      8993 Jun 29 05:01 log.nmbd
-rw-r--r--    1 root      root      1918 Jun 29 04:56 log.smbd
-rw-r--r--    1 root      root       405 Jun 29 04:56 nmbd.log
-rw-r--r--    1 root      root        65 Jun 24 04:03 smbd.log
-rw-r--r--    1 root      root        65 Jun 24 04:03 smbd.log.1
-rw-r--r--    1 root      root      3271 Jun 29 05:00 smbmount.log
-rw-r--r--    1 root      root      7431 Jun 23 04:03 smbmount.log.1
```

Additional Samba Topics

Samba Web Configuration Tool (SWAT)

SWAT is a Web-based administration tool for Samba. It is easy to configure and provides a simple interface for most Samba configuration tasks. On your Red Hat Linux system, the following steps had to be performed to get SWAT running. If you have a different UNIX variant, your steps will be different.

Edit the file **/etc/xinetd.d/swat** and change *disable* to *no* as shown in the following listing:

```
# default: off
# description: SWAT is the Samba Web Admin Tool. Use swat \
#                       to configure your Samba server. To use SWAT, \
#                       connect to port 901 with your favorite web browser.
service swat
{
                port= 901
                socket_type= stream
                wait = no
                only_from = 127.0.0.1
                user= root
                server= /usr/sbin/swat
                log_on_failure+= USERID
                disable= no
}
```

Restart **xinetd** with the following command:

```
# /sbin/service xinetd restart
```

From your browser, specify a *location* of *localhost:901* and enter the root user and password when prompted for them.

Figure 11-5 shows the SWAT interface. It includes links for *HOME, GLOBALS, SHARES, PRINTERS, STATUS, VIEW,* and *PASSWORD* and documentation on several important Samba topics.

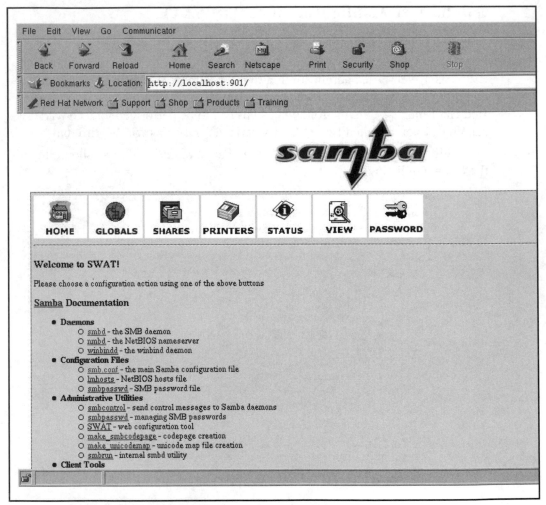

Figure 11-5   SWAT Showing Initial Window

From this point, you can view your current configuration and make configuration changes to Samba.

When you select *STATUS,* you are shown the information in Figure 11-6.

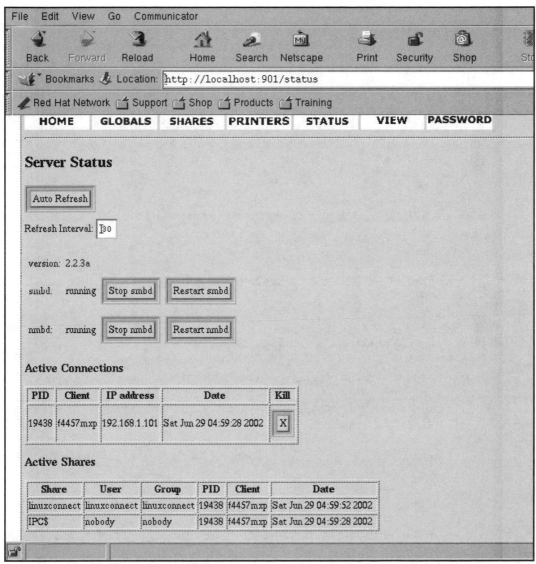

Figure 11-6   SWAT *STATUS*

You get such useful information as the state of the *smbd* and *nmbd* daemons, the *Active Connections*, and *Active Shares*.

There is also extensive online documentation for all Samba-related software at *www.samba.org*.

Samba Utilities and Programs

You have used several Samba utilities and programs in this chapter. The following list gives a description of the most often used Samba-related commands. There are manual pages for all these, which are part of most Samba installations:

- **smbd** - This daemon provides file and print services to SMB clients, such as the Windows system used in the examples throughout this chapter.

- **nmbd** - This daemon provides NetBIOS name server capability and browsing.

- **smbclient** - A program that gives the server access to remotely mounted SMB shares on other servers.

- **testparm** - A test program for **/etc/smb.conf**.

- **smbstatus** - Program that displays status information about current Samba connections.

- **smbpasswd** - Program used to change a user's SMB password on the local machine.

- **smbrun** - Program that runs shell commands for **smbd**.

- **smbtar** - Program to back up SMB shares directly to a UNIX tape drive.

- **smbmount** - Used to mount an SMB file system.

- **smbumount** - Used to unmount an SMB file system.

The online manual pages for these and other Samba-related commands provide more detail. Even in a simple setup, such as the one performed in this chapter, you want to run some of these programs.

Obtaining Samba

In the examples used throughout this chapter, we set up Samba on a Linux system that had Samba installed on it as part of the Red Hat 8.x Linux CD-ROM. Samba is included on the Red Hat Advanced Server distribution that is supplied with HP Integrity server. If Samba does not come on the CD-ROM provided with your UNIX variant, or if you want to be sure that you're loading the very latest Samba, you can obtain Samba from the Web.

www.samba.org is the place to start. From this Web site, you can select a "download site" in your country. You can also select "Web sites" on *www.samba.org* that provides a wealth of information on Samba, including the GNU General Public License mentioned earlier in this chapter.

There is extensive documentation on Samba-related Web sites, including detailed descriptions of the programs that I listed earlier and used in this chapter.

If you decide to download Samba, you'll probably be given an option of loading a precompiled Samba on your system or building and compiling Samba yourself. The choice you make depends on a lot of factors. If you have a good, reliable Samba distribution, as we did in this chapter when working with Red Hat Linux, working with a precompiled Samba may be best. If you're interested in learning more about how Samba works and is configured, and want the very latest and greatest version, download the source and compile it yourself.

Even if you have a great prepackaged Samba, as we did in this chapter, it is still worth visiting the Samba-related Web sites to view the extensive documentation available.

Chapter 12

ServiceGuard for Linux

ServiceGuard for Linux (what I'll call ServiceGuard in this chapter) is a High Availability (HA) application. It is used in conjunction with other HA techniques to produce a loosely coupled cluster. An application running on a primary system can failover to a backup system should a failure or other switch over condition exist on the primary system. ServiceGuard can detect failures of a CPU, LAN, application, and other components.

All the systems and all the application packages have IP addresses. When a failure occurs, the another system runs the high availability package and the IP address of the package moves with the package to the backup system. If only a LAN card fails in a primary system, ServiceGuard will fail over to a standby LAN card rather than the backup system.

You can have many systems in a ServiceGuard cluster, all of which can be active. You don't need to have systems in a standby state waiting for a failure to occur.

This chapter provides background on ServiceGuard to give you an overview of its operation. This is not a detailed setup guide for Service-Guard. There are excellent ServiceGuard documents on *www.docs.hp.com* including *Managing ServiceGuard for Linux*.

ServiceGuard Background

A ServiceGuard cluster is a networked group of Linux servers that transfer control of applications when hardware or software problems occur. There is hardware reliability designed into a Service cluster in the form of many redundant components, such as LAN cards, disks, networking connections, and so on. ServiceGuard handles much of the software reliability by transferring control of applications from a failed system to an operational system. ServiceGuard uses *packages,* which are Linux processes grouped together to facilitate the management and fail over of important applications. Packages include the resources needed to support a specific application including disks, networking, and linux processes. The best way to understand the makeup of a ServiceGuard cluster is through a diagram. Figure 12-1 shows a basic ServiceGuard setup.

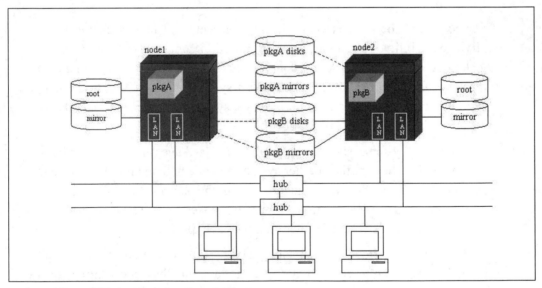

Figure 12-1   ServiceGuard Cluster

Figure 12-1 is a simple ServiceGuard cluster consisting of two systems. Note that there are many redundant components in the diagram. The disks for the operating systems (*root*) are mirrored. The shared disks that contain *pkgA* and *pkgB* are also mirrored. The package is setup with Logical Volume Manager (LVM) volume groups. The procedure for creating the storage required for a ServiceGuard cluster is described in the document cited earlier.

There are two LAN cards and two physical networks. The two networks are connected with a hub and not a router. Should one physical network fail, the hub provides instant connectivity to the second physical network.

When a failure occurs on the second node, the *pkgB* switches to the first system, as shown in Figure 12-2.

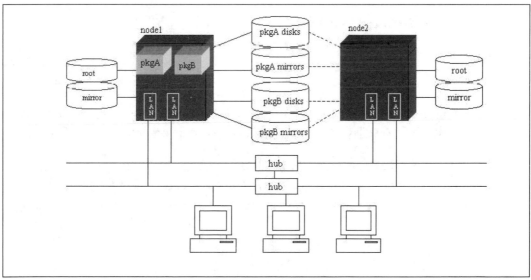

Figure 12-2   ServiceGuard Cluster After Failover

After the package switch takes place, the package and its associated IP address(es) are moved to the "adoptive" system. IP addresses are associated with each system and with each application package. When the failover occurs, the IP address of *pkg2* moves over to *node1* along with the application package *pkg2*. Users of *pkg2* connect to the same IP address after failover even though *pkg2* has been moved from *node2* to *node1*.

The application package contains all the information related to applications in the ServiceGuard environment. For each package, there is a *package configuration file* and *package control script*. The package configuration file contains all dependencies for the application, such as the package name, service name, subnet, and so on. The package control script is run to start or stop the application package. These are ASCII files.

In addition to the ASCII files used to define the package and start and stop it, there is a *cluster configuration file*. This file has in it parameters such as the cluster name, maximum number of configured packages, and so on. This file, along with the *package configuration file*, are combined to produce a binary file that is distributed to all the nodes. There are a series of commands to create a package and cluster. The **cmapplyconf** command is used to produce the binary file.

ServiceGuard Manager

ServiceGuard clusters can be managed through a graphical interface called ServiceGuard Manager, which is available for free on *software.hp.com*. ServiceGuard Manager gets configuration data from nodes in a cluster and is invoked with **/usr/local/sgmgr/bin/sgmgr -c** *clustername*. ServiceGuard Manager can also be run on HP-UX and Windows systems.

You can perform a variety of cluster-related tasks with ServiceGuard Manager including viewing a cluster as shown in Figure 12-3 for the cluster *morningstar.*

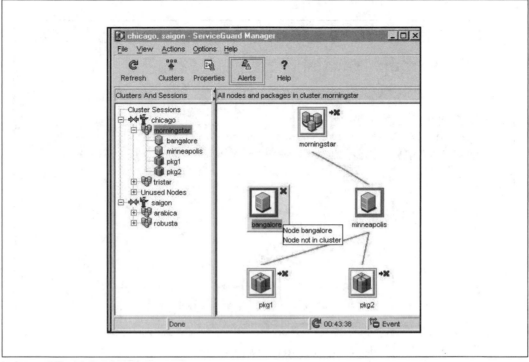

Figure 12-3   ServiceGuard Manager Showing the Cluster *morningstar*

This screen shows that the node *bangalore* is not in the cluster and two packages are running on the system *minneapolis*.

We can get more information about the systems in the cluster, as shown in Figure 12-4.

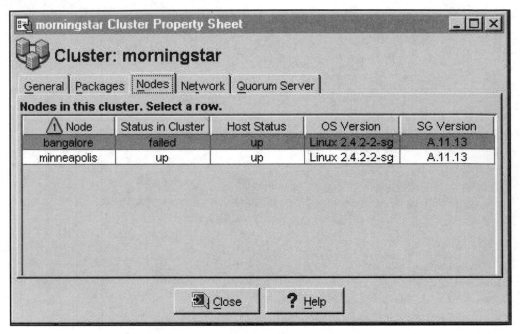

Figure 12-4   Nodes in the Cluster *morningstar*

This figure shows the status of the systems, including the fact that *bangalore* is *up* but that it *failed* as part of the ServiceGuard cluster. The *Cluster Properties* window shows information about the cluster, including a tab for its nodes as shown in the figure.

You can get specific information about the system *bangalore,* as shown in Figure 12-5.

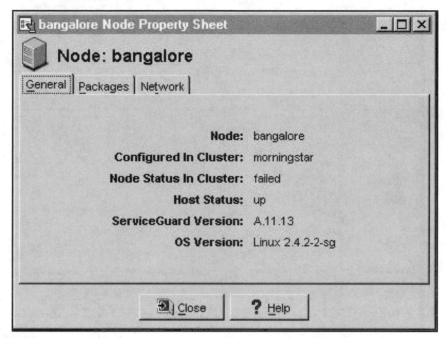

Figure 12-5   Status Summary on the Node *bangalore*

This figure shows information on *bangalore,* including the versions of Linux and ServiceGuard that the node is running. Using the tabs, you can also obtain information about the *Packages* and *Network*.

Figure 12-6 shows a summary of the ServiceGuard cluster.

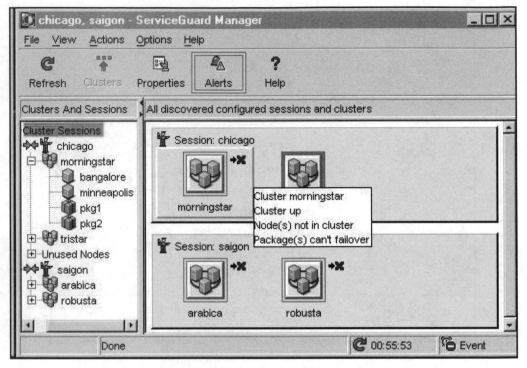

Figure 12-6   Specific Information on the Node *bangalore*

This figure shows the status of the clusters. You can see that the cluster *morningstar* is indeed *up,* but that the packages can't failover because the node *bangalore* is not *up.*

This was a high-level overview of ServiceGuard on Linux systems. To users of ServiceGuard on HP-UX systems, this functionality is nearly identical. To Linux users who haven't before seen ServiceGuard, this is a highly functional and widely used high-availability tool with tens of thousands of installations on HP-UX that is worth evaluating.

Chapter 13

HP-UX and Windows Installation on Integrity Servers

Although the focus of this book is Linux on Integrity servers, you can also load Windows Server 2003 and HP-UX 11i on Integrity servers. This chapter provides a quick overview of installing these two operating systems. The coverage of installing these two operating systems is not nearly as complete as the overall Linux topics in all the remaining chapters of this book, but you'll get a feel for these two operating systems on Integrity servers. At the time of this writing, you can boot one of these operating systems on an HP system. By the time you read this, you'll be able to run all three operating systems simultaneously on an HP system in different hard partitions (nPartitions.) Please keep in mind that in order to do this, you must have a system that supports nPartitions. The systems used in the examples in this book do not support nPartitions.

The first section covers HP-UX on Integrity servers, and then Windows is covered.

Installing HP-UX

This section covers installing HP-UX 11i on an HP Integrity server. At the time of this writing there is a version of HP-UX specifically for Integrity servers. The release we're loading is HP-UX 1i version 1.6 (B.11.22).

Begin the process to load HP-UX by placing the HP-UX *core oe install and recovery* DVD-ROM into the DVD-ROM on the Integrity server and then interrupting the boot process when we reach the window shown in Figure 13-1.

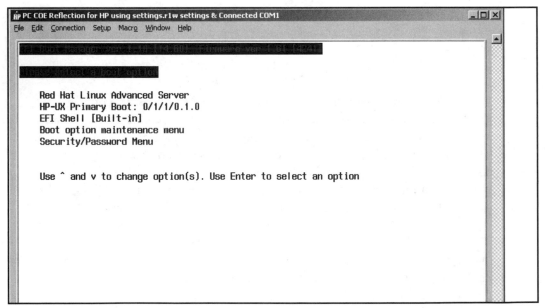

Figure 13-1   Select *Boot option maintenance menu*

From the menu shown in Figure 13-1, you could make a variety of selections, including booting a Red Hat Linux or HP-UX that you already have installed. You want to install from DVD-ROM, so you select *Boot option maintenance menu.* The next menu to appear is shown in Figure 13-2.

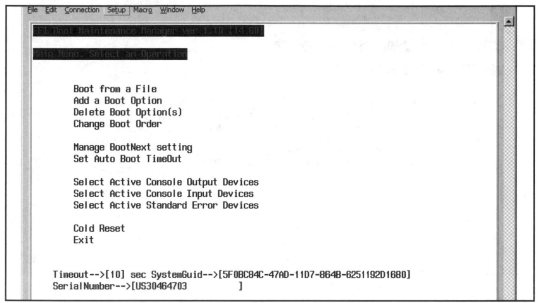

File Edit Connection Setup Macro Window Help

```
EFI Boot Maintenance Manager ver 1.10 [14.60]

Main Menu. Select an Operation


        Boot from a File
        Add a Boot Option
        Delete Boot Option(s)
        Change Boot Order

        Manage BootNext setting
        Set Auto Boot TimeOut

        Select Active Console Output Devices
        Select Active Console Input Devices
        Select Active Standard Error Devices

        Cold Reset
        Exit


    Timeout-->[10] sec SystemGuid-->[5F0BC84C-47AD-11D7-864B-6251192D1680]
    SerialNumber-->[US30464703            ]
```

Figure 13-2   Select *Boot from a file*

Many boot maintenance options are shown in Figure 13-2. You could perform a variety of tasks, such as adding and deleting boot options or changing the boot order. To install from DVD-ROM select *Boot from a file,* which brings up the menus shown in Figure 13-3.

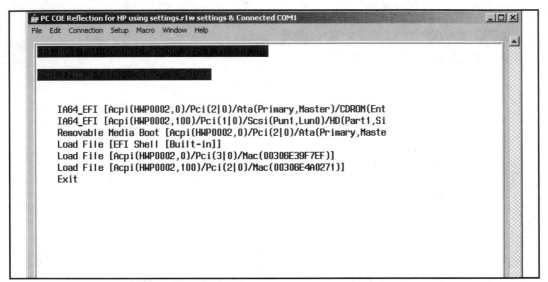

Figure 13-3   Select *CD-ROM*

You are now presented with a series of volumes off of which you could boot or go to the EFI shell. You have your HP-UX 11i DVD-ROM in the first entry in the figure that has *CD-ROM* in it. There are many volumes shown on which operating systems are already loaded. When *CD-ROM* is selected, the menu in Figure 13-4 is displayed.

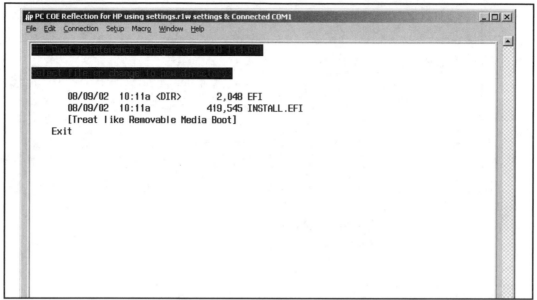

Figure 13-4   Select *INSTALL.EFI* to Proceed with the Installation

You want to load *INSTALL.EFI,* which is the second entry in the list. After you make this selection and enter the *console* line, the screen in Figure 13-5 appears.

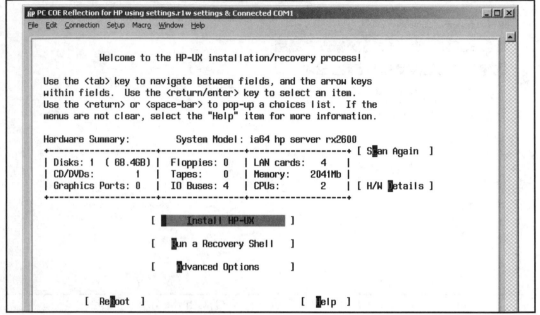

Figure 13-5   HP-UX Installation Screen with *Install HP-UX* Selected

At this point, you see the familiar screen of the HP-UX installation and recovery process. Loading HP-UX from this point is nearly identical to loading HP-UX on a Precision Architecture-based system.

Now select *Install HP-UX* and the screen shown in Figure 13-6 appears.

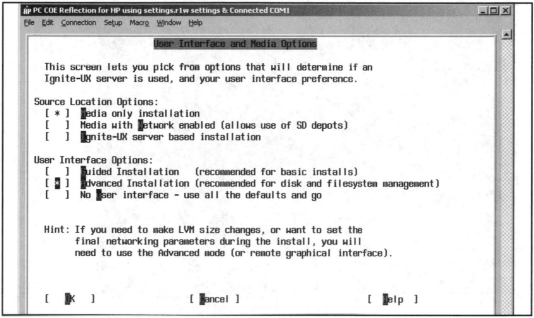

Figure 13-6   Options to Loading HP-UX

Now you can select from a variety of *Source* and *User* options. Since this installation is from DVD-ROM, select *Media only* and *Advanced Installation,* which brings up the window shown in Figure 13-7.

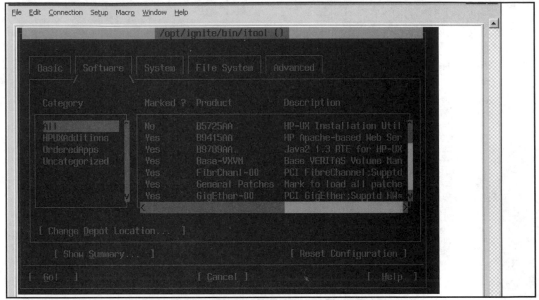

Figure 13-7   Making Selections When Loading HP-UX

Across the top of the screen shot are a series of tabs from which you can select and make modifications before installing HP-UX. The *Software* tab has been selected and you've selected *All* software to be loaded. Figure 13-8 shows the *System* tab.

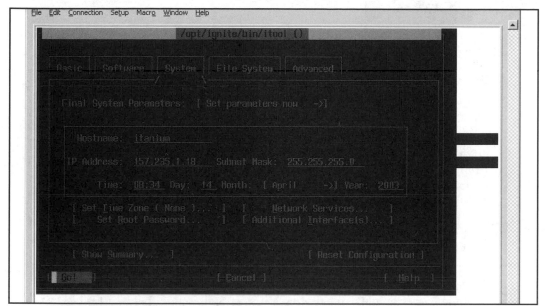

Figure 13-8   *System* Tab

This figure shows the system-related information that we've entered as part of the installation. You could select other tabs as well, such as *File System* to adjust the setup of the file systems. To complete the HP-UX installation, select *Go!*.

The installation process that we just walked through is nearly identical to a Precision Architecture-based installation once we reached the installation and recovery window.

The next section discusses how to install Windows Server 2003 on an Integrity server.

Windows Server 2003

Windows installs on an Integrity server just as it would on any other system. As with Linux, you select *Removable Media* and walk through the familiar Windows installation process so I won't cover installing Windows in this section. There are, however, some interesting aspects to running Windows on an HP Integrity server that are covered in this section. The first is *Special Administration Console (SAC)* which is covered in the next section. There are also some interesting configuration topics covered under *Installing and Configuring NetRAID* that include installing drivers and setting up storage on Integrity servers using the Itanium configuration DVD.

The following section covers SAC.

Special Administration Console (SAC)

Special Administration Console (SAC) is a command-line environment on Windows Server 2003. It provides a set of commands that can be used to perform many functions such as viewing and ending processes and working with the IP addresses of systems. It is separate from the Windows command line environment and can be used for remote management. SAC is part of Emergency Management Services, which must be enabled to use SAC.

SAC is available early in the boot process. You can use it to assist with management during normal system operation as well as in *Safe Mode*. Safe mode is a way of starting Windows using only the basic elements of the operating system. You can use the *F8* key when the system starts to go into safe mode. In the examples, you'll use SAC in normal operation and on the system console.

SAC provides a set of commands you can use to perform a number of management tasks that help return your system to a normally functioning state. These tasks include:

- Viewing a list of processes.

- Ending processes.

- Setting or viewing the Internet Protocol (IP) address of the server.

- Generating a Stop error to create a memory dump file.

- Starting and accessing command prompts.

- Restarting the server.

- Shutting down the server.

This section provides examples of issuing some basic commands in SAC on an Integrity system. Table 13-1 is a list of some of the SAC commands available at the time of this writing.

TABLE 13-1 SAC Commands and Descriptions

Command	Description
ch	Lists all channels. Use **ch -?** for help.
cmd	Creates Windows command-prompt channels. To use a command-prompt channel, you must provide valid logon credentials. You must log on to each command-prompt instance.
crashdump	Crashes the system. You must have crash dump enabled.
d	Deletes the current kernel log.
f	Toggles the information output by the *t-list* command, which shows processes only, or shows processes and threads
I	If no parameters are passed, this command lists Internet Protocol (IP) information. You can configure IP parameters to display or set the IP address, subnet mask, and gateway of a given network interface device by providing the network number, IP address, and subnet information. To do so, use the following format: <network#><IPaddress><subnet>
Id	Displays identification information about the server.
k <PID>	Ends the given process. PID is the process identification number you specify.
l <PID>	Lowers the priority of a process (and any associated child processes) to the lowest possible level.

Command	Description
lock	Restricts access to Emergency Management Services command-prompt channels. You must provide valid logon credentials to unlock a channel.
m <PID> <MB-allow>	Limits the memory usage of a process (and any associated child processes) to a specified number of megabytes. MB is the number of megabytes you specify.
p	Causes *t-list* command output to pause after displaying one full screen of information.
r	Restarts the computer.
s	If no parameters are passed, this command displays the current date using the 24-hour clock format. You can set the system time by providing the date and, optionally, the time in this format: *mm/dd/yyyy hh:mm.*
shutdown	Initiates a shutdown.
t	Lists the currently running processes and threads.
help or ?	Lists the available commands.

These commands are issued at the *SAC>* prompt. You can also set up the *channels,* which are direct connections to the Windows operating system specified by user and domain. SAC is also a channel. You can switch between these channels to perform your work. Table 13-2 shows some commonly used channel-related commands.

TABLE 13-2   Channel-Related Commands and Descriptions

Command	Description
ch	Lists all channels.
ch -si \<n\>	Changes to the channel *n*.
ch -sn \<name\>	Changes to the channel *name*.
ch -ci \<n\>	Closes the channel with the channel *n*.
ch -cn \<name\>	Closes the channel *n*.
ch -k \<name\>	Ends the channel *name*.
\<Esc\>\<Tab\>	Changes channels.
\<Esc\>\<Tab\>0	Returns to the SAC channel.
ch -?	Displays help information for channel management commands.

The following example shows issuing the **t** command that lists all processes and threads that are currently running:

```
SAC> t
memory: 2096632 kb  uptime:  0  0:08:35.990


PageFile: \??\C:\pagefile.sys
         Current Size: 2095104 kb  Total Used:   7584 kb   Peak Used   8768 kb

Memory:2096632K Avail:1749752K  TotalWs: 284936K InRam Kernel: 4096K P:11800K
Commit: 304904K/ 229384K Limit:4041240K Peak: 407112K  Pool N:21968K P:12200K

----Press <Enter> for more----
   User Time    Kernel Time    Ws   Faults  Commit Pri Hnd Thd  Pid Name
                             38072   14813                          File Cache
0:00:00.000   0:16:46.720     40       0      0  0    0   2    0 Idle Process
0:00:00.000   0:00:07.980    304    3890     96  8  202  55    4 System
0:00:00.010   0:00:00.040   1184     308    408 11   17   3  336 smss.exe
0:00:00.430   0:00:03.810   6352    2585   1560 13  334  10  384 csrss.exe
0:00:00.270   0:00:00.370   4008    4326   8688 13  428  20  548 winlogon.exe
0:00:00.340   0:00:00.620  17984    4747   9312  9  363  18  592 services.exe
0:00:00.200   0:00:00.210  21584    2933  14032  9  350  23  604 lsass.exe
0:00:00.070   0:00:00.050   8256    1101   2208  8  193  10  756 svchost.exe
0:00:00.020   0:00:00.050  10832    1404   3168  8  134  16  808 svchost.exe
0:00:00.000   0:00:00.030   9960    1296   5024  8  107   7 1004 svchost.exe
0:00:00.000   0:00:00.010   5832     737   1288  8   81   5 1064 svchost.exe
----Press <Enter> for more----
   User Time    Kernel Time    Ws   Faults  Commit Pri Hnd Thd  Pid Name
```

```
0:00:01.250  0:00:00.960 41536   18005  150408  8 1017  47 1076 svchost.exe
0:00:00.070  0:00:00.060 14288    1880    7528  8  136  11 1240 spoolsv.exe
0:00:00.040  0:00:00.050 12960    1677    3584  8  169  24 1272 msdtc.exe
0:00:00.010  0:00:00.020  8104    1058    1808  8   88   9 1416 llssrv.exe
0:00:00.000  0:00:00.010  3528     452     688  8   35   2 1460 svchost.exe
0:00:00.010  0:00:00.020  8672    1132    2312  8   77   9 1584 dfssvc.exe
0:00:01.140  0:00:02.150 36552   23669    9400  8  315  10 1912 explorer.exe
0:00:00.220  0:00:00.080 13368    1831    3040  8  156   6  456 wmiprvse.exe
0:00:00.020  0:00:00.040 11080    1526    3384  8  113   6  492 wmiprvse.exe
0:00:00.010  0:00:00.040 10440    1436    1448  8   72   5 1000 msiexec.exe
```

In the previous listing, information was displayed in pages and you hit *Enter* in order to view the next page of information. Next, you'll use **r** to raise the priority of process *1912* by one level from *8* to *9* and rerun **t** to view the new level of *1912*:

```
SAC> r 1912
SAC successfully raised the process priority.

SAC> t
memory: 2096632 kb  uptime:  0  0:10:19.010


PageFile: \??\C:\pagefile.sys
       Current Size: 2095104 kb  Total Used:   7584 kb  Peak Used  8768 kb

Memory:2096632K Avail:1751888K  TotalWs: 284424K InRam Kernel: 4096K P:11800K
Commit: 304400K/ 229072K Limit:4041240K Peak:  407112K  Pool N:21944K P:12208K

----Press <Enter> for more----
    User Time    Kernel Time    Ws   Faults  Commit Pri Hnd Thd  Pid Name
                              37624    14825                          File Cache
 0:00:00.000  0:20:12.080     40        0       0  0    0   2    0 Idle Process
 0:00:00.000  0:00:08.660    304     3890      96  8  202  55    4 System
 0:00:00.010  0:00:00.040   1184      308     408 11   17   3  336 smss.exe
 0:00:00.430  0:00:03.810   6352     2585    1560 13  331  10  384 csrss.exe
 0:00:00.270  0:00:00.370   4008     4326    8688 13  428  20  548 winlogon.exe
 0:00:00.340  0:00:00.620  17984     4747    9312  9  363  18  592 services.exe
 0:00:00.200  0:00:00.210  21560     2933   13912  9  346  22  604 lsass.exe
 0:00:00.070  0:00:00.050   8256     1101    2208  8  181  10  756 svchost.exe
 0:00:00.020  0:00:00.050  10832     1404    3168  8  134  16  808 svchost.exe
 0:00:00.000  0:00:00.030   9960     1299    4936  8  105   6 1004 svchost.exe
 0:00:00.000  0:00:00.010   5832      737    1288  8   81   5 1064 svchost.exe
----Press <Enter> for more----
    User Time    Kernel Time    Ws   Faults  Commit Pri Hnd Thd  Pid Name
 0:00:01.250  0:00:00.960  41504    18023  150312  8 1012  46 1076 svchost.exe
 0:00:00.070  0:00:00.060  14288     1880    7528  8  135  11 1240 spoolsv.exe
 0:00:00.040  0:00:00.050  12960     1677    3584  8  169  24 1272 msdtc.exe
 0:00:00.010  0:00:00.020   8104     1058    1808  8   88   9 1416 llssrv.exe
 0:00:00.000  0:00:00.010   3528      452     688  8   35   2 1460 svchost.exe
 0:00:00.010  0:00:00.020   8672     1132    2312  8   77   9 1584 dfssvc.exe
 0:00:01.140  0:00:02.150  36544    23669    9392  9  305  10 1912 explorer.exe
 0:00:00.220  0:00:00.080  13368     1835    3040  8  152   6  456 wmiprvse.exe
 0:00:00.020  0:00:00.040  11080     1526    3384  8  109   6  492 wmiprvse.exe
 0:00:00.010  0:00:00.040  10440     1436    1448  8   72   5 1000 msiexec.exe
SAC>
```

The *Pri* of process *1912* was indeed raised from *8* to *9*.

Using the command prompt channel, you can issue many commands that help you gather useful information about your system. In the following listing, we'll create a channel with **cmd**, view the available channels with **ch**, and then connect to channel *1* with **ch -si 1**:Á

Á

```
SAC> cmd
The Command Prompt session was successfully launched.
SAC>
EVENT:   A new channel has been created.  Use "ch -?" for channel help.
Channel: Cmd0008

SAC> ch
Channel List

(Use "ch -?" for information on using channels)

# Status   Channel Name
0 (AV)     SAC
1 (AR)     Cmd0008

SAC> ch -si 1

<channel-switch>
<name>Cmd0008</name>
<description>Command Prompt</description>
<type>VT-UTF8</type>
<guid>e560802d-6ebd-11d7-af15-505054503030</guid>
<application-type>63d02271-8aa4-11d5-bccf-00b0d014a2d0</application-type>
</channel-switch>


Name:                  Cmd0008
Description:           Command Prompt
Type:                 VT-UTF8
Channel GUID:         e560802d-6ebd-11d7-af15-505054503030
Application Type GUID: 63d02271-8aa4-11d5-bccf-00b0d014a2d0

Press <esc><tab> for next channel.
Press <esc><tab>0 to return to the SAC channel.
Use any other key to view this channel.
```

Now that we're connected to the channel, we can log in to it by specifying a *Username*, *Domain*, and *Password,* as shown below:

```
Please enter login credentials.
Username: Administrator
Domain  : hp
Password: **

Microsoft Windows [Version 5.2.3663]
(C) Copyright 1985-2001 Microsoft Corp.

C:\WINDOWS\system32>
```

Now that you're logged in, you can run Windows commands. The following example shows running **diskpart** and viewing *help* and various disk details:

```
C:\WINDOWS\system32> diskpart

Microsoft DiskPart version 5.2.3663
Copyright (C) 1999-2001 Microsoft Corporation.
On computer: ITANIUM



DISKPART> help

ACTIVE      - Marks the current basic partition as an active boot
              partition.
ASSIGN      - Assign a drive letter or mount point to the selected
              volume.
BREAK       - Break a mirror set.
CLEAN       - Clear the configuration information, or all
                 information, off of the disk.
CONVERT     - Converts between different disk formats.
CREATE      - Create a volume or partition.
DELETE      - Delete an object.
DETAIL      - Provide details about an object.
EXIT        - Exit diskpart.
EXTEND      - Extend a volume.
HELP        - Prints a list of commands.
IMPORT      - Imports a disk group.
INACTIVE    - Marks the current basic partition as a inactive.
LIST        - Prints out a list of objects.
ONLINE      - Online a disk that is currently marked as offline.
REM         - Does nothing. Used to comment scripts.
REMOVE      - Remove a drive letter or mount point assignment.
REPAIR      - Repair a RAID-5 volume.
RESCAN      - Rescan the computer looking for disks and volumes.
RETAIN      - Place a retainer partition under a simple volume.
SELECT      - Move the focus to an object.

DISKPART> list disk

  Disk ###  Status      Size     Free     Dyn  Gpt
  --------  ----------  -------  -------   ---  ---
  Disk 0    Online       68 GB   5337 KB         *

DISKPART>
C:\WINDOWS\system32>

DISKPART> select disk 0

Disk 0 is now the selected disk.

DISKPART> detail disk

HP 73.4G ST373453LC SCSI Disk Device
Disk ID: A1EF40E0-0295-01C3-A1F4-04622FD5EC6D
Type    : Unknown
```

```
Bus    : 2
Target : 2
LUN ID : 0

Volume ### Ltr   Label   Fs    Type      Size   Status   Info
---------- ---  -------  ------ -------  ------- -------- --------
  Volume    0    C       NTFS  Partition 68 GB  Healthy  Boot

DISKPART> exit

Leaving DiskPart...

C:\WINDOWS\system32>
```

In the previous example, you have one disk that you selected and on which you viewed details.

On a system with a NetRAID controller and multiple disks, we'll see more entries. The following example shows running **diskpart** on a system with several disks:

```
DISKPART> list disk

    Disk ###  Status      Size    Free     Dyn  Gpt
    --------  ----------  ------  -------   ---  ---
    Disk 0    Online       68 GB     0 B         *
    Disk 1    Online      137 GB  2015 KB         *
    Disk 2    Online      137 GB  2015 KB         *

DISKPART> select disk 1

Disk 1 is now the selected disk.

DISKPART> detail disk

HPNetRD  LD  1 NetRAID SCSI Disk Device
Disk ID: C4837A41-800D-11D7-8DD2-505054503030
Type   : Unknown
Bus    : 0
Target : 0
LUN ID : 1

    Volume ### Ltr  Label      Fs     Type       Size    Status   Info
    ---------- ---  ---------- -----  ---------- ------- --------- --------
    Volume 1    E   New Volume NTFS   Partition  137 GB  Healthy

DISKPART>
```

There are three disks listed. *0* is an internal disk that is mirrored, with RAID 0, to another internal disk with the NetRAID card. *1* is comprised of two disks that are combined into one partition that is striped with RAID5 also using the NetRAID card. *2* is also two disks that are combined into one partition that is striped with RAID5 also using the NetRAID card.

Next, you'll run **net** with several different options and then **exit** to close the channel connection:

```
C:\WINDOWS\system32> net start
   Network Location Awareness (NLA)
   Plug and Play
   Print Spooler
   Protected Storage
   Remote Procedure Call (RPC)
   Remote Registry
   Secondary Logon
   Security Accounts Manager
   Server
   Shell Hardware Detection
   Special Administration Console Helper
   System Event Notification
   Task Scheduler
   TCP/IP NetBIOS Helper
   Terminal Services
   Windows Management Instrumentation
   Windows Time
   Wireless Configuration
   Workstation

The command completed successfully.


C:\WINDOWS\system32> net config server
Server Name                      \\ITANIUM
Server Comment

Software version                 Microsoft Windows .NET
Server is active on


Server hidden                    No
Maximum Logged On Users          Unlimited
Maximum open files per session   16384

Idle session time (min)          15
The command completed successfully.


C:\WINDOWS\system32>net user
Software version                 Microsoft Windows .NET
Server is active on


Server hidden                    No
Maximum Logged On Users          Unlimited
Maximum open files per session   16384

Idle session time (min)          15
The command completed successfully.


C:\WINDOWS\system32> net user

User accounts for \\ITANIUM

-----------------------------------------------------------------
Administrator           Guest                      SUPPORT_388945a0
The command completed successfully.
```

```
C:\WINDOWS\system32> exit

SAC>
EVENT:    A channel has been closed.
Channel: Cmd0008
SAC>
```

Many Windows commands can be executed after a connection to the channel has been established in addition to the **diskpart** and **net** commands shown in the previous examples. The following example shows issuing the **help** command from the channel:

```
C:\WINDOWS\system32> help
```

```
For more information on a specific command, type HELP command-name
ASSOC          Displays or modifies file extension associations.
ATTRIB         Displays or changes file attributes.
BREAK          Sets or clears extended CTRL+C checking.
BOOTCFG        Sets properties in boot.ini file to control boot loading.
CACLS          Displays or modifies access control lists (ACLs) of files.
CALL           Calls one batch program from another.
CD             Displays the name of or changes the current directory.
CHCP           Displays or sets the active code page number.
CHDIR          Displays the name of or changes the current directory.
CHKDSK         Checks a disk and displays a status report.
CHKNTFS        Displays or modifies the checking of disk at boot time.
CLS            Clears the screen.
CMD            Starts a new instance of the Windows command interpreter.
COLOR          Sets the default console foreground and background colors.
COMP           Compares the contents of two files or sets of files.
COMPACT        Displays or alters the compression of files on NTFS partitions.
CONVERT        Converts FAT volumes to NTFS.  You cannot convert the
               current drive.
COPY           Copies one or more files to another location.
DATE           Displays or sets the date.
DEL            Deletes one or more files.
DIR            Displays a list of files and subdirectories in a directory.
DISKCOMP       Compares the contents of two floppy disks.
DISKCOPY       Copies the contents of one floppy disk to another.
DISKPART       Displays or configures Disk Partition properties.
DOSKEY         Edits command lines, recalls Windows commands, and
               creates macros.
DRIVERQUERY    Displays current device driver status and properties.
ECHO           Displays messages, or turns command echoing on or off.
ENDLOCAL       Ends localization of environment changes in a batch file.
ERASE          Deletes one or more files.
EVENTQUERY     Displays event log entries for specified criteria.
EXIT           Quits the CMD.EXE program (command interpreter).
FC             Compares two files or sets of files, and displays the
               differences between them.
FIND           Searches for a text string in a file or files.
FINDSTR        Searches for strings in files.
FOR            Runs a specified command for each file in a set of files.
FORMAT         Formats a disk for use with Windows.
FSUTIL         Displays or configures the file system properties.
FTYPE          Displays or modifies file types used in file extension
               associations.
GOTO           Directs the Windows command interpreter to a labeled line in
```

```
                    a batch program.
GPRESULT            Displays Group Policy information for machine or user.
GRAFTABL            Enables Windows to display an extended character set in
                    graphics mode.
HELP                Provides Help information for Windows commands.
IF                  Performs conditional processing in batch programs.
LABEL               Creates, changes, or deletes the volume label of a disk.
MD                  Creates a directory.
MKDIR               Creates a directory.
MODE                Configures a system device.
MORE                Displays output one screen at a time.
MOVE                Moves one or more files from one directory to another
                    directory.
OPENFILES           Displays files opened by remote users for a file share.
PAGEFILECONFIG Displays or configures Pagefile properties.
PATH                Displays or sets a search path for executable files.
PAUSE               Suspends processing of a batch file and displays a message.
POPD                Restores the previous value of the current directory saved by
                    PUSHD.
PRINT               Prints a text file.
PROMPT              Changes the Windows command prompt.
PUSHD               Saves the current directory then changes it.
RD                  Removes a directory.
RECOVER             Recovers readable information from a bad or defective disk.
REM                 Records comments (remarks) in batch files or CONFIG.SYS.
REN                 Renames a file or files.
RENAME              Renames a file or files.
REPLACE             Replaces files.
RMDIR               Removes a directory.
SET                 Displays, sets, or removes Windows environment variables.
SETLOCAL            Begins localization of environment changes in a batch file.
SC                  Displays or configures services (background processes).
SCHTASKS            Schedules commands and programs to run on a computer.
SHIFT               Shifts the position of replaceable parameters in batch files.
SHUTDOWN            Allows proper local or remote shutdown of machine.
SORT                Sorts input.
START               Starts a separate window to run a specified program or command.
SUBST               Associates a path with a drive letter.
SYSTEMINFO          Displays machine specific properties and configuration.
TASKLIST            Displays all currently running tasks including services.
TASKKILL            Kill or stop a running process or application.
TIME                Displays or sets the system time.
TITLE               Sets the window title for a CMD.EXE session.
TREE                Graphically displays the directory structure of a drive or
                    path.
TYPE                Displays the contents of a text file.
VER                 Displays the Windows version.
VERIFY              Tells Windows whether to verify that your files are written
VOL                 Displays a disk volume label and serial number.
XCOPY               Copies files and directory trees.
WMIC                Displays WMI information inside interactive command shell.

For more information on tools see the command-line reference in the online help.


C:\WINDOWS\system32>
```

Using SAC and the channels, you can connect to a Windows Server 2003 and perform command line-related work.